INVENTING TH⎍   ⎍RIA

INVENTING THE PIZZERIA

A History of Pizza Making in Naples

By Antonio Mattozzi
Edited and translated by Zachary Nowak
Illustrations edited by Donatella Mattozzi

Bloomsbury Academic
An imprint of Bloomsbury Publishing Plc

BLOOMSBURY
LONDON • NEW DELHI • NEW YORK • SYDNEY

Bloomsbury Academic

An imprint of Bloomsbury Publishing Plc

50 Bedford Square	1385 Broadway
London	New York
WC1B 3DP	NY 10018
UK	USA

www.bloomsbury.com

BLOOMSBURY and the Diana logo are trademarks of Bloomsbury Publishing Plc

First published in Italian in 2009

© Antonio Mattozzi, 2009 and 2015
English language translation and editorial material © Zachary Nowak, 2015

British Library Cataloguing-in-Publication Data
A catalogue record for this book is available from the British Library.

ISBN: HB: 978-1-4725-8617-9
PB: 978-1-4725-8616-2
ePDF: 978-1-4725-8619-3
ePub: 978-1-4725-8618-6

Library of Congress Cataloging-in-Publication Data
A catalog record for this book is available from the Library of Congress.

Typeset by Fakenham Prepress Solutions, Fakenham, Norfolk NR21 8NN
Printed and bound in India

*to my father
who dedicated his whole life to work,
and to the many Neapolitan pizzaioli of yesterday and today who are the true
protagonists of this story.*

CONTENTS

LIST OF ILLUSTRATIONS

LIST OF TABLES

ACKNOWLEDGMENTS

AUTHOR'S ACKNOWLEDGMENTS

I would like first to thank everyone who contributed to the success of the original Italian version of this book, *Slow Food Editore*, and Professor Alberto Capatti, director of the asSaggi series, who liked and accepted the original manuscript, along with the editors Giovanni Ruffa and John Irving. A heartfelt thanks as well to Dottor Mauro Giancaspro, director of the Vittorio Emanuele National Library in Naples. Dottor Giancaspro allowed us to use the Library's Sala Rari and moderated the first presentation of the original Italian edition. Discussing the book were Professor Guido D'Agostino of the Federico II University of Naples, with the participation of the journalist Luciano Pignataro (of the *Il Mattino* newspaper), the editor Giovanni Ruffa, and the unexpected (but very welcome) presence of the director Ugo Gregoretti.

I would also like to thank Professor Daniela Luigia Caglioti of the Federico II University of Naples for her invaluable suggestions at the outset of this project about archival sources to use. And of course I also thank all the employees and staff of the Italian State Archives in Naples, and the Vittorio Emanuele National Library, for their ability, availability, and courtesy. I owe a debt of gratitude as well to Dottor Gennaro Cavallaro, head of the Anagraphic Services of the Municipality of Naples.

I would also like to thank my former student, Professor Sergio Brancato of Federico II University of Naples, for the presentation of the book made at the Librerie Feltrinelli bookstore in Naples, together with the journalist Santa Di Salvo (of the *Il Mattino* newspaper) and the food writer Claudio Novelli.

Finally a special thanks to Zachary Nowak at Harvard University who took the idea to heart of translating this book and publishing it in English, and to my daughter Donatella, a passionate scholar of gastronomic history and of Neapolitan popular customs, who curated the iconographic material in the book with intense interest.

ILLUSTRATIONS EDITOR'S ACKNOWLEDGMENTS

I would like to thank Direttrice Imma Ascione for the permission to publish the documents from the Italian State Archives in Naples, as well as Dottoressa Mariolina Rascaglia of the National Library of Naples for the images from the Library's Fondo Lucchesi Palli, its Sala Napoletana and the Sezione Manoscritti. I would also like to thank Attilio Bachetti, Sergio Condurro, Salvatore di Matteo, Salvatore Grasso, Enrico Maria Lombardi, Franco Pepe, Umberto and Salvatore

Salvo, and Gino Sorbillo for having shared their family photos with us. In addition, a special thanks goes to Alfonso Mattozzi for the cover photograph, and to Maria Basciano Gasparri for having preserved important family memories. Thanks again to our friends at Gea Photo for their precious assistance. Finally, thanks to Slow Food Editore for the permission to publish the original edition's cover.

EDITOR'S ACKNOWLEDGMENTS

My thanks go to Antonio Mattozzi for having entrusted the translation of this gem of a book to me. I would also like to thank Donatella Mattozzi for the exhaustive iconographic research, and C. Scott Walker of the Harvard Map Collection. Scott created the maps for the book, maps which explain visually what Antonio describes in the text. Thanks too to Giuseppe Di Biase for having put this book in my hands so many years ago. The two anonymous reviewers' comments and suggestions made this a much better book, as did the patience and support of my wife Jill. My mother, Bonnie Karl, also deserves a hearty *grazie mille* for her proofreading of the whole manuscript. Finally, Jennifer Schmidt and Molly Beck were fundamental to this project and a joy to work with.

FOREWORD

Like most kids who grew up on the east coast of the United States, I had a favorite local pizzeria, called Attilio's. It was about the only place I could ride my bike to buy a slice, at only seventy cents. The aroma of slightly charred wheat wafted in the air to lure in neighborhood children downwind. Any time of day or night when the shop was open there was a muscular young guy named Geno with his hands in the dough, pressing it out, tossing it briefly, ladling on the thinnest swirl of sauce, deftly spreading grated mozzarella and sliding it from a peel into the oven. He did it without thinking and talked almost continuously in a lilting accent, mostly about the beauty of Neapolitan homeland. How he could have left such a place remained a mystery.

At the time, little did any of us suspect that Geno was the inheritor of a venerable tradition stretching back centuries from the ancient flat *panis focacius* of the Roman Empire, to the fanciful butter and sugar laden creations of the Renaissance, which even went by the name of pizza (Messisbugo's *Banchetti* from sixteenth century Ferrara contains a recipe) and thence to the classic pie of Naples. Pizza had of course adapted to American tastes, including pepperoni, sausages, and any manner of toppings that would probably have made his compatriots wince. But they were still honest pizzas, long before the day of smoked salmon, wasabi and pineapple.

It was not until reading this book that I came to appreciate the ancestry of Geno's trade, specifically nineteenth-century Naples where pizza was born. One visitor in the 1860s (Hippolyte Taine) described the street scene: "Steep narrow, dirty, and bordered at every story with overhanging balconies; a mass of petty shops, open stalls, men and women buying, selling, gossiping, gesticulating and elbowing each other ... a labyrinth of paved tortuous lanes buried in dust and strewn with orange peel, melon-rinds, fragments of vegetables, and other refuse ... All is bustling eating, drinking, and bad odors; it reminds one of rats in a rat-trap." Despite the crowded alleys, the poverty, impossible regulations and political debacles, let alone the sheer difficulty of making a living, this noble trade survived. It is a story both inspiring and eye-opening. It is now very clear why so many *pizzaioli* left for other shores and how pizza became not only America's favorite food but globally revered. It is also now clear why the pizza makers brought with them an idyllic memory of Naples: largely to efface the hardships their predecessors endured.

For anyone who loves pizza, and by that I mean everyone, this is a story stripped of myth and romance. It is an account of the tough and gritty business, the sweat and grime, the social and legal context that gave rise to what is unquestionably one of the world's most perfect foods.

Ken Albala, University of the Pacific

EDITOR'S INTRODUCTION

There is an unfortunate current of food writing—both popular and academic—that places undue attention on the food product or the oft-heroicized artisan producer, but relegates the actual workshop to the margins of the account, or even the footnotes. These accounts often center on the artisan, working alone, motivated by "passion" with nary a thought to filthy lucre. Fortunately recent books like Susan Terrio's *Crafting the Culture and History of French Chocolate* have shown how easy it is to be seduced by this tale, so often told about food-producing artisans today.[a] In this book, Antonio Mattozzi looks past the myths about pizza and its mythic makers to focus instead on the real people who made the delicious discs and the places where they worked.

Inventing The Pizzeria approaches a part of Italian food history that Anglophones may have little familiarity with. Many investigations of Italian food in English have explored the food ways of Italian immigrants in other countries, and whether these food ways were in fact transplanted (i.e. traditions brought from Italy) or hybridizations.[b] Other contributions in English to the literature on Italian food uneasily juxtapose Italian peasant food with elite cuisine. Intended as a corrective to the apparently class-less "Mediterranean Diet" puffery, these authors underscore that far from being the hearty meal of hardy farmers, the "cucina povera" (cuisine of the poor) was boring, repetitive, with a startling absence of things we think of as integral to the so-called "Mediterranean diet." Good bread, olive oil, and real wine (as opposed to the watered-down, often vinegary substitute called *vinaccio*, literally "bad wine") were only very occasionally part of the diet of the Italian peasant until the post Second World War period.[c] Pellagra and other diseases common to malnourished populations were as present as prosciutto, butter and cheese were absent. Parallel to this ran the cuisine of the peninsula's elite: while the use of spices, for example, changes, the cookbooks from Mastro Martino in the sixteenth century all the way down to the famous cookbook by Pellegrino Artusi in the late nineteenth all share a rich set of dishes that those that honed their scythes or rowed out early to

---

[a] Susan J. Terrio, *Crafting the Culture and History of French Chocolate* (Berkeley: University of California Press, 2000), Research similar to Terrio's, this time in the pizzerias of Naples, would make for a fascinating study.

[b] See especially Hasia R. Diner, *Hungering for America: Italian, Irish, and Jewish Foodways in the Age of Migration* (Cambridge, MA: Harvard University Press, 2001); Harvey Levenstein, "The American Response to Italian Food, 1880–1930," in *Food in the USA: A Reader*, ed. Carole Counihan (New York: Routledge, 2003), 75–90.

[c] For a good discussion of the "cucina povera," see Gillian Riley, *The Oxford Companion to Italian Food* (Oxford; New York: Oxford University Press, 2007), 150.

fish could only dream of. Historians, obviously uneasy with the unearned culinary privilege of the rich and powerful, focus their attention on the distance between the two cuisines, rather than their connections.[d]

In this book, Antonio Mattozzi deftly reconstructs the history of a particularly creative type of baker that, responding to the realities of demographics and the topographical straitjacket that the city of Naples was in, created a new food that was one of the first to be eaten by both the poor and (ultimately) the rest of the population too, both in Naples and the world over. This is an important contribution to the literature of food history, but also the social history of Naples and nineteenth-century urban history—and to what has been written on pizza itself. Precious few of the books about pizza's early history can claim any level of seriousness. One of the exceptions is John Dickie, who went a long way towards putting pizza in its proper historical context in his chapter on Naples in his book *Delizia*. Dickie, writing against the current of decades of just-so stories, showed how pizza was the food of the poor, and often suspected of being the vector of contagious diseases like the cholera that killed thousands of Neapolitans in the nineteenth century.[e] Carol Helstosky carried the story further in her global history of pizza, describing the first expansion of the post Second World War pizza into new provinces, creating a global Republic of Red-sauce Pizzas by the last quarter of the twentieth century.[f] These two serious investigations, though, are afloat in a sea of mythmaking. Even Franco La Cecla's otherwise admirable volume falls back into the same unsubstantiated stories about royal take-out. In this volume, Antonio Mattozzi highlights the fact that much writing on pizza falls under a narrative approach that "looks for the anecdote rather than the document, wittiness and a clever quip rather than the pure and simple narration of the facts, an approach that contaminates the real events with elements that are often legendary and fantastic."[g] In endless blogs, magazine articles and guidebook sidebars about pizza, the protagonists are either monarchs (often historically fond of the plebs and their cooking) or far-sighted makers of pizza that make the global spread of dish all but certain, a kind of culinary manifest destiny that does not even stop at the Pacific. *Inventing The Pizzeria* shows that nothing could be further from the truth.

This book by Antonio Mattozzi combines both serious analysis and more light-hearted commentary to trace the evolution of the pizzeria from a shop that was initially hard to distinguish from a bakery, and to focus our attention not on the steaming disc that people the world over love, but rather on the person who ran the pizzeria, the *pizzaiolo*. Mattozzi's careful analysis of their mention in all kinds of archival documents makes it clear that far from being the up-and-coming caterer of regal picnics, the pizzaiolo was initially at the bottom of the hills surrounding Naples (in among the crowded tenements) and at the bottom of the ladder of

---

[d]A recent work that seeks to bridge the gap is Fabio Parasecoli, *Al Dente: A History of Food in Italy* (London: Reaktion Books, 2014); see also Massimo Montanari, *Cheese, Pears, and History in a Proverb*, trans. Beth Archer Brombert (New York: Columbia University Press, 2010).

[e]John Dickie, *Delizia!: The Epic History of the Italians and Their Food* (New York: Free Press, 2008).

[f]Carol Helstosky, *Pizza: A Global History* (London: Reaktion Books, 2008).

[g]This is from the Mattozzi's preface in this volume.

artisans who worked there in the nineteenth century. Instead of the heroic (and equally mythic) artisan who worked only for passion, the pizzaiolo that Mattozzi paints for us is driven by the need to pay the rent and pay the waiters. Though focus on objective standards is always a goal, Richard Sennett has suggested that "social and economic conditions, however, often stand in the way of the craftsman's discipline and commitment."[h] As numerous disappearances from the archives testify, making pizzas in Naples was a risky, precarious business that few succeeded in. Though today's global presence of Neapolitan pizza seems to suggest otherwise, this success was far from being preordained. To the contrary, Mattozzi shows that after a century of existence independent from bakeries, the number of pizzerias had only barely doubled and was still around one hundred. In 1900, all of Naples' pizzerias were still inside the walls of the old city, and the only attempt at taking pizza "abroad" (to Rome, only 225 kilometers away) had failed miserably.

In addition to his dispassionate examination of the product and the producer, Mattozzi gives attention to *place*—a hot topic in food studies. His explanation of pizza's emergence is grounded in the particular environmental and socio-economic conditions of the city: hemmed in by the sea on one side and hills on three others, Naples pressed its inhabitants into a painfully small space. Mattozzi carefully traces out how the particular politics of the Kingdom of Naples created a city that in the mid-eighteenth century was Europe's third largest and also had Europe's highest population density. The incredible premium on space and high rents meant that inexpensive street food for residents who lived in kitchen-less (and often, window-less) abodes was bound to be popular. The teleological drive that seems to make pizza "meant to be" was undone by the real estate market. The same economic pressure that drove the poor out into the streets to find cheap, pre-cooked food also made it exceedingly difficult for that food's producers to have enough of a margin (or a high enough volume) to pay the rent at the end of the month. Mattozzi's pizzeria owners were in a perennially precarious position between running their own businesses and having to work for others. As if the rent were not enough to worry about, pizzerias also often fell to the wrecking ball. As Mattozzi explains, the late-nineteenth century version of "urban renewal" had exactly the same effect on Naples as it did on cities all over the world: the destruction of neighborhoods, bankruptcy of the small businessperson, and displacement of the urban poor. The "Risanamento" (renovation) program that the elite saw as cauterizing a dangerously diseased part of the city becomes, through this book's investigation of its effects on pizzeria location and ownership, a case study for nineteenth-century urban history.

While two of the most frequently-used words in this book need no translation at all ("pizza" and "pizzeria"), it is the third—*pizzaiolo*—that taxes the translator. Pizza maker? Pizzeria-keeper? Pizza vendor? Unlike the product and the place where it is made, the person making the pizza is a linguistic hole in the English vocabulary. I have ultimately left this word (and *pizzaiola*, as there were plenty of women who ran pizzerias) untranslated, and I think it is important to explain why. In addition to tracing taste back to the highly-specialized (and ever-"passionate")

[h]Richard Sennett, *The Craftsman* (New Haven and London: Yale University Press, 2009), 9.

artisan, there is also a vogue for giving climate, soil, and the specific varieties of grapes (or tomatoes, or forage, etc.), a central role—in other words, anything but hard, everyday human labor by people who were struggling against structural realties of the market or society. Terroir, or "the taste of place" as one commentator has ably translated it, makes a futile attempt to square the culinary circle by putting a static, absolute boundary around food's taste.[i] This book is an attempt to render the sights, sounds and tastes of the nineteenth-century pizzeria, and to describe its evolution, and Antonio Mattozzi is careful to avoid falling into the current rabbit hole of terroir. He dismisses any sort of terroirist, boosterish argument that pizza tastes a certain way in Naples (because of the water, because of the volcanic soil, because of age-old traditions that never change), preferring to examine the people who stoked the oven, kneaded the dough and garnished the loaves-squished-round before baking them.[j]

Inventing The Pizzeria is therefore Italian history, food history, urban history, but it is also social history. It emerges from the musty piles of papers to be found in the various Neapolitan archives, read back against the grain to tell stories that the bureaucrats who wrote them never intended to be told. Mattozzi's prose leavens the awkwardly old-fashioned legalese of these documents, drawing on a wide variety of them—police reports, complaints from neighbors, architects' inspections, accounts of fires, official censuses, lawsuits, marriage records, death certificates—to breathe life back into the pizzaiolo, or a composite that resembles of him or her. The result is a social history of the workers (and their workplace, the pizzeria) that have been all but forgotten with the global ascendancy of their product. That said, this cannot be considered a classic social history, as Mattozzi is very careful to remind the reader that the categories that the bureaucrats put people in were the invention of those same bureaucrats. Mattozzi spends considerable time discussing what William Sewell Jr. has called the central problematic of cultural history, "the question of how supposedly natural or settled identities have in fact been discursively established, maintained, and transformed."[k] Indeed, Mattozzi foregrounds the arbitrariness of the categories and the uncomfortable fit of the pizzaiolo within them: pizzerias were somewhere in between bakeries (because they had ovens) and restaurants (because customers were allowed by law to sit and socialize even after they had eaten), and those who worked in them were constantly moving back and forth between these other trades. Mattozzi also discusses two other kinds of pizzaiolo (street hawkers and back-alley producers) who further complicate the documentary record. The pizzaiola, the woman in the pizzeria, is also part of the story, though Mattozzi

---

[i] Amy Trubek, *The Taste of Place: A Cultural Journey into Terroir* (Berkeley, CA: University of California Press, 2008).

[j] For two other attempts to put the social back into taste and question the role of terroir, see Kolleen Guy, *When Champagne Became French: Wine and the Making of a National Identity* (Baltimore: Johns Hopkins University Press, 2003); and Simone Cinotto, *Soft Soil, Black Grapes: The Birth of Italian Winemaking in California* (New York: New York University Press, 2012).

[k] William Sewell, *Logics of History: Social Theory and Social Transformation* (Chicago: University of Chicago Press, 2005), 48.

explains how the documentary record (so focused on male owners) makes us underestimate their actual contribution.

This story is certainly about the pizza as well—but it is primarily about change over time in the places pizzas were made, and about the pragmatic people who worked so hard to make them. It is about high rent and overcrowding, not bucolic vineyards; it is about working-class men and women who labored at the bottom of the social ladder, not highly-respected artisans; it is about a delicious dish that had some good luck, not about success that was waiting to happen. To understand pizza, we have to look beyond the mythical heroes (be they Queen Margherita or "famous" pizzaioli); we have to understand the historically minor significance of ingredients with a special stamp or seal or logo that makes them expensive. We have to look into the nineteenth-century pizzeria, which would be dark but for the light of the oven stoked by the pizzaiolo. We have to see a category of worker that—at least for Anglophones—has been invisible heretofore: the pizzaiolo. I am pleased to have helped cook a delightful-yet-erudite book that adds much to the scholarship on one of the most popular dishes on the planet.

Zachary Nowak
Cambridge, Massachusetts, January 2015

Figure I: *Una Storia Napoletana: Pizzeria e Pizzaiuoli tra Sette e Ottocento* (*A Neapolitan History: Pizzerias and Pizzaioli from the Eighteenth through the Nineteenth Century*). The first edition of the book by Antonio Mattozzi was published in 2009 by Slow Food Editore in their AsSaggi series (edited by the culinary historian Alberto Capatti). On the cover: "Il Pizzajuolo" by Gaetano Dura. Watercolored aquatint, c. 1830. Courtesy of Slow Food Editore.

AUTHOR'S PREFACE

Even a child knows that Neapolitan pizza is one of the world's most popular foods, now found all over the globe. I have specified "Neapolitan pizza" and not simply "pizza," even if the latter term now generically means "Neapolitan pizza" by definition. Italian dictionaries published in the last decades of the nineteenth century always made clear that the word was of Neapolitan origin: "in Naples *focaccia* is called pizza." Why was it important to be so specific? Because pizzas have been made for a long time: all that was necessary was dough with a bit of water and some kind of flour, whether wheat, rice, corn, potato, or something else. Flatten it out and cook it on a flat surface made of stone or iron and you have a pizza or a taco or a gyro or whatever it is called in one of the many dialects spoken on Earth. In Naples this primordial dish was refined and changed and became a delicious meal which everyone liked and which was embraced with such voracious enthusiasm that it became (along with pasta) one of the symbols of Neapolitan cuisine.

This all happened in the first half of the eighteenth century but it took another two hundred years for pizza to escape the city limits of Naples, and a few more decades until the globalization (and unification) of tastes and of habits that have become universal patrimony. That pizza was limited to the area within Naples' city walls has been confirmed by many studies. We only need to refer to two of them. In 1884 the journalist and writer Matilde Serao, in her very polemical book[1] about Naples, put pizza on a list of the popular foods with which even a miserable *lazzarone*[a] could banish his hunger pains. Serao also described how an entrepreneur had tried to start a pizzeria in Rome (about 200 kilometers from Naples). Despite initial success due to the novelty of the food, he had had to close his doors because no one else was interested in the dish.

In 1956 another Neapolitan journalist, Roberto Minervini, in his elegant little book on the history of the pizza,[2] claimed that "it is notable how such singular misfortune hangs over the many attempts thus far carried out by some of our *pizzaioli*[b] to open up shop outside of Naples. Almost all either failed or have not prospered." These assertions of two great journalists of the past cannot but elicit

---

[a] As will be explained below, a *lazzarone* (plural *lazzaroni*) was the lumpenproletariat of the day.

[b] "Pizzamaker" is at best an awkward translation of this word, and fails to convey the fact that makers of pizza in Naples could be either a *pizzaiolo* (male pizza maker, plural *pizzaioli*) or a *pizzaiola* (a female pizza maker, plural *pizzaiole*). The latter indeed occurs frequently in the documents examined, and many poems were written to pizzaiole. While I will use these modern spellings throughout, an *i* in between two other vowels in eighteenth-century Italian became a *j*, hence the original quotes cited here often had the word spelled *pizzajolo* (or even *pizzaiuolo*). This book will use *pizzaiolo* as it the more common form and the one that is closer to Neapolitan pronunciation.

gentle smiles of compassion, given the planetary spread of the pizza in the last few decades. That said, it is an incontrovertible fact that this great culinary creation was the exclusive property of the city of Naples for over two centuries, just like the pizzerias in which it was developed and perfected.

Indeed, in order to establish itself so strongly, pizza needed—in addition to a long period of evolution—two great allies: the pizzeria and the *pizzaiolo*. The presence of both in Naples is yet another confirmation that the phenomenon of the pizza was born in the city. No other place in the world can document, throughout the nineteenth century, officially registered pizzerias: over sixty-eight at the beginning of the century and over 120 by the end. The third element in pizza's ascent (and perhaps the most important) is the environment, in the socio-economic and anthropological sense. This theme demands further comment.

THE ENVIRONMENTAL CONTEXT

Naples is one of the most beautiful cities in the world, with Vesuvius on one side and gentle hills on the other, forming a frame for a gulf that is renowned for an inviting coast, fertile soils, and a mild climate. The area around Naples provides the products that have made pizza the delicious fare that we know so well: tomatoes which originated in the Americas but which found a new "natural" habitat in southern Italy; mozzarella and other cheeses which were produced in the hills along the coast between Naples and Sorrento and were not called "Monti Lattari" (the "Dairy Hills") by coincidence; a kind of lard called *sugna*, an inexpensive condiment that was made by cooking the fat of a pig (an animal common to the Neapolitan hinterland) and which was used for simple pizzas; and olive oil from the numerous olive orchards of the peninsula of Sorrento. In addition to these ingredients, produce from market gardens was fundamental: basil, oregano, and garlic are the basis of the aromas of the two most typical Neapolitan pizzas, the Margherita and the Marinara. Finally, we have to rememeber the gulf's contribution: anchovies, *cecenielli* (anchovy fry, just born), clams, mussels, and the other mollusks that were often used on nineteenth-century pizzas. These products of the land and the sea had something in common that was fundamental for the spread of pizza: they were all very inexpensive, indeed some were considered "poor products," third-rate ingredients. As Alexandre Dumas said, even with a single *soldo*[c] one could buy a slice of pizza and survive to see another day.[3] This brings us to another important element in the popularity of pizza in Naples.

THE SOCIO-ECONOMIC CONTEXT

Naples was for centuries the capital of an important kingdom. Founded around the sixth or fifth century BCE by Greek colonists, it came into the political orbit

---

[c] The *soldo, carlino, centesimo, grano,* and *ducato* (plural *soldi, carlini, centesimi, grani,* and *ducati*) were Neapolitan coins of the nineteenth century that I have left in the original rather than trying to convert them to today's currency.

of Rome,[4] then the Byzantine empire, then became an autonomous duchy, then an important administrative city under Emperor Frederick II Hohenstaufen. In 1282 Charles I of Anjou made it the capital of the Kingdom of Naples, and it remained the capital until 1860, when the Kingdom of Italy came into existence. In the meantime it had been under the Aragonese monarchy (1442–1503), the Spanish vice royality (1503–1707), the Austrian vice royality (1707–34), and lastly the primacy of Charles of Bourbon and his descendants, who reigned (with a brief French occupation, 1806–15), until Italian unification in 1860.[d]

This historical summary is brief because the history of Naples has been studied and described in several thousands of books by numerous scholars, but also by the many foreign travelers (both famous and not so famous), who visited the city between the eighteenth and nineteenth centuries and who wrote down their interpretations of it—all of them true but each different from the next. This was a result of the fact that Naples and its inhabitants, its customs, its vivacity, and its vital force are so diverse that it is almost impossible to capture them in a sentence or even a single volume. The city's history is the result of all of these entanglements and superimpositions of cultures, dynasties, laws, and different habits, so that the social fabric is a outcome of the resulting hybridization. Naples has often been defined either as a palimpsest (an ancient parchment whose words have been erased and rewritten multiple times), or a kaleidoscope that takes on different forms depending on who is looking.

Naples was thus the capital of a feudal kingdom under the Angevins and the Aragonese but then in 1503, as a result of the European wars of that time, the city came into the orbit of the Spanish monarchy. Spain was the most powerful European power of the time, and the Spanish kings, in order to rule their vast dominion, relied on viceroys who concentrated power in their own hands. This situation led to a phenomenon that had enormous consequences for the kingdom, its capital, and its inhabitants: in order to be closer to the capital's power and to try to control it (almost always in vain), most of the feudal lords who had previously been spread throughout the region moved to the capital. They left their feudal lands to administrators who took care of their interests.

This determined a transformation that was first of all in the physical layout of the city, but also in the social structure of the capital. Many buildings were built—some noble palaces, some not—and even more importantly there was massive migration from the countryside, a flow of people that increased every time there was famine (something that was quite frequent). In the course of the sixteenth century the population of Naples increased from 100,000 to 350,000, giving the city the highest urban population density in Europe. Naples was second only to Paris in number of inhabitants, and the latter had a much larger surface area. Neapolitans were forced

---

[d] A visual summary of the dynasties who succeeded each other in the Kingdom of Naples is represented by the eight statues on the principal façade of the Palazzo Reale of Naples, and show the eight progenitors of the dynasties: Roger I of Sicily, Frederick II Hohenstaufen, Charles of Anjou, Alfonso V of Aragon, Charles V of Hapsburg, Charles VII of Naples (a Bourbon), Joachim Murat, and Victor Emmanuel II of Savoy.

to live in a much smaller space, closed in as the city was by the surrounding hills and the sea.

This torrent of newcomers made its mark, irreversibly, on the destiny of Naples. Apart from the nobles, their servants and other families who had resources enough to prosper in the city, the largest group of migrants was composed of poor, hungry farmers, dressed in rags, without jobs or a trade. They flowed into the capital only because they were in any event able to survive because of the government's guarantee to supply the population's basic food needs, especially grain and bread; these products' prices were carefully watched by the government and regulated to keep them at a "political" price (i.e artificially low).

In a city so full of people it was a matter of necessity for buildings to have six or even seven floors, whereas in other European capitals houses were two or perhaps three floors, maximum. This gave rise to real estate speculation that continues to this day. Every hole, every cavern, every nook, even street vendors' stands were occupied at night by a new social group which arose spontaneously in that age, the so-called *lazzari* or *lazzaroni*. The lazzari were dressed in tatters, barefoot, uneducated, unemployed, and homeless; they survived due to the mildness of the climate, the tolerance and kindliness of the rest of the population, but also their constant search for temporary odd jobs, as well as petty larceny or cons. They were always moving, so much that the great Wolfgang Goethe declared that he "had never seen another people more active than the Neapolitans,"[5] an opinion quite contrary to the prevailing one of a lazy, slothful population.

Another problematic phenomenon—unresolved to this day—was a result of the density and the real estate speculation: the *bassi*, the rooms at ground level on the street or around narrow, dark interior courtyards (called a *fondaco*, plural *fondaci*, in Naples) of these buildings. In other cities these would have been shops, warehouses, or stables; in Naples they were (and still are) used as habitations: one room, sometimes two, with no light at all except what came in from a street that in the old part of the city was just a back alley, no wider than two or three meters. These are the famous "alleys of Naples." In a city in which around half the population did not have a stable source of income but rather was forced to take to whatever work or odd job was available, using savviness and subterfuge to make ends meet, imagination and wisecracks developed rapidly. This brings us to the third important context, the anthropological one. Barrels of ink have been spilled describing the character of the Neapolitan. The marvelous natural setting, the fabulous blue sky, pleasing weather, and exceptional panoramas juxtaposed with the daily struggle for survival under difficult (albeit negotiable) conditions made the Neapolitan a cunning dreamer, romantic but pragmatic, kind and violent, but enormously creative. Imagination and creativity were lavished on the invention of new trades. One stood out for being so widespread: that of the *pizzaiolo* and the pizzeria.

Perhaps this long preface seems unnecessary, but it is a context that one needs to understand in order to understand why Naples and Neapolitans are (respectively) the place and the people naturally predestined to create one of tastiest and most popular dishes in the world. Just short of a half a million people were crammed into an area that was a tenth of the size of the modern city, half of these people living in precarious conditions if not outright poverty. It was a place where seeing tomorrow meant being talented at the art of survival. A rich iconography of this period is proof of the invention of new trades: sellers of macaroni, *franfelliccari* (a Neapolitan sweet) vendors, hawkers who sold sulphur water mixed with lemon juice (*acquaiuoli*), hawkers of various snacks (*bazzarioti*), octopus salesman, and those who sold a powerful distilled spirit (*acquavitari*) are just some of them.

Naples had another characteristic: most of the trades (be it commercial or artisanal), were done by hawkers, in other words while walking around the city crying out to advertise one's wares. Everything was sold like this because the capital necessary to open a shop (or even pay the rent for one), was out of reach for most of the hawkers. Thousands of hawkers were on view in the crowded city, one which offered the visitor exceptional beauty and extreme squalor. This contributed of course to folklore, that local color that became the main attraction for the thousands of foreign visitors to Naples in the eighteenth and nineteenth centuries.

The writers who have been interested in the history of Naples—historians and economists, but also journalists—have often not just narrated the history of the Neapolitan people, but have also described the personal lives, activities, and occupations of this variegated populace. The books, essays, and articles that have dealt with these topics are too numerous to count. Among them, however, more than a few were conceived with what we could call purely folkloristic taste in mind. In other words, they seem to have been written not so much to reproduce reality as faithfully as possible, as rather to excite and intrigue the readers and their fantasy. These accounts take readers to a "place that does not exist"—to a place that is at the same time real and imaginary, a place which seems (paradoxically) to be nonetheless perfectly locatable in Naples.

This is because the conditions and the history of the city and its people, the extraordinary beauty here, the city's immense cultural patrimony and—at the same time—its age-old social decay and its backward economic structures are so complex and interwoven as to appear absurd, as if suspended between fact and fiction. Indeed, life, habits, and social juxtapositions are so strident and extreme here that they seem intentionally contrived so as to push whomever trespasses towards the pleasantly reassuring terrain of literary invention. There is a particular narrative approach that follows this path: one that comes up alongside history but looks for the anecdote rather than the document, wittiness and a clever quip rather than the pure and simple narration of the facts, an approach that contaminates the real events with elements that are often legendary and fantastic. In this manner, certain things are presented as "facts"—things which are, on the contrary, simply made up.[6] This book's topic—the pizzerias and *pizzaioli* (pizza makers) of the nineteenth century—is among those which have been the friendliest to this sort of "history." Out of it has come a picture like that of a postcard, where it is hard to understand where the real ends and the plausible begins, so much are the two intertwined.

My intent, above and beyond bringing back the discussion to an acceptable level of documented history, is to contribute a tile to the grand mosaic of which the social

Figure II: "Fabbricante di Franferlicchi" (Maker of Franferlicchi) by Achille Vianelli.
Acquatint (85 x 105mm). Naples, 1832.
From the book *Scene popolari di Napoli: Disegnate da Achille Vianelli con Acquatinta di Witting*. Containing thirty-six etchings, this book is considered the only collection showing popular scenes by an artist of the Posillipo School.
Courtesy of Biblioteca Nazionale di Napoli, MiBACT (L.P. Racc. Nap. III.71).

history of this city is made. Naples, from the unification of Italy up to today, has always been at the center of attention for southern Italian scholars. This has been especially true in the post Second World War era with the general renewal of Italian cultural studies and the use of a more rigorous methodology. The protagonist of our history is a tiny social group, the *pizzaioli*, the people who made pizza. It is a trade that now in Italy alone has over 50,000 pizzerias with 250,000 practicing members; throughout the nineteenth century, though, that number never went over 100–20, but was likely closer to sixty to seventy. This is a laughable number for us today, accustomed as we are at seeing pizzerias on every corner of Naples, of any Italian city and indeed anywhere in the world. It might seem odd if it was not well known that pizzerias started Naples and stayed there to "ferment" (perhaps a word not used in this way in English, but an immediate and appropriate metaphor), for almost two centuries.

This premise was necessary to clarify the methodology of this essay: this is no folkloristic research, nor a celebration, nor a nostalgic congratulations, in the description of a theme that can easily fall into the trap of the commemoration of the stale cliché of "local color." These all fall right back on tracing Naples and pizzerias on that same old postcard, so often the case in the past and indeed even more today. On the contrary, this book will offer the reader a small cross-section of the nineteenth-century city, seen from a particular (albeit limited) point of observation, the "shop of the *pizzaiolo*." From here we will follow the difficult and laborious existence of this restaurateur, his (or her) relationship to the city, to its institutions, laws, police ordinances, the problematic social and environmental context, his status and his collocation in the society of the day, and his (perhaps) happy and (certainly) trying daily creative life. The choice of the nineteenth century as the principal period of the book is because this is the century in which the craft emerges, develops, and prepares itself (however unconsciously) for a leap onto the global scene in the following century

In reality, the development of the Neapolitan pizzerias is a longer phenomenon which runs roughly from the middle of the eighteenth century to the middle of the twentieth. During this whole time, however, pizzerias remained inside the city, where they had a role and an identity ever better known, but of which there were few possessors. Even though some pizzerias had been opened in America by Neapolitan emigrants at the end of the nineteenth and the beginning of the twentieth century, they were isolated phenomenon that did not have much importance. It was only at the midpoint of the twentieth century that Neapolitan pizza, finally pushing beyond the city limits, started to arrive further and further away. It gained momentum and culinary importance until it became that great wave that crashed into literally every corner of the world. The total globalization of pizza and pizzerias has been a reality only of the last few decades of the twentieth century.

The choice of the nineteenth century is due not only to this having been the fundamental period for the process of identification of the craft of the *pizzaiolo*, but also for two other historical events that opened and closed the century. Despite being quite different, both left a profound mark on urban life in Naples: the first was the Neapolitan revolution and the decade of French rule, which renewed the workings of the state and modified social and economic relationships. The second was the dramatic urban renewal in the city center (called *il Risanamento*, "the renewal'), which brought a radical redistribution of pizzerias there.

There are many inevitable problems of such a restricted temporal arc for research, among them the difficulty of finding the very few remaining documentary records. In addition, the pseudo-cultural "historical" incrustations mentioned above do not permit one to distinguish easily between history and invention, between reality and fantasy. Above all, this study investigates something that today is an anthropological phenomenon of planetary dimensions, but which in the past was regarded as being yet another example of "local color." The *pizzaiolo* was seen as just another one of the many Neapolitan crafts, exercised by a category of worker long held to be one of the lowest in the social scale, and even in the field of restaurateurs.[7]

For this research I have primarily drawn on the documents of the Ministry of Police in all of its many "articulations"—the Cabinet, the Prefecture, and the Chief of Police—preserved in the State Archive in Naples, as well as some other sources that I will cite individually. There are two reasons for the use of the police documents. The first is that pizzerias were part of the vast category of "public businesses" and as such were subject to the supervision and the licensing of the police. This is still true today for any business that has a certain number of people on its premises at any given time. The second reason is that during the Bourbon period (except for one brief exception), the police were responsible for the prevention and extinguishing of fires. Because of this, all businesses that had to do with fire, with ovens or in any event with flammable materials were under their jurisdiction and subject to their constant inspection. Indeed, it was the police that were responsible for granting permits to pastry shops, bakeries, pizzerias, and sellers of fried food, but also to those who sold firewood, coal, hay, wine and spirits, not to mention all artisans who worked with metal.

But the consultation of these documents offered another unexpected advantage: it provided, in addition to the data collected, the opportunity to look into a life that appears (sometimes almost palpably), in the various reports that the officers in the neighborhoods sent to their superiors daily. These documents allow us to have a vision of public and private life that is both vivacious and concrete. From literary sources, on the other hand, the nineteenth-century writing about pizzerias operating in Naples offer only a few articles written by men who wanted to illustrate "local customs" (like Gaetano Valeriani, Emanuele Bidera, and Emanuele Rocco) and some references by writers or journalists of the latter half of the 1800s: Alexandre Dumas, Francesco Mastriani, Matilde Serao, and Salvatore Di Giacomo.[8] The former treated the topic above all as an example of local color, whereas the latter writers—though approaching pizzerias from another point of view—described the phenomenon only briefly, never investigating them in depth.

Even less—really hardly anything—was written on the subject in the first half of the twentieth century. Only in the 1950s were a few monographs written, casting their gaze not on the history of *pizzaioli* as a social category, but rather on the phenomenon of the spread of pizza.[9] In those days, just after the end of the Second World War, pizza had begun to travel beyond Europe's borders, destined to become not only one of the most eaten foods in the world but one of the few known every-where by its original name. Today, everyone looks at pizza—and eats it. Pizza has been so thoroughly integrated into eating habits (both Italian and otherwise), that not a day goes by that there is not another article published in the newspaper or a magazine, an article that repeats the same old stories, but not pizza's history.

The three maps included here represent the distribution of the pizzerias across urban space in Naples during the nineteenth century.ᵉ The period under examination is bounded by three dates: 1807, 1860, and 1900. In 1807 the first census of the activities of the Neapolitan population was done on the orders of the king, Joseph Bonaparte. The census records sixty-eight pizzerias—of which fifty-four entries also have the address, as well as given and surname of the owner—spread across the various city neighborhoods. The "photograph" of these locations is visible in the first map, made in 1826 (the changes in the layout of the city between 1807 and 1826 were few). Notable in this map is the almost total absence of buildings of any sort in the coastal part of the Chiaia neighborhood (at the bottom left), as well as in the San Carlo Arena neighborhood (at the top left). The three "historic" pizzerias that will be discussed in Chapter 7 are marked with a star, and are on all three maps.

The second map represents the situation in 1861, the date of the first census after the unification of Italy (1860). There are now more than 100 pizzerias. In both the first and the second maps the pizzerias that were demolished during the massive urban "renewal" begun in 1889 are marked with an x inside of a circle.

In the third map the city appears to have been redesigned, with new arteries that have taken the place of scores of alleyways and old buildings, all demolished. The map shows new pizzerias along these new streets, a number of which (marked by stars) are still open today. The city has expanded: the Chiaia neighborhood, which in 1807 did not have a single pizzerias, in 1900 has fourteen. The San Carlo Arena neighborhood (here in the upper right), which also had no pizzerias in 1807, has four in 1900. There is also a pizzeria in the Vomero neighborhood (center left), one that is still active today. Pizzerias have also begun to appear in the new Vasto neighborhood (north of the train station, on the right). In the first decades of the twentieth century the situation changed not so much in the number of pizzerias, but in their distribution across the city's space. After the Second World War, on the other hand, there was a strong increase both in the rate of urbanization in Naples and the in the number of pizzerias.

ᵉ The following maps were created by C. Scott Walker, and the archival images are courtesy of the Harvard Map Collection. While the distributions given here are from 1807, 1860, and 1900 censuses, the actual maps are Andrè De Jorio's 1826 *Plan de la ville de Naples*, De Jorio's 1845 updating of the map and the 1890 *Nuova Pianta di Napoli* published by the Stabilimento Richter. While the maps were not made in the exact same years as the censuses were done, all three more or less accurately represent the city in those years.

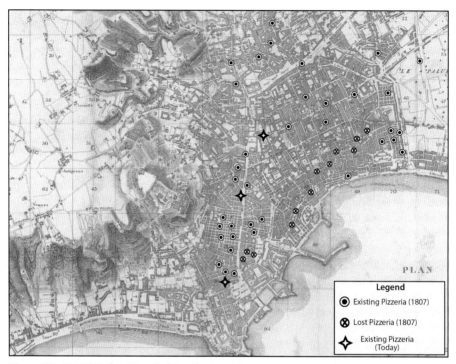

Figure III: 1807 Naples Pizzeria Distribution Map

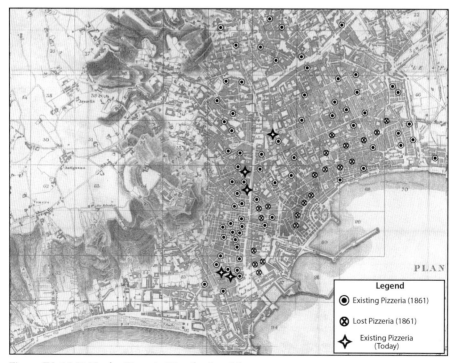

Figure IV: 1861 Naples Pizzeria Distribution Map

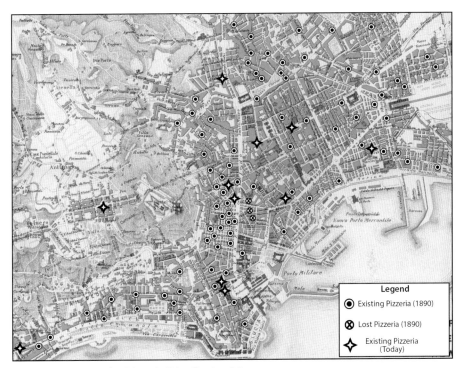

Figure V: 1890 Naples Pizzeria Distribution Map

The origins of pizza and the pizzeria

The precise date that the first pizzeria opened in Naples is not known, nor do we know when the first pizzaiolo was called by that specific name.[1] Their appearance falls under that category of social phenomena—in this case the search for new foods and new tastes—that initially escape the notice of chroniclers and are noticed and observed only when they are already established.

There were surely other types of pizza already produced in the eighteenth century, but they were most likely simple focaccia-type flatbreads prepared in taverns or in bread ovens with various ingredients, cooked on metal sheets or fried in pans. The actual trade of pizzaiolo, one which required a certain kind of shop and had to be done by specialized personnel, developed only in the middle of the eighteenth century. One way we can be sure about this chronology is to examine the hundreds of craft and trade guilds in Naples at that time, even humble guilds like the snack hawkers, undertakers, stable boys, macaroni sellers, fish fryers, the *franfelliccari* (hawkers of a typical Neapolitan dessert), oil vendors who traipsed around the city and tripemongers, to name just a few. Nowhere on these lists do we find pizzaioli: this absence means two things.

The first is that this specific professional category underwent a rather long process of identification because it was included and confused with the wine shop keepers, the tavern keepers and above all with the generic category of bakers. Pizzaioli shared with all these trades the passion and the ability to do one essential thing: prepare food. Perhaps then it was this initially vague identity, in addition to the small number of pizzaioli in the eighteenth century, which hindered the creation of a guild like so many other categories had.

The second thing that the absence means (a result of the first) was that by the time this process of identification had been completed, the guilds had lost their function. They did not draw new members, as they did not offer particular advantages for workers and were therefore already in decline. Leaving aside the guilds, we can see in a 1799 document that both pizzaioli and shops where pizzas were made and eaten were already in existence. This shop would only be called a "pizzeria" well after the middle of the nineteenth century, which underlines the slow development of this sector.

WHY NAPLES?

Matilde Serao, as cited in the preface, had the following to say about pizzerias outside of Naples:

One day a hardworking Neapolitan had an idea. Knowing that pizza was one of the culinary delights of Naples, and knowing that there were many Neapolitans in Rome, he decided to open a pizzeria in Rome. The copper of the bowls glistened, the oven burned continuously and all the pizzas were present: pizza with tomato, pizza with mozzarella, pizza with anchovies and oil, pizza with olive oil, oregano and garlic. At first a crowd came: then it waned. The pizza, removed from its Neapolitan environment, seemed off-key and was a symbol only of indigestion. Its star grew dark and set in Rome; an exotic plant, it died in solemn silence in the Eternal City. And indeed it is true: pizza is in that category of foods that are inexpensive and which is the breakfast or lunch of a large part of the Neapolitan population. The *pizzaiolo* has a shop where, during the night, he makes a large number of these flattened out discs, from a dense dough that burns but does not cook, and is covered with almost-raw tomatoes, with garlic, with oregano, with pepper: these pizzas are cut into many pieces that cost one *soldo* each are entrusted to a boy who walks around to sell them on the street, on a movable table. There he stays the whole day, with these slices of pizza which freeze in the cold, which turn yellow in the sun, eaten by the flies. There are also slices that cost two *centesimi*, for children going to school; when the supply is gone, the pizzaiolo fills the table back up, until late at night. There are also boys at night who carry a large convex tin container on their heads. They carry slices of pizza in them and give a special yell, saying that they have pizza with tomato and garlic, with mozzarella and salted anchovies. Poor women seated on the steps of their *bassi* buy some and have dinner, with this slice of pizza.[2]

In this page the insightful but combative writer summarizes quite efficiently almost all of the themes that someone who wants to analyze this particular aspect of nineteenth-century Neapolitan life has to tackle:

1. The particularity of pizza and the pizzeria to Naples.
2. The fact that pizza was for a very long time "adored" only by Neapolitans and not by others.
3. The umpteenth confirmation that the type of pizza that would be called "margherita" existed long before the supposed date of its birth, which instead goes back decades before 1889.
4. The popular, or even blue-collar, character of this dish.

The chroniclers of the age are in agreement that the Neapolitan "plebes" did not love to cook, but rather preferred to spend their miserable earnings in some greasy spoon, or buying something from one of the hundreds of food vendors who perambulated the city. What the chroniclers missed is that everyday the poor had to face the problem not just of buying food but of cooking it, because of the near-absence of not only bathrooms in the *bassi* and the *fondaci*, but also kitchens. The latter was sometimes improvised by a small cast-iron stove, placed on bricks, out on the street. If we remember that as late as 1902, Francesco P. Rispoli could note that "often the working man does not make food at home, where the angst and the discomfort hardly allow him to sleep, but rather looks to satisfy this necessity at a nearby dive,"[3] it is easy to imagine the living conditions of most Neapolitans. This endemic situation, noted by all chroniclers and foreign visitors, was present in the whole period from the Spanish vice royalty through the Bourbon monarchy and even after the unification of Italy.

Indeed in Serao's time, pizza, or at least a slice of it, was the lunch or dinner of many Neapolitans. Salvatore Di Giacomo, in one of his many articles (always brimming with moral tension), recounted the story of a needy family that had made a deal with a pizzaiolo. Each night, in exchange for a small coin, he gave them the crusts left by other customers during the day; these constituted a lavish dinner for the family.[4] Pizza was often listed as one of the "foods of the poor" by Neapolitan doctors and other promoters of hygiene—including Achille Spatuzzi and Enrico De Renzi to name just two—who began to be interested in the eating habits of the lower classes of Naples before and after Italian unification.[5] The success of pizza in Naples must be attributed to the simplicity of its preparation and to its delicious taste, as well as to poverty, to over population and to the extreme population density in the city.[6]

All of these factors are surely interdependent: because pizza at that time was a very inexpensive product (well known to be made from "poor" ingredients), in order to amortize the overhead of his shop's rent as well as the wages of one or more boys (called *garzoni*) and of course earn his own income, the pizzaiolo had to produce a large number of pizzas every day. The sheer number and the density of people in Naples meant that not only could someone with a shop in the well-trafficked street, Via dei Tribunali (near the courthouse), or near the port, make hundreds of pizzas a day, but so could a pizzaiolo in one of the side streets. Even though the profit from each was small, the number of pizzas allowed the business to be economical. Thus an autocatalytic cycle was created: the low cost allowed the penetration of pizza into any social class, and a large part of the population could get by on pizza given its low cost and its availability.

Naturally the small margin was made up for by the service, the ingredients, and furnishings and fixtures, although this is in a more advanced phase with shops that had side rooms, to be discussed below. The small margin on each pizza also explains why these poor pizzaioli worked until late at night. One other point of departure that Serao's comments on the pizza offer us is the actual denomination of this food, "pizza." The pizza is at the heart of the problem: even if the aim of this book is to trace out the history of the pizzerias and the pizzaioli in the nineteenth century, it is only natural that it investigate their product, the pizza itself.

"PIZZA": THE ORIGINS AND MEANINGS OF THE WORD

Today when we say "pizza" we know what everyone means: the "Neapolitan pizza" that is made at home or eaten in pizzerias, in Naples, in London, in Milan but also in New York. Pizza is a loaf of soft, fresh dough that Italian pizzaioli say is "crushed" (*ammaccata*), that is to say stretched out into a flat, round disc. It is then garnished with oil and tomatoes, and then with mozzarella, oregano, garlic, anchovies or whatever else is desired, and then cooked in an oven. But the word "pizza" in Italian is a generic term that refers to anything prepared and then crushed flat. In the literature of the past we can find numerous references to pizza, often indicating different things, both edible and otherwise: there is the "rustic pizza," the "sweet pizza" (a cake), various types of focaccia, but even certain kinds of cheese and, in more recent (although rapidly disappearing) times, the container that held movie reels. There is even an expression in Italian, "to reduce something to a pizza," in other words to squash or flatten something. The word can also be used to mean "boring" or "stuffy," either attributed to a person or a thing that is annoying or boring, and in Italian one says "What a pizza!" (*Che pizza!*). A word that means one of the most exciting dishes in the current gastronomic universe can also define something diametrically opposed.

Perhaps precisely because of the multiple meanings, there have been numerous investigations into the etymology of the word: *pistis, picea, pizzo, bizzo, pèza, petta, pitta* ... from Latin, from Greek, from a Germanic root or something else entirely. These conjectures across space and time have made people think that maybe pizza goes all the way back to the dawn of time, to prehistory or even to its invention by some mythological divinity, as some sort of dough made of water and flour, cooked on a flat surface or in a rudimentary oven. In poems, in mythological stories, in the ancient and medieval chronicles we find this word in its various forms, with one of its many meanings, including food-related ones.

But the questions that interest us are: when was Neapolitan pizza born? When did pizzerias first open? Who were the first pizzaioli? This is the heart of my research and these three interrogatives should not be separated, or else we risk talking about one of the other possible pizzas. Edmondo Cione, in a delicious chapter about Neapolitan pizza, gives this response to the same question:

> If by "pizza" we mean a generic flatbread that in some countries is called "pizza," I think that we need to go all the way back to primordial human civilization [...] to the Neolithic, or even to the Paleolithic [...] but it's not about these pizzas that we want to speak, but rather that Neapolitan specialty worthy of Jove's table, where it would have appeared had it not required the tomato [...] which had been introduced to Europe from Peru in the sixteenth century but only really cultivated in the seventeenth. On the other hand, I don't believe that pizza was well-known even in the eighteenth century given that I've never found any mention of it in all of the literature in dialect.[7]

In reality the word "pizza" can be found in a number of different texts of the past but it always refers to a type of focaccia different from pizza. We can skip the more scholarly citations (which go back to various historical periods and which are all listed in dictionaries, etymological and otherwise), as well as certain recent monographs and the hundreds of journalistic articles on the subject. The one exception is a quote that is often cited, from G. B. Basile's *Pentamerone*,[8] that Benedetto Croce called "the oldest, richest, and most artistic of all the books of popular fables." In the book Basile includes a novella called *Le due pizzelle*; the word "pizza" is used two other times in the text, once in the introduction to the second day, and also in the novella *Pinto Smalto*. In the novella about the two "pizzelle," though, the word refers to a little focaccia that the mother of the protagonist takes "from inside of a basket with a hook [...] because the day before she had made some bread." In the other two instances the word occurs in a string of made-up words: "ànola, trànola, pizza fontànola," used in a children's game and then in a magic spell. It is clear that this is not a reference to the subject of this investigation. Further back in time but closer to the current meaning, the word is used by a mid-sixteenth-century Neapolitan poet named Velardiniello in his poem entitled *History of One Hundred Years Ago* in which he praises the ages past.[9] Velardiniello says that the pizza then "seemed like the wheel of a cart." This sounds like pizza hawkers who, to call attention to the size (if not the quality) of the product they carried around for sale, yelled out that their pizzas seemed like "carriage wheels."

The question of the earliest possible appearance of the pizza seems to have been resolved by the fact that food historians have confirmed that the use of the tomato in Neapolitan cuisine only goes back to the end of the seventeenth century. In fact, even if it had been introduced a century earlier, it had long been believed poisonous (not to mention an aphrodisiac); these were twin reasons for banning the tomato, which belongs to the botanical family *Solanaceae* (along with deadly nightshade and the extremely poisonous mandrake).

It is not surprising then that the tomato makes only a fleeting appearance in Antonio Latini's book *Lo scalco alla moderna*, published in 1692–4. Latini emphasizes the "extravagance" of the recipe by calling it "Spanish-style Tomato Sauce."[10] The tomato disappears from view, not appearing in any eighteenth-century recipes until Vincenzo Corrado's *Cuoco galante* in 1773. In this first edition and all subsequent ones the tomato is presented almost exclusively as a container for various fillings.[11] Only in the seventh edition (1828) of an anonymous cookbook called *La Cucina Casereccia* was there a recipe for tomato sauce, or more specifically "meat sauce with added tomato" (an early Neapolitan ragù).[12] Not until Ippolito Cavalcanti's 1837 cookbook, *Cucina teorico-pratica*, did tomato sauce find its true partner in pasta, with the first recipe mentioning the two together, "vermicelli with tomatoes."[13]

Even more evidence of the late arrival of the tomato can be found in a receipt for expenses of the Monastery of Montecassino in 1727, on the occasion of a pastoral visit from the pope, published with other documents by Nunzio F. Faraglia who was researching an important essay on the history of prices in Naples. Even in this list, among all of the numerous products—even the smallest, like parsley, oregano, and other herbs—tomatoes are completely absent.[14] Given what has already been mentioned above, and that the tomato is a constitutive element of Neapolitan pizza as we know it today, it follows rationally that the birth of this delicious dish must have occurred in the decades that are just before the middle of the eighteenth century.

THE HISTORY OF PIZZA THROUGH DICTIONARIES AND WRITTEN ACCOUNTS

While it is possible when investigating pizzerias and pizzaioli to turn to documents that have survived—many have been destroyed for various reasons—and are consultable in Naples' archives, the history of pizza itself and its spread is imaginable only through literary sources. These however reveal themselves to be less than credible in that often they describe an exaggeration or "mythologization" of the dish, not its reality. It was not just pizza that inspired this approach, and it was not just journalists or writers of gazettes to take it, but also writers and scholars. "In Naples, as everyone knows, every-thing becomes glorious" wrote Gino Doria in reference to Salvatore Di Giacomo. Doria highlighted the fact that this great poet "in his articles on happenings in the city (good, bad, or neutral), in his descriptions of court cases and in any manifestation of his journalistic activity, sowed the seeds of poetry unconsciously."[15] Given that, it seemed wise for this research to examine (in addition to journalistic accounts) diction-aries—surely more discreet and objective. Naturally it is not the first time that this has been done, but in this case the use of these sources will be chronological. Through both dictionaries and written accounts we can try to follow the tracks of not only pizza's development, but also its spread outside of Naples' city limits.[16]

The starting point is the Neapolitan-Tuscan Dictionary of Abbot Ferdinando Galiani, published posthumously (in 1789) by the academic Mazzarella Farao. For the word "pizza" the dictionary says, "it is a generic name given to all kinds of cakes, focacce, or flatbreads; and thus one appends an adjective to distinguish between them. Here are the principle ones: *pizza fritta* [fried pizza], *pizza a lo furno co' l'arecheta* [pizza in the oven with oregano], *pizza rognosa* [?], *pizza sedonta* [?], *pizza stracciata* [torn-up pizza], *pizza di cicoli* [pizza with pieces of rendered lard], *pizza dolce* [sweet pizza] [...] For any of these the Nuns of our Monasteries are famous." He then adds "It would have been worthy of our zealousness for our homeland to pass down to our descendants an exact description of the preparation of the various types of pizzas. But given that cuisine is a branch of chemistry [...] we did think it appropriate to have them in this dictionary [...]. We believe that the word derives from Latin *pistus*, which since ancient times meant spreading out the dough, whence the words *pistores*, *pistura*, etc... We observe that Italians call our [Neapolitan] pizzas 'schiacciate,' because indeed the most simple of them are simply a piece of dough flattened between the hands and then, with some topping or garnish, put in the pan or the oven."

Aside from my disappointment for the missing description of the preparation of the various pizzas listed, the description of the learned scholar leads us to other deductions: the word "pizza" did not yet have an unequivocal meaning that it would later have, but indicated other types of dishes. In addition, "pizza" did not immediately suggest "pizzeria" or "pizzaiolo" to the author, but rather a convent. This means that the other kinds of pizza were better known but also that pizzerias were still of relatively recent origin, or perhaps that they were still avoided by the higher social classes as being too plebian. The description also shows that "pizza," today a universal word, was then still the exclusive linguistic property of the Neapolitans. The "Italians" called it "focaccia," "schiacciata," "stiacciata." We will see further on, well into the nineteenth century, in the applications that the pizzaioli submitted to the authorities at various bureaucratic levels, we often find the word "focaccia" and sometimes even "torta,"[a] perhaps in order to make the craft seem less plebian.

In 1797 the abbot D'Alberti di Villanuova published his *Dizionario universale critico della lingua italiana* in Lucca, in which only the word "focaccia" (not "pizza") appears. In a second edition of 1804, the word "pizza" is defined as "a sort of dish, or a type of focaccia." It is clear that the word pizza had gone beyond the boundaries of the Kingdom of Naples but the dictionary does not explain what exactly it is. The *Vocabolario domestico napoletano e toscano compilato nello studio di Basilio Puoti*, published in 1841, does not help us much more, although it does definitively identify the pizza: "pizza al forno = flattened dough cooked in an oven = focaccia." Pizza must have been well known in Puoti's school as one of his most illustrious students, the historian of literature Francesco De Sanctis, mentioned it in his memoirs. He wrote that in 1833 (when he was sixteen), "At that time in the evenings we would go to eat pizza in certain rooms at the Largo della Carità."[17] This testimony highlights again that pizzerias had become places to meet and socialize in addition to simply places of production and consumption.

We also find other published mentions of pizza in the 1840s and 1850s:

1. In the evocative article by Emanuele Rocco in the collection edited by De Bourcard, *Usi e costumi di Napoli*, the author punctiliously describes the particulars of the pizzaiolo's shop, with its counter, the bowls with various ingredients, the "little rooms where one eats," the upper room, the oven (always burning) and of course the pizza. "Pizza cannot be found in the dictionary of the Academy of the Crusca, because it is a specialty of the Neapolitans, or rather of the city of Naples."[18] The explanation is important as all of the inhabitants of the Kingdom of Naples—Calabrians, Apulians, Sicilians—were then called "Neapolitans." "The focaccias and the other flatbreads are somewhat similar, but they are the embryo of the art. The most ordinary pizzas, called 'coll'aglio' (with garlic) and 'l'oglio' (oil) have as a condiment oil, and on it one sprinkles, in addition to salt, oregano and finely minced cloves of garlic. Other are covered with grated cheese and garnished with lard, and then a few leaves of basil are added on top. To the former pizzas one often adds small fish; to the latter, thin slices of

---

[a] While *focaccia* always refers to a savory bread, "*torta*" in Italian means either a sweet or savory cake.

Figure 1.1: "Il Pizzajuolo" by Filippo Palizzi. Etching print (160 x 250mm), Naples, 1858. This print accompanies the text dedicated "to the Pizzajuolo" by Emanuele Rocco in the famous book *Usi e Costumi di Napoli e Contorni*. The two-volume work, edited by Francesco De Bourcard, described and illustrated scenes from the daily life of Naples' lower class. The best writers and painters of the day contributed to the compilation. Courtesy of the Biblioteca Nazionale di Napoli, MiBACT (L.P. IV. 6.5.2).

mozzarella. Sometimes sliced prosciutto, or tomatoes, are used."[19] "In the small hours of the night, troops come to occupy the lurid little rooms of the pizzaiolo [...] Stuck back in one of the little halls, the first person to come to them is not the pizzaiolo but rather the boy from the wine shop next door, who asks them 'Which wine do you command?'"

The arrival of a boy from the wine shop next to the pizzeria, offering wine, seems odd; as we will see further on, it was because pizzerias were forbidden to sell wine unless they were licensed as trattorias.

2. The pages that Emanuele Bidera dedicated to the "bottega del pizzajuolo" in the chapter about "minor occupations" (again proof that there was little consideration given to those who made pizzas) in his book *Passeggiate per Napoli e contorni* of 1847. In the description, Bidera talks about the rooms of the pizzeria where "before me seemed to be an apparatus with the whitest eggs (probably mozzarella, which in Galiani's dictionary were described as "of the size of an egg") and red eggs (tomatoes), that form a mosaic, various species of little fish, and types of dairy products." In the interior room there was an oven that seemed to be "the forge of Vulcan with cyclopses that

moved about the ardent furnace." This last part reminds us that in Naples (for a change) reality had to be garnished with a bit of mythology.

3. *Il Corricolo* by Alexander Dumas describes not the pizzaiolo's shop but rather the pizza hawker (*pizzaiolo ambulante*), who walked around the city and sold pizza in the winter and in the summer became a melon vendor. The walking pizzaiolo was the most noted of the trade, especially for those who were charmed by the colorful, everyday Neapolitan life, with its many walking vendors and their yells. Strangely, while there is a rich iconography of pizza hawker as well as of taverns and trattorias, there has yet to be found a single depiction of a pizzeria of the times (despite numerous studies). Going back to Dumas, it is important to note that in addition to his vivacious description, his text shows perspicacity in perceiving pizza as a complete and inexpensive meal. Just after mentioning the pizzaiolo, Dumas adds that "a pizza that costs two *centesimi* is enough for a man, a pizza that costs two *soldi* can satisfy a whole family."[20] This too is part of the success of pizza in Naples.

4 One discordant voice in the otherwise harmonious choir of pizza-praisers is that of Gaetano Valeriani. In his short story "Porta Capuana," written in 1847 and published in a collection edited by Mariano Lombardi, *Napoli in miniatura*, he asserts that a taste for pizza cannot be "a theme of envy." He describes it as "a dough made of wheat, without yeast [*sic*], and thus extremely indigestible. [...] Sometimes raw tomatoes are put on top, sometimes fish, sometimes cheese [...] and prepared like this they are put in an oven, burned rather than cooked, taken out and eaten. Heaven help us! All one's digestive forces are in difficulty for half a day with this undigested weight occupying them." There are two possibilities here: Valeriani had run into some incompetent pizzaiolo, or he had an instinctive aversion to this food as it was so far from his ancestral tastes—he being a native of Ferrara and therefore only a Neapolitan by choice.[21]

One thing is sure: in the hundreds of accounts and mentions by foreign visitors, aside from Dumas, not a single one discusses this food in depth. If it is mentioned at all, pizza is simply named, without specifying its meaning or its widespread availability. These oblique citations are not simply by the superficial observer, a visitor who simply repeats the usual clichés about local color, the people of Naples and the *lazzaroni*. Even Carl August Mayer (called "the most faithful chronicler of Neapolitan customs" by Gino Doria), a German traveler who lived in Naples at the end of the 1830s, left out pizza.

Lidia Croce, who edited many of Mayer's pieces and published them in 1948 in a book entitled *Vita popolare a Napoli nell'età romantica*, said in her introduction that Mayer's "interest was on all those aspects of the daily life of the people of Naples, and he described with exactitude that which he saw, observed and lived during his long stay in Naples." In Mayer's description of Strada Toledo bursting with people, with carriages, with stationary and perambulatory vendors, the author reports some of the cries: "*Oh che bella cosa!–Pesci! pesci!–Oh che bella pizza–Gelati, signori, gelati,*

Figure 1.2: "Il Pizzajuolo" by Luigi Buonocore. Etching print (105 x 150mm), Naples, 1847.
From *Napoli in miniatura, ovvero il popolo di Napoli e i suoi costumi, opera di patrii autori pubblicata per cura di Mariano Lombardi.* The book collected various accounts of the city's neighborhoods and popular figures, and was illustrated with forty-eight images. Courtesy of the Biblioteca Nazionale di Napoli, MiBACT (L.P. Racc. Nap. III.69).

un grano il bicchere!–Galli! galli!–Belli portugalli! Tutti strillano ..." ("Oh what a
beautiful thing—Fish! fish!—Oh what a beautiful pizza!—Gelato, ladies and gents,
gelato one *grano* per cup!—Chickens! Chickens!—Beautiful oranges! Everyone cries
out."). In checking the original German,[22] we can see that Mayer lists all of the items in
the original Italian, providing a German translation of each in parentheses. Only next
to the phrase "Oh che bella pizza!" is there no translation; evidently it was something
that was completely unknown to Mayer's country people and therefore untranslatable.

Moreover the chapter on foods, not translated by Croce, despite listing various
Neapolitan specialties like mozzarella and ricotta, never cites pizza, which would
certainly have attracted his meticulous gaze. Why? Perhaps the same reason as
macaroni. Despite having eaten it for centuries prior, Neapolitans started to be
referred to as "macaroni-eaters" (*mangiamaccheroni*) only between the eighteenth
and nineteenth centuries, whereas before they have been called "lettuce-eaters"
(*mangiafoglie*).[b] Evidently the same thing happened with pizza, which despite origi-
nating in the eighteenth century was only universally identified with Naples around
the end of the nineteenth century. Before that only Neapolitans talked about pizza,
wrote about it and identified themselves with it.

AFTER THE UNIFICATION OF ITALY

Getting back to dictionaries, which grew more numerous after the unification of
Italy in 1860, we note that all those published in Naples give the usual definition
for pizza as a *focaccia* or *schiacciata*: P. P. Volpe (1864), L. Manzo (1865), E. Rocco
(1869), R. D'Ambra (1873), R. Andreoli (1887), and several others. The dictionaries of Niccolò Tommaseo and Luciano Scarabelli (published in Turin (1871) and
Milan (1878)) give the meaning of the word pizza as "a cheese shaped like an egg"
in the first case and "a kind of cheese in the form of a focaccia" in the second.[23]
Finally in 1905 in the *Dizionario Moderno* by Alfredo Panzini (called "a punctilious
purist but curious about novelties"), pizza is defined as "the vulgar name of a very
popular Neapolitan dish, probably derived from *pinsa*, from the verb *pinsere* =
pestare = to crush." The word "pizzeria" also makes its first appearance in Panzini,
given as "the shop where one makes and eats pizza and other Neapolitan delicacies
like mozzarella, loafs filled with anchovies, etc." Never before had the word
"pizzeria" appeared in a dictionary.

In the early years of the twentieth century a number of dictionaries "for young
people" were published, aimed at spreading the national language among Italian
youth to substitute it for local dialects. Two of these were the *Vocabolario comparato
del dialetto napoletano con la lingua italiana* by Ferdinando Di Domenico (1905)
and the *Vocabolario Napoletano-Italiano per gli alunni delle scuole primarie e
secondarie inferiori* by Gaetano Ceraso (1910). Both listed both "pizza" and the
word "'o pezzaiuole" (il pizzaiolo). The 1922 edition of the now-classic Italian
dictionary, published by Zingarelli, declares the etymology of pizza as uncertain,

---

[b] Neapolitans had been enormous eaters of greens until the late eighteenth century, hence the nickname.
For a further discussion, see Franco La Cecla, *Pasta and Pizza* (Chicago, IL: Prickly Paradigm Press), 2007.

and for "pizzaiuolo" explains that "he who makes and sells pizzas, in Naples." In 1944 P. Sella, for "focaccia," says: "in Neapolitan it is called pizza." Another author, Peruzzi, adds that "Until recently this word was typically Neapolitan [as] when Salvatore Di Giacomo, writing in Italian, used it, he put the word in cursive and gave the Neapolitan spelling, *pizzaria*."[24]

As we can see in the mid-twentieth century, *pizza* and *pizzeria* were exclusively Neapolitan words. But we have reached the Second World War and soon pizza would go beyond not only the city limits but also spread throughout Europe and the Americas—though as we saw before it had already been "exported" sporadically, limited to zones where there were Italian emigrants. In those years many etymological dictionaries were published, although it is difficult to find two that have the same etymology for "pizza." Each author used his or her erudition to find in this or that linguistic context the root or provenance of the word.

The fact that there are few connections with ancient flatbreads, and that pizza is a relatively recent introduction, leads us to reject en masse etymological explanations for continuity. But this is in any event not the place to cover such difficult arguments. It is preferable, while respecting various interpretations, to cut short the discussion and stop at the conclusion of the Zingarelli dictionary (and others): "of uncertain origin." The discussion would be as inconclusive as the date of birth of pizza or the name of its inventor, if ever there was one single one.

Many essays have been written on the etymology of the word "pizza." Discussing or even simply listing them would require a lot of space, and in any event, the fact that the various interpretations contradict each other would render any discussion not only inconclusive but also outside of the scope of this book, which is ultimately about pizzerias and pizzaioli. Professor Alberto Capatti, the former president of the University of Gastronomic Sciences in Pollenzo (promoted by Slow Food), in his essay on pizza, noted that the word "pizza" was found for the first time in a manuscript in the archive of the Cathedral of Gaeta (a city south of Rome). The word had the generic meaning of "product of a bakery." Capatti claims that "the word 'pizza' has poisoned etymologists and tormented food historians" and that "the etymologies proposed and discussed are innumerable—from Greek, from Latin, from the Germanic languages—without clarifying the fundamental question of which product it corresponds to."[25]

As an example of the lack of a definitive conclusion, I will cite four authors. G. Princi Baccini, the renowned and esteemed scholar of Germanic philology, claims in *Germanic Etymon and Italian Itinerary of Pizza* that the word is of Germanic origin.[26] This thesis is rejected by Johannes Kramer, the German-speaking etymologist, who brings the origin back to Italy, listing all of the regional variations. He does not exclude, however, an Eastern European origin (from the Illyric word "pita"). This in turn provoked responses from two other respected scholars, Mario Alinei and Ephram Nissan, who with careful argumentation derived the word from the various languages spoken around the vast area of the Middle East— Aramaic, Semitic, Syriac, Greek, Byzantine—that arrived in Italy through the Balkan peninsula.[27] The etymology of the word "pizza" remains, in the end, of obscure origin.

2

Censuses and statistics: Pizzaioli in their social context

THE FIRST DOCUMENTS

On August 12, 1799, among the other dispatches sent to the Head of Police from the Royal Secretary of Justice and Clemency, we find a request from a certain Gennaro Majello. Majello, writing in the third person, explains that "with humble supplications, prostrate at the feet of Your Majesty, explains how for calamities suffered in the time of the self-styled Republic, having kept his shop closed for many months without procuring a single kernel, practicing the trade of Pizzajolo, could not open his shop for fear the French would eat dinner without wanting to pay, has had to suffer the burden of the expenses of his shop (which are not indifferent), as well as those of his numerous family." To face this situation, Majello, after having sold everything in his house that he could sell, had still incurred many debts, "amounting to around 450 *ducati* owed to many creditors" who threatened to send him to jail. He asked for clemency "in order to be able to satisfy the aforementioned debts" and that way be able to come to an agreement with his creditors—as well as avoiding jail.[1]

Unfortunately, neither the street where the pizzaiolo lived nor the location of his shop are in the request for clemency. In another earlier document there is an address: in 1792 a certain Giuseppe Sorrentino had rented a shop in Borgo del Loreto where, "despite the announced interdiction," he had had "an oven for cooking focacce" built. From the inspection done for the granting of the license it was clear that "the ceiling was held up by old timbers and beams; the space was separated by a simple divider wall from two stalls full of hay and straw. What is more, the shop was not far from the large tower of the Castello del Carmine, where "there were stored more than twenty *cantaja*[a] of gunpowder." The double fear of a possible fire with

---

[a] *Cantaja* is the plural form of the word *cantaio*. It was a Neapolitan measurement of weight equivalent to about 89 kilograms.

the subsequent risk of a devastating explosion moved "His Highness to comand [Sorrentino] to desist immediately" from cooking with the oven.[2]

Returning to Majello we can see that his letter of supplication bears his signature, a rather self-assured autograph; this means that the man had a certain familiarity with writing. The document also tells us—very important to our theme—that in Majello's shop "one ate dinner." In other words it was a pizzeria in the fullest sense, where pizzas were not only made but also consumed. The document also says that the rent was "not indifferent," a constant reality of the Neapolitan market. High rents would be the rule of the whole period we are examining, and likely were the principal cause of the high turnover in pizzerias and other similar businesses, as we will see below.

In the context of historical periodization, this document brings us to the dramatic post-revolutionary period. The French army—an army of occupation likes any other—lost its dominant position and a violent counter-revolutionary reaction began, first from the masses and then from the Bourbon monarchy. After about two years of trials, death penalties, expulsions and confiscations, intended to eradicate the "Jacobin disease" but which led to the almost total disappearance of the Neapolitan intellectual elite (in the capital and the provinces), the city slowly returned to normality. Businesses and individuals went back to normal and new shops and new pizzerias opened.

But Napoleon, now emperor as well as King of Italy, overran Europe and his martial shockwave made King Ferdinand IV of Naples flee to Sicily for the second time. This time in Naples there was not an occupying power but rather a change of dynasty: in place of the Bourbon king of Naples, Napoleon's brother Joseph Bonaparte was put on the throne in 1806. Taking the place of a despotic regime that had become strongly reactionary, the new regime was just as authoritarian but also very reformist. Many political, financial, fiscal, administrative, and judicial reforms were promulgated. Feudal privileges were finally abolished: "The Middle Ages had finally ended" wrote Benedetto Croce, listing the innumerable reforms made by the two French kings, Joseph Napoleon and his brother-in-law Joachim Murat (who succeeded him in 1808).[3]

Naturally this is not the place to discuss the legislation of this period, but we cannot ignore some of the ordinances that are pertinent to our discussion. Even before being nominated king by his brother, Joseph Bonaparte, only several weeks after arriving in Naples, promulgated an edict reorganizing the General Police. A "General Commissioner" was appointed for the city of Naples; in 1808 a decree changed the name to "Prefect of Police of the City of Naples." The Prefect was directly responsible to the Ministry of the General Police and had under him twelve "commissioners," each responsible for one of the twelve neighborhoods[b] the city was then divided into. Among the various responsibilities of these functionaries was that of "monitoring the fairs, markets, food shops, vendors who perambulate the city, etc." In addition, these twelve had the duty to "take measures opportune for

---

[b] The Italian word here is *quartiere*: it can be translated literally as "quarter," awkwardly but accurately as "administrative district" or loosely as "neighborhood."

the prevention or halting of fires." In 1810 a Fire Brigade under the control of the Prefect was organized.

In May 1807 a "law on tax stamps" was issued, in which the need to affix a special tax stamp was decreed: any and all public or private documents needed a stamp, including *patenti*, a kind of license that anyone who practiced a profession or trade needed to have in order to work legally. Each *patente* needed a stamp of a different value depending on the importance of the job: the range went from twenty-five *ducati* for wholesalers; fifteen *ducati* for lawyers, doctors, pharmacists and notaries; ten for all merchants including silk and cloth stores as well as sorbet sellers with a storefront; five *ducati* for any kind of craft or trade "including coffee and acquavite sellers with a shop"; and two *ducati* for the license for bakers.[4]

In enforcing this law, the General Commissioner of the Police of Naples on November 12, 1807 sent the Minister of Finance Roederer a list of names and numbers of all shopkeepers who had a storefront, and "given their art, trade or type of store are not subject to [taxation] by the City Council nor by the craft guilds." It is quite a long list, with the names and addresses of 1,867 shopkeepers divided into categories: 348 hotelkeepers, seventy-eight trattoria owners, 206 coffee sellers, fifteen sorbet dealers, fifty-five pizzaioli, seventeen fryers, 212 liquor vendors, twenty pastry makers, 114 tavern keepers, and many others—all in the thirty-four different categories in need of a tax stamp on their licenses.[5] Our present investigation is of course most interested in the list of pizzaioli, published here. Note that in this list we find neither Sorrentino nor Majello, whom we had encountered earlier.

The particular detail in the letter accompanying the list that it contained those shopkeepers "not subject to [taxation] by the City Council nor by the craft guilds" is probably the reason that we find none of the most famous locations of Neapolitan pizzerias: Port'Alba, Largo della Carità and above all Sant'Anna di Palazzo, which Raffaele De Cesare, writing about the era of Franceso II (1859–60) said "was more than a century old."[6] These pizzerias were probably also taverns or wine shops and as such were subject to another licensing process. To be a tavern keeper, one had to be a member of the relevant guild whereas wine shop keepers had to pay a tax of 30 *carlini* to the City Council.

Comparing this document with the "Statistical Outline of the Population of Naples and its Suburbs" (discovered in the Bibliotheque Nationale in Paris by historian Giuseppe Galasso[7]), we see that eleven pizzerias are missing in addition to the three we have already mentioned, though both documents are from 1807. In fact, in the Parisian document there are sixty-eight pizzaioli, whereas in the Neapolitan list there are fifty-five (fifty-four as one is listed twice, perhaps by mistake). The difference is easily explained when one considers that the two documents have different functions: the French list was created in order to better understand the population and its activities, whereas the Neapolitan list was for taxation on shopkeepers who—it is important to remember—were "not subject to [taxation] by the City Council nor by the craft guilds."

The importance of this document for our present investigation is that it allows us to trace out a first draft of the distribution of pizzerias in the city at the beginning of the nineteenth century. One could make a map not only of pizzerias but also of the pastry shops, sorbetterias, etc., in that the lists contain not only names but also the addresses of the businesses subject to taxation.

PIZZERIAS IN NAPLES IN 1807

Looking at the list of pizzerias in Table 2.1, we immediately see that the pizzaioli are listed by their neighborhood. If we mark these on a map of the period, we have a pizzeria distribution that perfectly corresponds to the population density of the various neighborhoods. We note that there are ten neighborhoods listed, instead of the twelve that the city had been divided into; the two that are missing are Chiaia and San Carlo all'Arena. These two areas had no pizzerias precisely because they were zones with the lowest population concentrations, a fundamental variable (as we have seen) for the survival of a pizzeria.

Table 2.1 Pizzaioli with a shop in 1807

Surname and Name	Neighborhood	Address
Di Mase Vincenzo	S.Ferdinando	Strada Campane, 7*
Pecoranio Antonio	S.Ferdinando	Vico Chianche, 16*
Riccardo Andrea	S.Ferdinando	Strada Carminello, 8
Quagliariello Agostino	S.Ferdinando	Strada di Chiaia, 20
idem	S.Ferdinando	Strada S.Pantaleone, 1
Izzo Gennaro	S.Ferdinando	Vico lungo Trinità degli Spagnoli, 17
Sirij Luigi	S.Ferdinando	Strada Speranzella, 115
Le Noci Domenico	Montecalvario	Vico S.Sepolcro, 23
Paparcone Domenico	Montecalvario	Strada Pignasecca, 24
Ottaviano Gaetano	Montecalvario	Vico Barretta, 28*
Izzo Michele	Montecalvario	Salita Montecalvario
Bozza Domenico	Montecalvario	Vico S.Matteo, 47
Brusciante Filippo	S.Giuseppe	Vico I Gravina, 4
Di Mase Gioacchino	S.Giuseppe	Strada Toledo, 24
Ramaglia Gioacchino	S.Giuseppe	Strada Toledo, 100
Novembre Giuseppe	S.Giuseppe	Largo S.Tommaso, 4*
Piacente Nicola	S.Giuseppe	Vico Carrozzieri a Toledo, 12*
Fedele Orsola	S.Giuseppe	Strada Corsea, 92*
Franceschetti Alessandro	Avvocata	Strada S.Efremo Nuovo, 80
Spadaro Vincenzo	Stella	Strada Misericordiella, 8
Profilia Scuotto	Stella	Strada Stella, 72
Mellone Alessio	Stella	Strada Imbrecciata alla Sanità
Apresta Raffaele	Stella	Cavone di S.Vincenzo
Paparcone Carmine	Vicaria	Strada Porta Capuana, 5
Saporito Saverio	Vicaria	Borgo S.Antonio Abate
Di Massa Nicola	Vicaria	Parrocchia Tutti i Santi
Gioia Raffaele	Vicaria	Strada Porta Capuana, 10

Romito Maria Rosa	S.Lorenzo	Strada Gesù delle Monache, 12
idem	S.Lorenzo	Strada Porta S.Gennaro, 27
Casato Antonio	S.Lorenzo	Strada Purgatorio, 48
Benevenia Arcangelo	S.Lorenzo	Vico Purgatorio, 3
Rosolia Michelangelo	Mercato	Strada Barrettari, 74
Taglialatela Elisabetta	Mercato	Strada Barrettari, 25
Marramarra Vincenzo	Mercato	Strada Annunciata, 1
Gargiulo Gaetano	Mercato	Strada Lavinaio, 60
Persico Domenico	Mercato	Borgo di Loreto, 112
Massa Pietro	Mercato	Str. Madonna delle Grazie al Lavinaio, 20
Ruggiero Antonio	Mercato	Borgo di Loreto, 203
De Caro Domenico	Mercato	Strada Conciaria, 1
Zambrano Catiello	Mercato	Salajoli all'Orto del Conte
Di Giacomo Angela	Mercato	Borgo di Loreto, 225
Vecchione Felice	Pendino	Vico Pozzari*
Capuozzo Rosa	Pendino	Fontana de' Serpi, 12*
Di Pietro Paolo	Pendino	Loggia di Genova
Ottajano Paolo	Pendino	Strada Pendino
Ottajano Gaetano	Pendino	Strada Vicaria Vecchia, 16
Soreca Lucia	Pendino	Strada Vicaria Vecchia
Pendino Elisabetta	Pendino	Strada Nuova Marina
Nardelli Berardino	Porto	Strada di Porto, 20*
Fusco Gennaro	Porto	Strada Ecce Homo, 4
Esposito Salvatore	Porto	Vico Monaco, 4*
Guadino Vincenzo	Porto	Strada Nasti, 25*
Fieno Giosuè	Porto	Strada Porta di Massa, 2
Aprea Antonio	Porto	Strada di Porto, 125*

* Streets that no longer exist because of the "Risanamento" project (see below).

If we now turn to Andrè De Jorio's 1826 map of the city,[c] it is evident that Chiaia was inhabited only along two long streets. The first (on the coastal side) went from the Riviera di Chiaia to Piedigrotta, and had only two rows of houses, many of which were aristocratic residences. The second, towards the interior, left from the Gradoni di Chiaia and ended San Nicola da Tolentino and the Petraio area, a zone that bordered on the countryside. The case was much the same for the San Carlo Arena neighborhood, situated in a corner on the opposite site of the city where there was still more green space than buildings. The neighborhood included only one part of the northern stretch of the Foria road. It also contained a small part of the little concentrations of people in Borgo dei Vergini, the Salita dei Miracoli and the Salita dei Cristallini.

---

[c] This is the first map of the three reproduced at the beginning of the book.

These areas were totally different then from the enormous concentration of the "lower" neighborhoods (Mercato, Pendino, and Porto) which (not coincidentally) were the worst hit in the various epidemics of cholera. Also extremely dense were the so-called "upper" neighborhoods (San Ferdinando, Montecalvario, and San Giuseppe) which represented the administrative center of the city, in that the Royal Palace, the ministries, and (apart from the court) all of the other administrative offices were located there. The majority of pizzerias were concentrated in these six neighborhoods; today only in the three "upper" ones do we find some of the pizzerias (just a few) that were registered as such in the 1807 list, though almost all of them were open until the end of the nineteenth century. For the "lower" neighborhoods, on the other hand, the disappearance is near-total.

The first round of demolitions for the *Risanamento* took place at the end of the nineteenth century, when scores of buildings—and along with them many pizzerias—were demolished. Among these was the pizzeria at Vico delle Campane 7. This little street, parallel to Via Santa Brigida, began at Via Toledo (more or less where the entrance to the Galleria Umberto I is today) and ended at the castle (Castelnuovo), where Via Verdi is now. It had a certain importance, being as it was almost directly in front of Teatro San Carlo. It connected to Vico della Cagliantessa and part of Vico Chianche, which after 1850 was called Vico Rotto San Carlo. For the whole nineteenth century this street was lined with pizzerias and trattorias, as well as the hotel of Signor Moriconi, made famous by Wolfgang Goethe during his Neapolitan stay (and later identified by Benedetto Croce in an article published in *Napoli Nobilissima*).

The pizzeria at Vico Chianche 16 (later Vico Rotto San Carlo) had much the same importance, and the spectators at Naples' most famous theater—along with artists, singers, and writers—frequented both late at night. In the book previously cited, Raffaele De Cesare wrote "two other busy pizzerias were those in Vicolo delle Campane and Vico Rotto San Carlo, where the humble spectators of the theater had their dinners and discussed their impressions of the performance."[8] These streets and their buildings were all razed to make way for the new Galleria Umberto I. Only part of Vico Rotto San Carlo remained, a cul-de-sac (today the Piazza Matilde Serao) created by the Galleria.

Speaking of vanished pizzerias, those of the San Giuseppe neighborhood were very important, as they were also near the theater and administrative districts. Those of the Porto neighborhood were also numerous and quite busy, especially those that were located in Porto Street. In 1894—just before the area was razed—Benedetto Croce wrote an unforgettable piece about the street, then still bustling with people of all kinds, full of stores, of stands, of merchandise for sale.[9] For almost all the other pizzerias of the list, the theme is similar: even if they were not physically destroyed, the transformation of the layout of the city made during the end of the nineteenth, and first decades of the twentieth century, sent many into a decline that ended in disappearance. But others opened in the new areas of the expanding city—in the Amedeo, Vasto, and Vomero neighborhoods. Slowly not only the topography of the city began to change, but also the centuries-old mixing of social classes that had earlier characterized the city: a mixing where nobles and

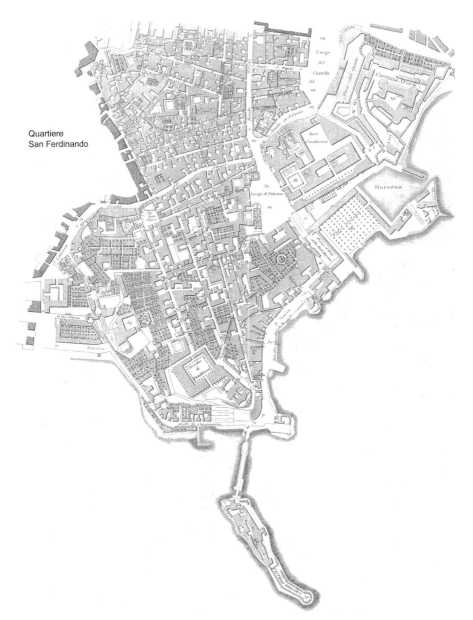

Quartiere
San Ferdinando

Figure 2.1: Detail from the Map of the San Ferdinando neighborhood. Naples, 1804.
From the exquisite *Mappa topografica di Napoli divisa in dodici quartieri* (Topographic
Map of Naples Divided into Twelve Neighborhoods), created by the cartographer Luigi
Marchese.
Courtesy of the Italian State Archives of Naples (Raccolta Piante e Disegni card.1 n°8
Publication authorization n. 21/2014).

plebs, bourgeois and artisans, laborers, and merchants lived together in the same street or even the same building.

In conclusion, today only a tiny number, not even a dozen, of those nineteenth-century pizzerias remain—and of those only a few "famous" ones. The historic map of today's pizzeria sector, both for the pizzerias themselves and the families of pizzaioli, date for the most part from the interwar period, that 1920s and 1930s. Some of the names of pizzaioli have, as we shall see, older origins.

THE EXPANSION OF THE 1800S

In an essay cited above, the historian Giuseppe Galasso compared three censuses of the city of Naples: the French one from 1807, which was certainly done with precision; a second census in 1844, considered more or less reliable among those of the Bourbon period (in which the methods of calculation were various and less precise); and the census of 1871, with Italy then unified. For our present micro-history, of all the data reported in those three censuses, we are only interested in references to pizzaioli with a shop. From the comparison we see that in 1807 there are sixty-eight reported, while in 1844 not a single one is mentioned; this is probably because they were incorporated into other similar categories (trattorias, taverns, wine shop keepers). In 1871, 120 are registered, almost double the 1807 number.

Taking the earliest and latest data (1807 and 1871) as reliable given that they were done with very precise methodologies, the fact that in just a bit more than sixty years the number of pizzerias doubles jumps out at the observer. This is proof that the trade was more and more established, that it had spread into all of the city's neighborhoods, and that pizza had started to become (along with macaroni) the emblem of Neapolitan-ness. Pizza was then eaten and relished by the social classes that had perhaps initially disdained it. It is important to note, however, that growth was not constant and progressive. We can with surety affirm that for more than thirty years, the number of pizzaioli remained almost the same, whereas a boom occurred in the 1840s and 1850s. This boom corresponded to a period of notable cultural and social dynamism whose political consequences were liberal uprisings and the subsequent national unification. All of this had a positive effect on economic activity in general and thus also on pizzerias. In these decades we can find records of changes in the sector: the opening of new pizzerias, the renovation of long-abandoned old ones and the transformation of pastry shops into pizzerias. At the same time numerous trattoria and tavern keepers requested permission to add a pizzeria and even some bakers asked to be allowed to open pizzerias in their bakeries. It was a boom, and we will look at some examples.

In 1842 Giuseppe Corrado opened a pizzeria at Vico Lungo Montecalvario 42. In 1844 Domenico Rippa opened one at Largo Chiodaroli a Pendino 4. In 1845 Nicola Ottaiano started a pizzerias in Strada di Porto 9; this particular location became important immediately. In 1847 Giuseppe D'Arrigo opened a wine shop and pizzeria at Strada Magnocavallo 27. In the same year a certain Gennaro Sarnelli asked for permission to open a pizzeria at Strada Selleria al Pendino 35, a shop which had been closed for ten years. Antonio Sepe, who owned a wine shop in Strada Santa Monica 24, asked to add on a pizzeria.

In 1851, Luigi Paparcone—member of an old family of pizzaioli already present in the census of 1807 but whose traces are lost after the 1860s—reopened a pizzeria at Vico Neve al Pendino 29, a shop with a well but which had been closed for two years. In 1852 Angelo De Marco turned a pastry shop in Vicaria Vecchia 19 into a pizzeria, and Raffaele Iovine [a flour seller] did the same in Strada Trinità Maggiore (today Via Benedetto Croce) 4. The same pastry store-turned-pizzeria story occurred in Via Loggia di Genova 27, where Franceso Rossi has bought the shop of pastrymaker Felice Gaetano. Camillo Giordano, on the other hand, asked to be allowed to use his pastry shop at Via Verde alla Selleria 4 as a pizzeria, but only in the afternoons.

In 1852 Michele Mattozzi renovated the old pizzeria in Largo San Demetrio (part of Via Banchi Nuovi, today Piazzetta Teodoro Monticelli) at number 16–17; this became the "mother" of all of the "Mattozzi pizzerias" opened in the last 160 years. Another pizzeria to remember is the one that Mariano Liccardi made out of a pastry shop in Via Porta Nolana 20. Angelina Caiazzo, in Strada Cedronio 13, did the same with the former kitchen of a pastry shop in 1857; another woman, Anna Della Monica, requested permission for two ovens, one to cook bread and the other "to cook focacce" at Vico Monteroduni 4 and 23, respectively. In 1855 Luigi Papercone (whom we have already met) opened a brand new pizzeria in Strada Foria (in an area still sparsely populated) in a shop with no street number "in front of Santa Maria degli Angeli alle Croci, property of Signor Vittoria."[10]

We could add many more to this list, opened both in the last years of Bourbon rule or the immediately following unification. In the latter period the number of pizzerias continued to grow despite the fact that the expectations of continued development were proving themselves illusory.

PIZZAIOLI IN STATISTICS AND CENSUSES

The examples given here confirm the increase noted in the census of 1871. It bears repeating that this census was done with updated criteria and therefore the data contained is certainly more reliable than that of the Bourbon censuses. These were quite imprecise not only because of the different system used by the census recorders to take account of the movement of the population (something under-lined by many historians), but above all (at least for the sector that interests us) because it was done using estimates or by personnel that were not diligent. This assertion is based on a factual observation which is worth mentioning. During the second Bourbon period (1815–60) an "Office of Statistics" operated in Naples. Its function was to take censuses and collect various statistics on the city, its neighbor-hoods, its hospitals, its prisons, etc. Among these there was also a set of statistics on "the classes of the population," or rather the statistics on the professions and trades practiced in the capital. This was along the lines of the census done by the French in 1807. Despite the French interlude, the merits of having introduced a more modern administrative system were implicitly recognized in that various reforms were left untouched, especially those that had to a certain extent renewed the rusty hodge-podge of the state machinery.

There are still twelve copies of these statistical outlines in the National Library in Naples, transcribed on twelve summary tables that cover the period from 1816 to 1834. Each table is a large square, decorated with artistic flourishes and colored ornamentation (different each year) that are the frame to the series of data displayed. This richly decorated copy was the "bella copia" destined for the eyes of the king. Keeping in mind that there were sixty-eight pizzerias in the French statistics of 1807, we can see that in National Library series there is a large error under the entry "pizzaioli with shop." In the first seven Bourbon reports this number remains more or less constant. In the three compiled before 1819 there are sixty-six pizzerias, then only one added to the next four surveys, between 1819 and 1827. In 1828 there are seventy-two pizzaioli with shops but then suddenly in 1829 there was a miraculous multiplication and the seventy-four that should have been recorded that year became 740, ten times more than the year before. It is obvious that the pen of the compiler added one extra "0" to the count.

We have no idea how many people caught the misprint, but evidently someone looked at the report not solely to admire its beauty, but to read its content. That person saw the error and told the person responsible, who (most likely) decided

Figure 2.2: "Classes of the Population," manuscript with coloration, decorated with gold (560mm x 750mm), Naples, 1828.
Kingdom of the Two Sicilies, General Direction for Censuses and Statistics.
Courtesy of the Biblioteca Nazionale di Napoli – MiBACT (Palat. Banc. 82/4).

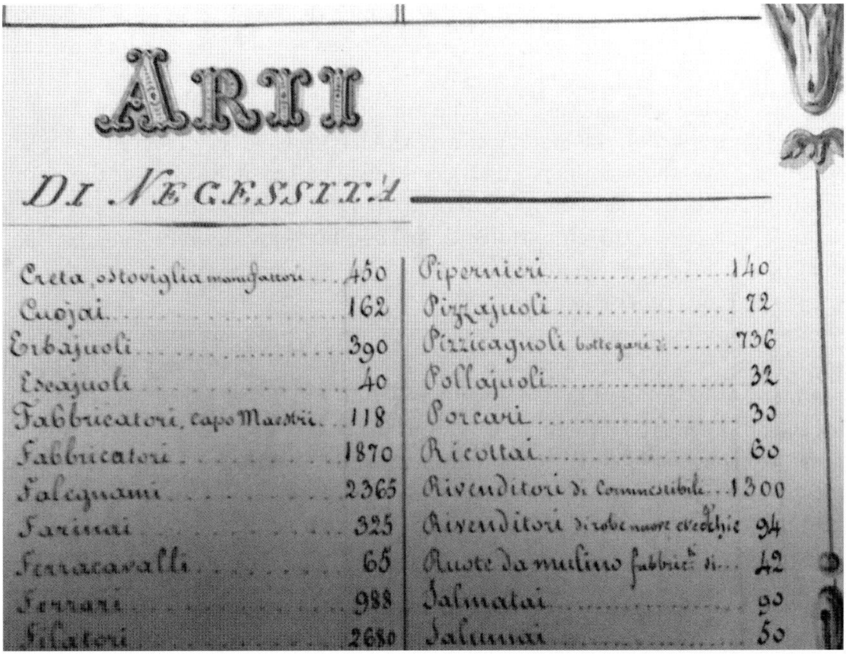

Figure 2.3: Detail: 72 Pizzajuoli.

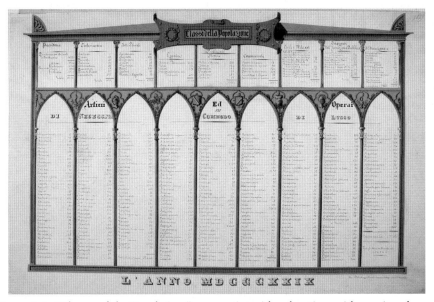

Figure 2.4: "Classes of the Population," manuscript with coloration, with a series of arches that divide the statistical tables (500mm x 750mm), Naples, 1829.
Kingdom of the Two Sicilies, General Direction for Censuses and Statistics.
Courtesy of the Biblioteca Nazionale di Napoli, MiBACT (Palat. Banc. 82/6).

surreptitiously to remedy the error by diminishing the number, little by little, to its actual value. In 1830 there were 700 pizzaioli, then in 1832 (as if struck by a fatal epidemic) their number declines to 450. In 1834 their number is 400. After that we cannot be sure what happened to the number, as both the "belle copie" and the summaries preserved in the State Archive (which both have the error) run only until 1834.[11] Probably the compilers quietly continued to gradually correct the mistake that had been made. One is tempted to think that this is the reason that the entry for "pizzaiolo" disappear from the statistics in 1844 but—as Giuseppe Galasso rightly points out in his essay—many other entries are missing because the trades were incorporated into other categories.

During the Bourbon period, then, the number of pizzerias remained stable for around thirty years. There was then a notable rise in the 1840s and 1850s, parallel to an increase in population and a general period of affluence and well-being. Just after the unification of Italy there was a further period of growth, and the opening of new pizzerias led to their doubling in number. The situation remained the same until the end of the century, when, after repeated cholera epidemics, a number of neighborhoods were gutted and new streets and residential zones were built. Instead of growth, we can see this period as one of a total reordering of the distribution of pizzerias, with a decline in some areas and increase in others.

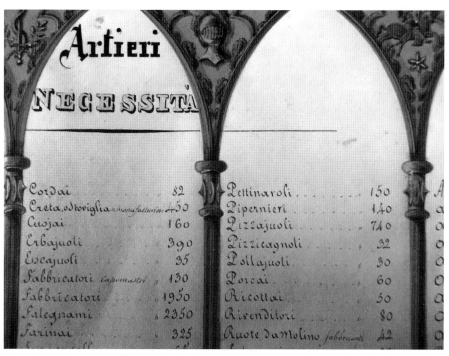

Figure 2.5: Detail: 740 Pizzajuoli.

THE SOCIAL STATUS OF THE PIZZAIOLO

But who was the pizzaiolo, socially speaking? What place did he occupy in the social ladder of the time? Naturally, here we are talking about the artisan himself, the owner and not the boy waiting tables or selling pizza while walking around the city. Today the owners or the managers of a pizzeria are accorded a dignity and a role in the field of food service that they certainly did not have 200 years ago. At that time his position was at the bottom of the heap, socially. His life was one of hard work that was likely not well compensated economically speaking, given that we can find him located in the last class of shopkeepers. These conclusions can be drawn from factual data. In the 1807 law about tax stamps that we saw above, bakers (with whom pizzaioli were lumped together) had to pay only two *ducati* instead of the five, ten, or even more of other professions.

What is more, in 1810 a new law was promulgated, one that "abolished the tax on industry" and ordered a "right to a license for the exercising of commerce, arts and professions."[12] The text of this law is quite interesting in that it contains a very specific list of the professions and trades. Its particular articulation of these allows us to penetrate the universe of the businesses of the time in relation to the presumed profit margins that each was thought to offer. The workers were divided into seven classes each with a corresponding fee to pay. The list went from the first class, which had the producers and wholesalers; their license fee cost seventy-five *ducati* annually, a considerable sum in those days. The second class fee was twenty-five *ducati* and thereafter the fee went down to fifteen, ten, eight, six, and finally four *ducati* for the seventh (and last) class. In order to make a comparison we can extrapolate from this list several categories of people who worked in the food service field, or "subsistence" as it was then called.

We can see that the second class includes, amongst others, the sorbet-sellers, the oil-sellers, and the wholesale wine merchants. In the third class (paying fifteen *ducati*), were the wine shop owners, restaurateurs, owners of trattorias in apartments,[d] and makers of the festive Neapolitan sweet *torrone*. In the fourth class (ten *ducati*) were the *casadogli* and *cacioli* (retailers of cold cuts and cheese, respectively). In the fifth class (eight *ducati*), were the bakers and pastry shop owners, chocolateers, fruit sellers who had a storefront, butchers, sausage and cured meat makers, tavern keepers, and restaurateurs with a shop. In the sixth class (six *ducati*), the coffeemakers, fryers, pastry makers, cured sausage makers, chicken sellers, and fruit vendors. In the seventh and last class (four *ducati*) were those who sold acquavite (a distilled drink) retail, the mineral water with a fixed stand, the sellers of cooked offal, the greengrocers, the fruit vendors with a stand, macaroni sellers, and pizzaioli. For the infinite variety of perambulant vendors (hawkers) or those with just a little stand, there was a total exemption.

As we can see the pizzaioli were on the very lowest rung, together with the macaroni sellers and the vendors of cooked offal, but at the time belonging to this category was a privilege given the great mass of unemployed people, beggars,

---

[d]This strange category will be discussed in Chapter 4.

lazzaroni and the like. Nor would the situation (despite highs and lows) change much in the course of the century. In 1877 the English journalist, Jessie White Mario, in her expose *La miseria a Napoli* would write an incisive analysis of the Neapolitan situation. In 1892 Marcellin Pellet, the French consul in Naples for some years, would highlight in his essay "Naples contemporaine" that the city, with its half-million inhabitants "had a 100,000 needy officials."[13] The list of critics would become long if we add Serao, Francesco R. Rispoli, F. S. Nitti, and many others.

These citations do not seem relevant, but serve to underline the enormous exertion and daily travails that whole generations of artisans and shopkeepers had to bear in order to continue their work and survive in this city. Naples was buried in a perennial contradiction between development and underdevelopment—still true today—despite the many changes that had occurred. This renders the "resistance" of the humble category of the pizzaiolo even more important; with their persistence and work ethic they knew how to pass on the secrets of their trade to the next generation. In doing so, they laid the foundations for a phenomenon that on one hand led to the spread of one of the tastiest modern dishes, and on the other hand created one of today's largest revenue generators.

Returning to the two laws cited above (passed only three years apart), it is important to reiterate the fact that both put pizzaioli in the lowest category of possible earnings. Corresponding to this position was a low place in the social ladder, as well as the pizzaiolo's way of life.[14] It is well known that among pizzaioli, wine shop owners, and other similar professions (coffee makers, liquor dealers), the habit of living in one's shop, in nearby "bassi" or in a small room above the shop, was widespread.

This was the norm of the time in all European cities but while in London and Paris—capitals that Naples was then compared to—the phenomenon declined and then disappeared, in Naples it lasted much longer, due again to the particular urban terrain of the city. On the individual level there were certainly economic differences among pizzaioli, a small social stratification that went from a pizzaiolo who owned other real estate to the pizzaiolo who as forced to change shops multiple times or even to work for someone else, having accumulated debts.[15] But no matter where on the spectrum of the trade, the social status of pizzaioli was certainly not high.

This same social position rendered less likely written accounts of their lives, although it is clear that they were like others in the working class. Following the custom of the times, many pizzaioli brought nestfuls of children into the world. These children then worked in the shops of their fathers, and if only a few went on to become pizzaioli, it was a sign that the pizzeria was not successful. The literary accounts are in agreement with our "popular" conception of the working pizzaiolo. Francesco Mastriani sketched a disarming description in his novel: "Because of his natural shabbiness or because of his trade he followed, he was always dirty; his shirt, rolled up to his elbows, was always stained with splashes of wine he was accustomed to drink in the morning: his hands were always oily from the greasy focaccia."[16] This is a description aimed at sketching out Mastriani's character, the protagonist in a tragic history of an ingenuous and honest pizzaiolo who ended his days on the gallows because of an egregious error in the judicial system (something quite common in those days).

Perhaps some documents with a description of the pizzaiolo's lodgings, his furniture, his personal objects would have come down to us had there been bankruptcy proceedings in their trade. At least heretofore, no such proceedings against pizzaioli have been found, not because they were always able shopkeepers but rather because it was a business for which all of the products were of low value and used daily—apart from the oven and its accessories, which in any event perhaps belonged to the landlord of the shop itself—so that it was difficult to go into debt so deeply as to merit judicial action.[17] There were certainly debts and bankruptcies, but they were never so large as to prevent another pizzaiolo from taking them over, together with the business. It is also easy to imagine that it would have been difficult to recover loaned money from people who were protected by their own poverty.

The absence of the pizzaiolo in his shop in graphic representations unfortunately presents an obstacle to accurately evaluating his dress. Judging from the numerous reproductions of the pizza hawker, their clothes were probably rather shabby and mismatched. Only a few appear a bit more decent, which makes one think that they might be the owner of a pizzeria, one of the "well-off" few. This better-dressed pizzaiolo is depicted with a dignified waistcoat, undirtied pants, nicer shoes and an almost elegant cap that has a tuft hanging down on one side. With his apron rolled up on his waist, he seems to be in a moment of temporary absence from his counter and oven, showing his wares on the stand outside the shop, something one can see even today in some working-class neighborhoods.

In the last two decades of the nineteenth century something new was added to the application for obtaining a license: in addition to the personal particulars (date of birth, etc.), of both parents (absent in the first decades of the century and limited to the father in the last decade of the Bourbon period and immediate period after unification), the profession of the applicant's father was recorded. There are only thirty-nine of these applications, and thus the statistical significance is limited. That said, the data indicate a trend.

Of the applications examined, the father's profession was as follows: five pizzaiolo were orphans, three were sons of pizzaioli, three had a father who was a day-laborer, two were winesellers' sons, two had wine shop keepers as fathers, two sharecroppers, and two carpenters. The remaining professions were: vendors of cooked cod, snack hawkers (bazzariota), cobbler, mule driver, stablehand, stage-coach driver, shipping clerk, plumbers who maintained public water conduits, fruit vendors, civil servant, a type of porter (industriante), street musicians, oyster salesmen, stablehands of the royal stables, fishmonger, painter, coppersmith, and tailor. Some of these occupations—like the bazzariota, a generic snack hawker, or the industriante, who was a versatile—yet normally unemployed porter—belonged to the numerous ranks of Neapolitans who (despite working hard) were only rarely able to climb out of poverty. That said, the other occupations listed here also belonged to that class that made up the majority of the population of Naples.

We are talking about the end of the nineteenth century, though, and something has certainly changed in the city and in the trade of pizzaiolo. Precisely because the

Figure 2.6: "Venditore di Ostriche e Frutti di Mare" (Seller of Oysters and Seafood) by Saverio Della Gatta. Drawing made with stencils. Naples, c. 1820.
In Naples from approximately 1750–1900 there was an extraordinary production of lithographs and etchings, in addition to tempera and watercolor paintings, all showing scenes from everyday life. These were called "Bambocciate napoletane."
Courtesy of the Biblioteca Nazionale di Napoli, MiBACT (L.P. Racc. Nap. III.60).

social origin of those who wanted to open pizzerias was rather modest, attempting this profession was a sign—if not of actual social advancement—at least of economic progress.

PIZZA HAWKERS AND "OGGI A OTTO"

In discussing pizzaioli we cannot forget two figures connected to the trade, but with other roles: the pizza hawker (*pizzaiolo ambulante*, who sold pizza but did not make it) and the seller of pizzas "a oggi a otto," who made pizzas but sold them in return for a payment after seven days. In reality the pizza hawker is only an extra in our cast, as he was a pizzaiolo in name only. His work was limited to selling pizzas of which he knew only the toppings, not the recipe. That is to say that he only knew he was selling pizza "with tomato, oregano and anchovies" or "with tomato, mozzarella and basil," or those even more simple pizzas "with garlic, oregano and tomato" and "lard, cheese and basil." These last two were the cheapest and thus the ones most sold by the perambulatory sellers, who advertised their wares by crying out about their quality, taste, and (especially) price. The price was often lowered, especially when there was not much demand and the pizza risked becoming pieces of ice in the winter or being eaten by flies in the summer (as Serao so clearly described).

Certain owners of pizzerias avoided these inconveniences by furnishing the hawkers with "stoves," a sort of metal container that held a certain number of pizzas and preserved for a time their heat and fragrance. The pizzaioli in question were those that tried to augment their production through this system of external sales; they had a constant relationship with the pizza hawkers, who were almost their employees. Most of these vendors however carried their pizzas on a simple, less expensive piece of wood which, when they stopped to sell a pizza (or a slice of one), they could rest on a foldable sawhorse. They were always ready to close it back up and head off on the hunt for other customers.

As is easy to imagine, we are talking about a trade for which there were no skills required; nor did it take even a minimum of capital, as almost certainly the vendor got his pizzas from a pizzaiolo without paying for them right away, but rather paid his bill at the end of the day. Nonetheless, this is the kind of pizzaiolo most often represented in the iconographic material of the nineteenth century. Not only that, but in all the illustrations the man represented is never listed as "the pizza hawker" (*pizzaiolo ambulante*), but rather simply "the pizzaiolo." Evidently it was the figure that was the easiest to depict, especially by those painters and draftsmen who sought to illustrate the customs and local color of Naples. These artists use as their subjects the most numerous people: the hawkers, a veritable crowd among the Neapolitan trades. It was also these vendors who most attracted the attention of foreign visitors, for whom the reproductions were in any event destined.

This abundance of iconographic material—which derived in turn from a superabundance of human material, because Naples was full hawkers (including pizzaioli)—has generated two misinterpretations, one about pizzaioli and the other about pizzerias. About the former we can cite that great detractor of pizzas, Gaetano Valeriani, whose pizza sat in his stomach. After having written about the indigestability of pizza, he added "There are two kinds of pizzaioli in Naples, one that has a shop […] and the other that walks around the city […] You hate a pizzaiolo who from afar deafens your ears; […] this pizzaiolo sells his pizzas in slices for whatever coin he can get; […] these pizzas for the people often combine the disgusting with the indigestible."[18] After Valeriani there were not a few authors who considered this category of walking vendors—for whom one article for sale was as good as another—the real and true pizzaiolo. Dumas notes this implicitly when he says that the [walking] pizzaiolo sells pizzas in the winter and melons in the summer.

The second misinterpretation was in dividing pizzerias into two distinct categories: those with only a workshop (which should be considered the original ones), and those with tables, which arrived a bit later. In the former (according to one interpretation) only pizzas for hawkers were made. In the second, pizzas were eaten seated at a table, like one does today. This distinction does not seem to be, however, a rigid one. The "shop-pantry" model seems more adapted to a product already well-defined and able to be produced in a sort of assembly line worthy of

Figure 2.7: Raffaele Viviani in "Toledo di notte" (Toledo by Night). Gelatin photo (170 x
33mm). Naples, c. 1918.
The celebrated actor and playwright playing the role of a pizzaiolo in one of his
comedies. On his head he is carrying a *stufa* (stove), the cylindrical tin container used to
keep pizzas warm.
Courtesy of the Biblioteca Nazionale di Napoli, MiBACT (L.P. Foto 97).

a modern organization, like some of the American chains in the second half of the twentieth century. We cannot forget however that pizza in the eighteenth centuries was still a product in evolution, probably still prepared in taverns which then slowly turned into pizzerias.

An origin that is so indefinite thus renders improbable such a clear-cut distinction. More likely we can image that, as the dish became more widespread, new shops were opened that did not always have rooms able to host customers who preferred to sit. Given that pizza even today is a food that one can fold and eat standing up in

Figure 2.8: "Pizzajuolo" by Carl Jacob Lindstrom. Lithographic print on ivory cardboard, with watercolor (180 x 230mm). Naples, 1836.
From *Costumi e Vestiture Napoletani disegnate ed incise da Carlo Lindstrom,* a work which contained forty etchings of various popular figures. During his Neapolitan sojourn, the Scandinavian painter also made a book called *Panorama delle scene popolari* using a decorative elongated format.
Courtesy of the Biblioteca Nazionale di Napoli, MiBACT (Sez. Nap. Misc. VIII. C.1/19).

the street, those shops that did not have much space were perhaps limited to selling pizzas in front of the shop itself like macaroni sellers. Many Italian pizzerias do this today, selling slices to passers-by, though naturally with more hygienic display cases.[e]

These same shops then added to their revenues by furnishing pizza to hawkers. At the same time, though, they began to open new shops that were renovated taverns and as such already had tables and either chairs or benches. These new places hosted a clientele that went not only to eat pizza but also to socialize, talk with friends, be with family, or flirt with a lover. This conviviality within the means of everyone became so widespread that in order to offer more privacy, almost all pizzerias (even when they had no "upper room"), had wooden partition walls of various heights. These created little rooms in which the clientele could stay more comfortably. Naturally no one could prohibit the owners of these more important pizzerias to increase sales by working with perambulatory pizzaioli, who remained a very common figure for the rest of the nineteenth century and even beyond.

Another figure ever present in the history of pizzerias in Naples, but who had a more recent appearance, was the vendor of pizza "a oggi a otto" (today for eight). They emerged around the mid-nineteenth century and were pizzaioli who made pizzas and sold them for payment later, a form of credit that lasted a week. It is almost surely this type of pizzaiolo that Dumas, discussing "a oggi a otto," says sold week-old pizzas.[19] In a city with a population that was in a continual struggle for survival and suffered a constant lack of cash, even a credit of a few cents (the cost of a pizza) would be convenient and enjoy a certain favor. That said, it could not be the mainstay of a pizzaiolo with a shop who, had he done this on a large scale or with a certain proportion of his production, would surely have faced bankruptcy. This was the origin of these pseudo-pizzerias which were not real pizzerias and could not be, in that they had neither oven nor tables nor anything else. They were "bassi" (lodgings in the ground floors of buildings), often with no running water, in which large Neapolitan families had lived for centuries.

On a certain day of the week (always the same one), the man of the house (but even more often the woman, if the man worked or was dead or simply not around) after having put out the ingredients, made the dough. She/he placed an improvised counter in the street and then brought out the "focone," a large cylindrical burner with iron feet, fired by coal. The daily production was, perforce, quite limited, first and foremost because only fried pizzas could be made with the *focone* and the pan for frying. The number of pizzas was also quite limited, given that the clientele was restricted to the neighborhood and had to be both known to the pizza fryer and reliable as well.

Above all because the work occupied only a few morning hours of one (or at most two) days, it was ultimately one of the many occasional jobs that made up this minimal economic system that has been defined by sociologists as "alley economies" whose "principal characteristic is that of being a closed, clandestine economy, based on a block of houses or an combination of blocks that form an economic island."[20]

Stories have frequently been spun around this figure, especially after the particularly rich description in Giuseppe Marotta's *L'Oro di Napoli*. Marotta had

---

[e] In Italy today, these are called *pizzetterie*.

the intuition to call his comely character "donna Sofia," inadvertently anticipating the actress in Vittorio De Sica's film, played by Sophia Loren. From then on the Neapolitan pizzaiola was identified with Loren's character, the pizzaiola being a reoccuring character in the history of the city. Some journalistic accounts have even suggested that the "bassi" were the embryos of the first pizzerias, as if they were not two totally different phenomena. The two locations of production have in common only the name of the product and the socio-economic context in which they began.

It is important to highlight this distinction: the name of the product but not the product itself. Even though both produced pizzas, in the *basso* version the only pizza that could be made was fried pizza, one that could be made anywhere, even at home. In Neapolitan pizzerias, on the other hand, they made the real Neapolitan pizza, the one cooked in an oven, and one which needed a specially equipped room and trained personnel. Naturally we cannot exclude the possibility that some part-time street pizzaiolo fell in love with the trade and started a real pizzeria but— apart from these special cases—the two things need to be distinguished one from another. What they shared was the social context and the density of the population of Naples; aside from that the two phenomena had completely different trajectories and aims.

PIZZAIOLE

In this particular way of making and selling pizzas (the *basso* version), women were certainly more numerous than men. Often, whether because her husband was out of work, in jail, or even dead, it was left to the woman to keep the family afloat. Unfortunately there are no traces of this work in the documents considered here because selling pizzas like this was precarious and occasional—even homemade, in that it took place in the *basso*. The house at ground level could become a little shop with minimal changes. All that was necessary was to take the tools of trade—the table and the little burner—outside, and to stretch out the dough made earlier, and garnish it with the ingredients that were typical to fried pizzas; ricotta, mozzarella, and salami.

But women did not just limit themselves to doing this type of "house" work, they also worked in the more standard pizzerias. Indeed, sometimes they ran them. In an era in which the role that was reserved for women was exclusively subaltern, it was the same women who often continued their husbands' businesses after their death, or after his departure from the city for one reason or another. As we can see from the documents listed in the sources at the end of the book, the names of women who worked in the pizzeria trade are numerous. In the 1807 list five of the fifty-four pizzerias where the owner is named are women, and of these five, one is even the owner of two different pizzerias. Surely not all of these women were pizzaiole in the fullest sense of actually working the dough, as we are talking about a period in which the trade was arduous and quite tiring—in the nineteenth century there were no days off, no holidays, or protections for workers like those we have today.

Despite the fact that they were quite obviously skilled, they lacked the most important thing for running a business: legal status. A woman could run a business only if she were a widow or unmarried or, if she were married, if she had the permission of her husband. It is not a coincidence that in the census of 1871 of the 120 pizzaioli with a pizzeria, only three were women, and two of them were widows. During the Bourbon period (but excluding the brief French "parenthesis" of 1806–15), there were seven women working in the pizzeria trade. After the unification of Italy (1860), their number grew notably. Here too we find widows who were pizzaiole: Rosa De Chiara (1885), Carolina Monaco (1888), Maria Nocera (1900), Elisabetta Teodanno (1885). There were also wives of pizzaioli who worked in other pizzerias, though these women were perhaps only legally the owners: Maria Pennino (1876), Luigia Germano (1883), and Angela Pedata (1890). One thing is certain, and that is that tradition gave women the tasks of preparing fried pizzas, serving the tables, or preparing other dishes in those pizzerias which also had other things on the menu. This does not, however, take away their right to be part of the history of pizzerias. One exceptional (though unique) example is the pizzeria at Via Tribunali 35: other than brief periods, there was always a woman who took part in the running of the pizzeria.

3

Licenses and the law

ORDINANCES AND POLICE REGULATIONS

Returning to historical events, it is important to remember that in 1815 there was a dynastic change. After Napoleon's defeat, Joachim Murat was executed and the former king, Ferdinand IV regained his throne. He took the name Ferdinand I after uniting the Kingdom of Naples and the Kingdom of Sicily as the new "Kingdom of the Two Sicilies."

This time there were no executions or exiles, though several months after the king returned, a special decree abolished the Fire Brigade instituted by Murat. This service was given to the demolitions unit of the army, although the Police of Naples still had a supervisory role. It was now the responsibility of the neighborhood commissioners both to prevent and put out fires, in addition to keeping public order, inspecting shops, checking the quality of food (often put up for sale despite the state of decomposition), and all the other normal activities of the police. Apparently this work of prevention was not carried out well, as in November 1821 the Prefect, complaining that the decree had "long since fallen into oblivion," ordered the reprinting of it. He also encouraged the enforcement of the decree, "given that the period [of the year] when the lard was rendered and sausages were smoked," in addition to the start of the work of the "sanguinacciari" (who made a sort of dessert from pig's blood mixed with chocolate).[1]

Unfortunately, apart from the statistics already cited, there was a long period up to the 1830s in which documentation relating to pizzerias is almost entirely absent. Among the few documents that have survived is a report from Commissioner Pendino from 1821. The document discusses inspections made in "trattorias, taverns and pizza bakeries" for copper utensils discovered to be "either untinned or worn down" and cites (along with several taverns) "the pizza bakery of Pasquale Salvati," though it lists neither address nor any other information. The year after the fire prevention inspections began again we have the first description of a pizzeria, one belonging to Teresa Santelia, "pizzaiola at Strada Tribunali 35." The description is from the police architect assigned to do the inspection, and he stated that the shop had "three rooms with masonry ceilings" and in the first there was "a wall whose distance from the oven renders it tolerable for use." Evidently the architect was referring to partition walls of wood that separated the booths. Nothing is said about the second room, while in the third there is an oven "of recent construction, whose vent was cleaned ten days ago."[2] It is interesting to note that the architect was due five *carlini* (coins) for his work, though there was an "exemption for the poor," who were among the shopkeepers.

In July 1822 a certain Rose (the last name is illegible), a pizzaiola at Largo San Paolo 72 had "a copper wheel and two tiny frying pans, also of copper" seized from her.[3] Nothing is said about Gioacchino Barone and Raffaele Cuomo, pizzaioli with shops in Strada Barrettari at numbers 74 and 26, respectively. These were clearly shops that were in existence in 1807 even if the numbers listed here do not correspond perfectly. The phenomenon of moving numbers is not so much due to new shops being opened but rather to the imprecision of the inspectors. In addition to getting the street numbers wrong, they also mangled names.[a] Sometimes even the last names underwent temporary changes, even in the same dossier: a different last name in the request, the inspector's report, and the document granting permission.

If the documentation for the pizzaioli in this period is scarce, it definitely is not for related activities, the wine shop keeper and the tavern keepers. They were subject to much more frequent checks by the police, in part because their shops were often frequented by people wanted by the law. This is not to say that the other categories of shopkeepers always had a peaceful relationship with the police: it was a continuous contest with the police to get around laws, rules, and various fees, and the dilapidated bureaucratic machinery could not always keep up with the various tricks—created by real economic necessity—of the shopkeepers.

On August 4, 1826, for example, the mayor of the capital was forced to ask for the help of the neighborhood commissioners to accompany the "inspector of the grain trade" and sanction those who refused to pay the "right of the piazza" (a tax for permission to occupy part of the street or piazza with a stand).[4] In June of the following year the Prefect sent a letter to all the commissioners inviting them to inspect all of the wine shops as word had gotten to him that the wine shop keepers were putting bags of copper inside their barrels "in order to render the wine stronger to the palate."[5]

This is not counting all of the fines imposed for failing to renew a license or (for the wine shop keepers) for refusing to pay the annual fee of thirty *carlini* to the City Council. The situation became farcical, if not dramatic, about the ban on remaining open during holidays, something shopkeepers did because of a tragic economic situation. In January 1815 an ordinance was issued that ordered that on Sunday and all holidays "the artisans or workers of all classes" abstain from work and keep "their factories or shops" closed. The justification hearkened back to ancient philosophers, and stated that "considering that the first obligation is that of fulfilling religious duties," holidays were times which required abstention of manual labor. The only shops not subject to the ordinance were grocers, who had to stay closed only on "the feast of the birth of our Lord" and "Easter of the Resurrection." The law specified that artisans or merchants who had to pass through their shop to

---

[a] This meant that a Francesco could become a Francesca at the movement of a quill.

reach their domicile "could keep half of the door open" but "with the absolute ban on selling even the smallest item."[6]

Therefore there were closed workshops, but with sellers of food open. For the wine shop keepers—who in any event belonged to the second category—there was a unique exception. On holidays, to prevent people from thinking of their own pleasure (or getting drunk or doing something scandalous) on a day "dedicated to our Lord," these shops had to be closed "from the second hour until one at night." During this long interval they could sell wine only "distributing it by way of a little window into receptacles that the customers brought with them, but without the wine sellers distributing [the containers]."[7] From one until five at night they could open their wine shops, but with the obligation of keeping "the doors opened and perfectly illuminated in all of their internal recesses in order to have the wine shop contribute to a better safeguarding of all of the people transiting the streets in the hours here indicated."[b]

SKIRMISHES BETWEEN SHOPKEEPERS AND POLICE

These bans, as we have said, were embraced by neither the shopkeepers nor the wine sellers. In February 1828, in another letter to the commissioners, the Prefect complained that "the precepts of the Church regarding the abstention from manual labor on holidays" had been disregarded "in that the shops of the traders, the makers of combs and scissors, cobblers, hatters and other similar classes remain open in the aforementioned days." He invited the commissioners to intervene "to make them desist from the aforementioned problem."[8] The fines for wine shop keepers not closing on holidays are practically uncountable, and the correspondence between the Prefect and the commissioners, including all the letters and various notices, is ample. What is surprising is the criterion and the means by which the inspectors ascertained that an infraction had occurred.

The inspections were made by overlapping checks: the inspectors from one neighborhood checked on the shops in two neighborhoods other than theirs, perhaps to avoid cronyism. This was all well and good, but in wandering through all of the innumerable streets and alleys of the two unfamiliar neighborhoods the inspector limited himself to indicating only the addresses of the shop found open, not the first or last name of the shopkeeper—perhaps to make the job quicker or to keep the element of surprise by maintaining a low profile. After the rounds the inspector made a list of the street addresses of the shops found to be in contravention of the law, and then sent it to the Prefecture. There, the officials—having no idea whom to notify with the fines—had to send the lists to the neighborhood commissioner with a request to attach the names of the shopkeepers whose shops corresponded to the addresses noted. It is easy to image the confusion that resulted; below are some examples.

---

[b] For the whole Bourbon period in Naples, time was measured in another way. The new day began at nightfall, hence the expression "from one until five at night" meant more or less "from seven in the evening until midnight" for us today.

In a document from around 1840, when Ferdinand II had sought to reorganize the administration of the kingdom, the commissioner of the Vicaria neighborhood sent back a list of the names requested, adding: "I'm obliged to have Prefect note that in Strada Poggioreale there is no street numbering, and therefore perhaps the inspector believed he was taking down numbers for Strada Poggioreale, while in fact they were numbers from Largo Cavalcatoio or Via Casanova. I've indicated here the names and the shopkeepers in these two streets." Notes like these need no commentary.

From the commissariat in the Pendino neighborhood we have these clarifications: "Via Pendino 8 is a gendarmerie station, and is a small closed door. The wine shop is at number 11, not 8." We can find other examples: "At Via Pendino 51 there is no wine shop; that number was noted by mistake [...] but at number 62 there is a wine shop [...] now closed but it remains to be ascertained whether the owner transferred the business elsewhere or simply closed definitively." "In Via Violari the wine shop at number 33 was found to be in contravention though by mistake number 32 was written down [...], the same with the Old Spice Shop at number 18 instead of number 17." "In Vico Cassari at Loggia di Genova 39 it was recorded that there was illegal drinking of wine, but in reality this is a workshop and not a wine shop." The following report was from the San Ferdinando neighborhood: "At Supportico Astuti 28 [...] there has been a seller of vegetables for the last three months." From the commissioner of the Porto neighborhood: "Strada Porto 45. When found in contravention [of the law] there was a wine shop here, now bankrupt. What has become of the shopkeeper has yet to be ascertained. [...] For 'Strada Porto 6' the address should read 'Strada Maio di Porto 6.'"

The ballet of the numbers continued, so every report is an estimate, a ballpark guess. Perhaps the errors were not even entirely the fault of the police officers. The commissioner of the Vicaria neighborhood, in his report to the Prefect, complained about "the guile of the offenders, who have invented a method, in part to obscure the numbers of their shops, others covering them by the doors." The commissioner of the San Ferdinando neighborhood wrote that the shopkeepers often removed the numbers from their shops "in order to incapacitate the public officials in their work of noting contraventions."[9] Perhaps even more often the street numbers were erased by time and neglect, as anyone who is looking for a street address today in the old center or the Quartieri Spagnoli neighborhood can see.

It is clear that there were many errors if the pizzeria of Pietro Calicchio at Sant'Anna di Palazzo, and another one at Vico Campane 7 were fined. Both were pizzerias and therefore enjoyed—along with the wine bottlers, which sold only wine in bottles—the privilege of staying open. There was also the strange case of a wine shop keeper, Maria Parise, who "passed on to a better life long before the fine, which came after her death certificate."[10]

Many examples of poverty emerge from the various appeals presented to the authorities. Raffaele Fabbrocino, who had "the impressive number of nine children in addition to his consort" in order "to live honestly" worked hard to sell "a little bit of wine by the barrel" (in other words by the glass, rather than by the bottle), in a shop at Vico San Carlo alle Mortelle 20. The numerous children (all young) constantly went in and out of the "basso" where Fabbrocino (because of his poverty), had both his shop and his domicile. Fined for having his doors always open, he asked for clemency and the annulment of the penalty. Two months after having been asked by the Prefect for more information, the commissioner of the Chiaia neighborhood responded that Fabbrocino did indeed live with his wife and his children in the shop. He added that Fabbrocino was "squeezed by wretched earnings, and at present has been evicted from said shop for back rent" and that Fabbrocino had gone to live in the Montecalvario neighborhood.[11]

The wine shop keeper Salvatore Varriale was fined for a similar situation for his shop at Largo Pignasecca 8. In his appeal he claimed that he closed the shop on Sundays but his children "seeing themselves closed in, they shout to go outside, not having any other exit but that of the wine shop" and that he "makes so little money from his labors, implores that he be relieved of these heavy fines in order that with this same money he can feed his poor children who languish with hunger."[12] Costanza Cimino, who had a wine shop in Via Nuova Poggioreale 50, was arrested after not having paid a number of fines. Her appeal claimed she had been reduced to a miserable state, something that was confirmed by the commissioner of the Vicaria neighborhood, who added that "at present she works as a domestic in a tavern in Borgo Sant'Antonio Abate."[13]

LICENSES, INSPECTIONS, AND RULES

Poverty, guile, and approximations therefore resulted, even though the police commissioners sought to discipline the trade with reoccurring ordinances. These seem to have had the effect of shouting in the wilderness, given the countless rebukes of the Prefect, complaining about the noncompliance with the laws. In 1828 a new one was promulgated in which it was ordered that all merchants and those who had a trade or art of any kind—and therefore also seamstresses, hat makers, private tutors, bloodletters, and anyone else who wanted to put a sign or a plaque "on their shop"—first had to obtain the permission of the Prefecture. In another law (this time in 1828 but repeating an ordinance of 1823), it was ordered that no one could build "a new oven or kitchen" or open a shop to sell "acquavite, charcoal, wood or any other combustible material" without first having obtained the permission of the police authorities. The request had to be accompanied by the inspection of an architect "who certifies that the construction will be neither dangerous nor opposed to any existing regulations."[14]

In January of 1830 a new ordinance was issued which began by stating that despite the multiple requests for professional inspections, shopkeepers continued to "open wine shops and other stores without the authorization of the police," whereas those in possession of such authorizations had not bothered to renew them. The ordinance directed that "wine shop keepers, tavern keepers, pizzaioli, trattoria owners, restaurateurs" had to present their expired authorization within one month to their neighborhood commissioner to renew it or request a new one. The ordinance added that "permission to exercise more than one trade mentioned in this present law in the same shop will not be granted" except for certain exceptions that in any event had to be authorized.[15]

Even though they were often ignored by those regulated by them, these ordinances have a certain importance for this research on pizzerias. Reading the numerous architectural evaluations that were attached to the requests allows us a description of many pizzerias, and confirms that in many of them there were "camerini" made from wood, even within the first large room. In addition, these surveys tell us that given the type of activity and the presence of an oven, many pizzerias had two or more rooms, sometimes even with a second floor, but in any event as a bare minimum a single room that was quite large.

The regulation that did not allow more than one trade to be exercised in any one shop confirms what Emanuele Rocco said in the essay cited above: the patrons, "stuck back in one of the little halls, the first person to come to them is not the pizzaiolo but rather the boy from the wine shop next door, who asks them 'Which wine do you command?'" For the whole Bourbon period the sale of wine by pizzaioli was prohibited because selling wine would have been functioning as a wine shop. Shops were not allowed to house two trades, and therefore pizzerias serving wine were illegal. The only exception permitted by the ordinances was when a pizzeria had a license as a trattoria, something found over and over in the records for the 1840s and 1850s. One exception that illustrates the rule is the request, in July 1852, of a certain Margherita Giustiniano. Having been authorized "to use an oven to cook pizzas" at Vico San Pasquale a Chiaia 26 who "implores permission to serve, to those customers who frequent [the pizzeria] to eat pizza, some wine, given the location far from wine shops." Here we find an exceptional situation in an area that was still not densely inhabited and therefore one without many shops.

After the unification of Italy, when commerce was liberalized, pizzaioli were able to have people taste their dishes accompanied by wine that they themselves sold. It was not rare for public officials to continue to associate wine with wine shops; certain authorizations read "pizzeria and wine shop" and then the next year "pizzeria with the sale of wine." Proof of this confusion of one trade with another is given by an order to close shop during an epidemic of cholera in 1884, issued to a pizzeria at Via Banchi Nuovi 16–17. The ordinance had been intended to temporarily close wine shops, but in the general confusion it was applied to the pizzeria, as we can see from the appeal of pizzaiolo.[16] As we will see below, the administrative confusion in the former capital had changed only slightly.

4

Inside the pizzeria and behind the counter

PIZZAIOLI BETWEEN COPS AND OWNERS

The battle that the police conducted on a daily basis against the shopkeepers who broke the various laws passed by different parts of the government in Naples—of which we have seen only a small sample—is common to all countries in all eras. What happened in Naples, especially during the Bourbon period, seems to have been exceptional, whether because the character of the Neapolitans, their socio-economic condition, or for the excessive arrogance and highhandedness of the "ferocious ones" (*feroci*) as the beat cops were called. What is certain is that the most minimal breach could get one arrested, sometimes even the smallest suspicion. There are so many cases in the files that they could fill a whole book, but here we will examine two that are relevant to our topic.

In July 1852 sixteen year-old pizza hawker Carmine Palmentieri was arrested in Via Toledo on suspicion of being a pimp. He was the son of Raffaele Palmentieri, who had been a pizzaiolo at the pizzeria at Strada Speranzella from 1842–4. Carmine was arrested while standing in at the corner of Via Nardones, perhaps while taking a break from work. To get him out of jail the pizzaiolo Salvatore Sangiorgio (probably Carmine's boss, with a pizzeria in Vico Barletta allo Spirito Santo), had to make guarantees for him. In the meantime other people came forward to offer guarantees for Carmine, evidently struck by the fact that the police had abused their power and arrested a young, innocent working boy.

In June 1843 Antonia Ruffo, the wife of a waiter in a pizzeria, Antonio Esposito, was arrested. Antonio worked and even slept at night in the pizzeria at Vico Baglivo Uries 6. Antonia was stopped as she walked down a street in the Porto neighborhood, apparently because (as the report states) it was "a whores' street." She was taken to Santa Maria della Fede—both a jail and a hospital for prostitutes—where she underwent a "surgical examination" but was found to have no diseases or infections. Ruffo was apparently arrested for both her location and because of a report lodged by her husband, from whom she was separated. In this case as well it was the owner of the pizzeria in Vico Baglivo, sixty-four year-old Aniello Buonomo, who had to be her guarantor; she was released to his custody after he had promised to make her live as an honest woman "under pain of himself being immediately arrested in the case of [her] transgression."

The behavior of some of the neighborhood commissioners was quite different from that of their subordinates, perhaps because of a different cultural or class origin, or perhaps simply a gourmand's sympathy for pizzaioli. Even when besieged by protests from the owners of property near pizzerias, they turned a blind eye. There were often complaints lodged against shops with ovens and burners—pizzerias, fry shops, taverns—because they disturbed their neighbors with the odor of frying or the danger of fires. On September 18, 1841 the Prefect received a complaint from the owners of an apartment at Strada Sette Dolori 20 (today Via Pasquale Scura), requesting that he close the oven (run by Pasquale Paparcone) working below their residence as "the locale has wooden beams and is in danger of catching fire."

The Prefect sent the protest to the commissioner of the neighborhood, who responded that the oven was quite old, and added that he remembered "thirty-five years back, as a young boy I lived at the [nearby] Salita Sette Dolori, and I ate the pizzas that the shopkeeper at number 20 made." He then added that "just because these two [people] have acquired apartments above this shop does not mean they have to do everything to take away business from the pizzaiolo, whose shop is also a residence." The commissioner admitted that the ceiling of the pizzeria was made of beams but concluded that the oven was "well taken care of with a hood and attached chimney."

Despite the invitation of the Prefect to inspect the pizzeria, the commissioner dithered until the two owners made further complaints. Finally he called the police architect in, who naturally suggested the appropriate remedial construction. It then came to a counter protest from both the pizzaiolo "against the insinuations received" and the actual landlord of the pizzeria space, who received eighty *ducati* annually from the rent. The latter, on account of the "large expense" that was necessary, asked that he be allowed to put off the construction until the next year, and answered the threat of closure by saying that "it is not right that an owner lose his rent without reasons." But, by this time, many months had passed and the construction had to be undertaken. The next May the architects hired by the police reported to the Prefect that the owner "had had Sicilian-style brickwork done" and that "given this precaution we believe that this shop be allowed to continue though with the obligation to have the chimney cleaned every fifteen days."

Another protest was lodged against the pizzaiolo Giovanni Bianco, at Largo Trinità degli Spagnoli 17, again because of the danger of a fire. The commissioner of the Montecalvario neighborhood (to whom the protest had been forwarded) responded that though the pizzeria was not in his territory, he had gone there nonetheless with police architects. They ascertained that although there were exposed wooden beams, there was no risk of fire because it was quite old and in any event state of the art. Their only recommendation was to keep the firewood and wood shavings away from the oven. When the dossier got to the actual

Figure 4.1: Pizzeria Gennaro Mattozzi, Largo Carità. Naples 1940.
A waiter and some customers eating pizza folded "a libretto."
Courtesy of Donatella Mattozzi.

commissioner of the neighborhood of San Ferdinando (where the pizzeria was in fact located), the tone changed and the recommendation became an obligation "under threat of arrest and closure of the shop."

In 1845 Nicola Ottajano, member of a family that worked in pizzerias during almost the entire nineteenth century, decided to open a pizzeria at Strada di Porto 9. This time it was a nearby shopkeeper who had a warehouse of *acquavite*, and thus for whom the proximity of the oven represented a grave danger. Again it was the commissioner of the neighborhood (Porto) who, along with an architect, went in person to inspect the shop in question. Despite a favorable report, a second look was necessitated by the other complaints that had arrived in the meantime. Ultimately the permission was granted and the business was run magnificently by the Ottajano family until the demolition of the street, as described above. The Montecalvario commissioner, despite being benevolent with the pizzaiolo at the Trinità degli Spagnoli, revoked the license of a fry shop in the Vico Lungo Gelso for the many protests of numerous proprietors who declared that "there was a risk of loss of annual income."[1]

REAL ESTATE INCOME

Annual income from real estate property is an old Neapolitan problem. In Naples, investing in real estate has always been the only business practiced by all of the city's various classes, even by those who were only modestly well-off, and with only mediocre property. The large population and the limited space meant that rent from property had a relatively high yield; this meant that those who had a house or a shop had a secure income, but one that was perhaps not high enough to live on. "In Naples there is still the prejudice that whoever owns property should not do anything else. Being a landlord is here almost a profession. One is content to live, or to struggle through life, with a small income from rents instead of increasing one's income through a professional or commercial activity," asserted Professor Alberto Malghieri, a public official for the municipality in 1889.[2] This "hobo" attitude, which was focused on getting money out of property (whether large or small), led to another serious problem still around today: the neglect in both management and maintenance of property which has contributed to urban decay in Naples.

The high cost of rent in Naples created another unusual phenomenon: every fourth of May (the day that contracts expired), the city became a traffic jam of carts and wagons that transported those few pieces of furniture and furnishings that the less well-off class—in other words, the majority of the population—possessed. Michele Mattozzi, who started the first of the many pizzerias owned by this large family and whose movements we can follow through the municipal marriage registries, was father to eight children. Despite their number, all of them (except for the first two, born in a house at Via Mezzocannone 28) were born in different houses. Two of the children lived only a few months each, and were born in one house and died in yet another. For eight children there were nine addresses, all of which were in the same neighborhood (Porto).

This is only one example of the many analogous cases. The reasons were on one hand the high rents and the meager economic resources of the population, and on the other the second-rate accommodations that offered neither real livability nor comfort, especially in certain areas. Francesco P. Rispoli maintained that "the high rents for lodgings and for shop space for industry or commerce do not in any way correspond to the economic conditions." Citing a French investigator who had studied the conditions of the working class in the Unites States, he added that in New York, "the most expensive city in the world," lodgings cost around half what they did in Naples. He also claimed that this was not to mention the fact that they were larger "commodious, clean, well-lighted, and furnished with heating devices, a bathroom and running water [...] while in Naples ..."[3]

Apart from the late nineteenth-century "Risanamento," it would take until after the Second World War for a partial renovation of the urban built environment. Given these conditions, the hunt for income in the context of the chronic shortage of lodgings was not limited to the owners of houses but even their tenants. Evidently eager to add a few *carlini* to their daily earnings, applications for permission to rent out rooms or beds were sent to the police commissioners from all social categories for all sorts of spaces, including "bassi." In 1843, applications to rent out space were made by "a walking cane maker, a fishmonger, a mason, a seller of acquavite, a scribe, a butcher, a wine shop keeper a painter, a butcher's boy, a porter, a stockbroker, a blacksmith, a waiter, a cobbler, a cheesemonger, a domestic servant, and a carpenter." It is easy to imagine what sort of accommodations they would have been able to offer.

Getting back to the struggle between proprietors of apartments and nineteenth-century pizzaioli, another protest was registered in 1843 against the old pizzeria at Vico Campane 7 because it had "a ceiling of low wooden beams, piles of wooden shavings, wooden tables, and other combustibles." The owners of the apartments above the pizzeria were worried because the shop was below their property, which "stretching out to [Via] Toledo is of quite significant value." There was the usual back and forth of accusations, but the pizzeria had to close in the end and could open only when the remedial construction (which took about a month) was done.

Another complaint by a landlord was made about a pizzaiolo in Via Speranzella 150; the landlord asked that the shop be closed because of the risk of fire, in this case because the "*camerini*" had been built too close to the oven. The complaint against Carmine Di Matteo, tavern keeper and pizzaiuolo at Strada Lavinaio 160, was that he fried "in a public street and inundated the same with a horrible stench." This has already made the complaining landlord lose a tenant, while others threatened to break their rent contracts. In the complaint even the agents of the police were accused of not proceeding against Di Matteo because of "tips." "Everything in the complaint is completely false" was the defense of the commissioner of the Mercato neighborhood in his report to the Prefect. Other complaints were made, leading finally to an inspection which, however, confirmed the legal operation of the shop. Given the spirit of the times, it is hard to say for sure whether the inspections were in good faith or were indeed influenced by "tips."

FIRES

Of course there was no shortage of fires and not only in pizzerias but in bakeries, stables, and even in private homes. These were the result of ignoring ordinances issued by the police in which the first recommendation was to keep chimneys clean. In June 1849 there was a fire in the cellar under the pizzeria of Pietro Calicchio at Salita Sant'Anna di Palazzo 1. This was one of the most famous pizzerias—if not *the* most famous—and as we have already seen, it was mentioned by the journalist Raffaele De Cesare, who said that in the 1890s the street was known as "of Pietro il pizzaiolo." Perhaps because of the nearness of (and visits from) the royal palace or because of the ability of the pizzaiolo, the necessary closure of the pizzeria must have worried the authorities a great deal. In a report by the commissioner of the San Ferdinando neighborhood to the Prefect, we can read that "the vice-mayor of this area convened with me a commission of architects among whom is the police architect Signor Baccigalupi and the chief of the fire brigade Signor Del Giudice, in order to excogitate a means to secure this locale from fire."[4]

Inconveniencing so many important people for a pizzaiolo was certainly not normal for the time. Evidently it was pressing business for the Prefect and other authorities to have the pizzeria reopen as soon as possible. If we remember that De Cesare maintained that Ferdinando II—in addition to macaroni, his favorite dish—loved "all of those unrefined foods which Neapolitans are so eager to eat: cod, sautéed vegetables, caponata spread, mozzarella, pizzas, and vermicelli with tomato sauce," it is not unreasonable to hypothesize that the pressure on the Prefect came from above.[5] The meeting resulted in a report (unfortunately lost) in which everything necessary to secure the pizzeria from future fires was listed; as soon as the work was done, the pizzeria was reopened.

Fate had something else in store for Francesco Giannocca, or "Giannoccola" as he is sometimes referred to. For twelve years he run a pizzeria at Vico Nunzio 3, near Largo della Carità. In the evening of September 1, 1857, a fire broke out in the chimney of his pizzeria. The police commissioner, two inspectors, a clerk, two corporals, and a squad of gendarmes quickly arrived; as all worked to put out the fire, someone cried out that smoke was coming out of the third and fourth floor of the building next door (at number 4). More people rushed to the scene and masons were summoned to break the floor "of the aforementioned stories and rip out the canvas ceiling coverings to impede the spread of the flames." They had reigned in the fire when the captain of the fire brigade, a fire truck, and a platoon of the royal Swiss guards arrived with a rather obvious delay: "they were all immediately dismissed."[6] It seemed that it was all over, and having fined the pizzaiolo and threatened him with the closure of the shop, everyone was getting back to their normal business when flames again came out of the top floor. Everyone rushed back to work and "the beams had to be ripped out" of this apartment as well. With this, the fire seemed finally to be under control. Giannoccola had it much worse than Calicchio. He received a heavy fine and lost the eighty *ducati* that he had given as a deposit to the landlord, Giuseppe Cavalcanti. He also had to pay for rebuilding and remain closed for two months: in the end, perhaps exasperated and bitter, he left the pizzeria. In May 1858 it was rented to Raffaele Carpentieri, who stayed there for many years.

Today the risk of fire is almost nonexistent: pizzerias installing ovens have to follow certain security regulations that certainly did not exist in the nineteenth century. The technology of oven construction has changed as well. In any Neapolitan pizzerias there are also filters in the oven hoods that dramatically reduce the sootiness and harmfulness of the smoke. One thing is certain: in the memories of the oldest pizzaioli, from the immediate postwar era down to today, there have only several small fires that were easily put out by the pizzaioli themselves.

DESCRIPTIONS OF PIZZERIAS

These documents, in addition to allowing us to relive past episodes, are valuable in that they give us descriptions of the actual rooms where pizzerias were located. They do not refer to the marble counters with their bowls of ingredients—more or less like today, with oregano, minced garlic, grated cheese, sliced mozzarella, and the like—but rather the floor plans of the pizzerias, with layouts of the rooms and the "*camerini*" (booths).

We have already seen the pizzeria at Via Tribunali 35, made up of three rooms, so we will move on to others. The shop in Salita Sette Dolori (mentioned above) was rather large: on the left was the oven "sitting on a base and furnished with a hood" while on the right there were "booths for the convenience of the customers, booths that exist by virtue of the wooden partition walls attached to the wall." The pizzeria at Larghetto Trinità degli Spagnoli 17ᵃ was a "basso" covered with beams with a room upstairs for customers. There were no booths in this pizzeria as the main room already offered a certain amount of privacy. The pizzeria at Vico Baglivo Uries 6–7, run in 1844 by Leopoldo Calicchio (one of the children of the famous Pietro), was actually two shops with two back rooms. In the back there was an oven and a fireplace "covered with two separate hoods that came together in a single chimney." This was because the shop was both a pizzeria and a trattoria. In the pizzeria in Via Speranzella 150 there was "a partitioned-off area with tables for the customers, next to the oven"; these were the booths (as we saw before) that because they were too close to the oven, had been the reason for the complaint of the nearby landlords. In this complaint they had written that "the ceiling of the shop is [exposed] wooden beams" and "what's more, numerous booths made from wood have been built on the right side and are next to the oven."

In a report written in 1863 after an inspection of Nicola Ottajano's shop at Strada Porto 9, no booths are indicated but the pizzeria is described as having six rooms: the first two were for the customers, the third had the oven, and the other three were storerooms for the "material necessary for the trade," such as wood, lard, and other things. These "other things" were not specified, the architect was only interested in combustible objects but, given that this was a very busy pizzeria

---

ᵃIn Naples the numbering of a street often continued into the piazza-like spaces (a *largo*, plural *larghi*) where the street widened; thus this refers to the same pizzeria from the 1807 list.

because of its location on a heavily trafficked street, they were probably ingredients. These would have been sacks of flour, containers of various products like tomatoes or dairy products, tools for mixing the dough and other tools and ingredients, all in large quantities given the high daily production.

The pizzeria of Antonio Liccardi at Strada Vicaria Vecchia 8 was also quite large. It is described as having been made up of three rooms; between the first and second there was a set of stairs leading to two other upstairs rooms. Antonio's twenty year-old son Mariano, on the other hand, had rented a pastry shop in Strada Nolana and had turned it into a pizzeria. Mariano's shop had three rooms, the second of which had an oven whereas the third was next to a garden. There's no inspection report for the pizzeria on Largo San Demetrio (perhaps because it was already quite old) but in response to a specific query from the Prefecture, the neighborhood commissioner wrote that the shop had a masonry ceiling. In addition we can deduce from an application to put up a sign that read "Rooms for dinner," as well as the request several decades later from a pizzaiolo to be permitted to sleep in an upstairs room, that there was another room above the principal one.[7] The shop of pizzaiolo Vincenzo Sorano, at Via Loggia di Genova 67, had only one "very long" room. The first half was for the customers, fitted out with "wooden booths" whereas the other half had the oven and a wide masonry hood that covered "almost all of the second section of the aforementioned room." Many other pizzerias in the sample available had two or three rooms.

PIZZERIAS AND TRATTORIAS

The historic pizzeria at Vico Rotto San Carlo 16 (the new name for the old Vico Chianche a Toledo) merits its own section. In May 1857 Giuseppe Niglio applied to be the new holder of the license, having taken the pizzeria over from Pasquale Ferrara. Several days later a certain Antonio Cangiano made a request to start a trattoria on the first floor of entrance of street number 15, "using the hearth to cook meals in the shop below, where there is a pizzeria."

The police architect was sent and he noted that the locale on the ground floor was made up of various rooms; in the first were "booths for the customers" and in the others there was a pizza oven with a hood and chimney. Next to it was a "hearth for burning coal, which is for the trattoria." From the adjacent door marked number 15, one could go up to the second floor, which had "two large rooms and one small one" where the trattoria was. The food, once ready, were taken upstairs "thanks to an internal passageway by the door of the pizzeria." It seems then like a kind of partnership in which, however, it was not clear who took care of the kitchen for the trattoria.

This is not to say that there was any shortage of pizzerias run by the same shopkeeper and in the same place. Already in 1840 (when the archival material becomes more abundant) we find a certain Salvatore Sangiorgio, the same man who had been the guarantor for the young pizza hawker Carmine Palmentieri. Sangiorgio asked permission for a pizzeria license, a license for cooked food, and a license to hang a sign in Strada Nuova Capodimonte, "at the house [owned by] Signor Fiore."

That same year Gennaro Ruocco applied for a license "for the old bakery at Vico Campane 7 and across the street, at number 65, that of a restaurateur." He also requested permission to hang a sign on which was written "Ristoratore e Pizzajolo" (Restaurateur and Pizzaiolo). While Sangiorgio was granted permission, Ruocco's application was rejected; the authorities responded that it was not legal for one shopkeeper to have two businesses, so Ruocco had to put the pizzeria in his brother Antonio's name.

As we can see, the ordinances were sometimes effective: a single shopkeeper could have two businesses only if they were similar and practiced in the same shop. Exceptions were made when the shops were next to each other, but in this case the actual shop rooms had to be separate. In 1842 Domenico Esposito asked for the licenses for a trattoria and pizzeria at Strada Porta Sciuscella 18, with a sign "Trattoria and Pizzeria of Monzù Testa." This was the old pizzeria of Port'Alba that was not cited in the 1807 list. The combination of pizzeria and trattoria was pre-existing, as Esposito had attached two prior licenses authorizing Giuseppe Pacella to have a pizzeria and a trattoria, just as the ordinance demanded. A similar request for the renewal of a license for a pizzeria-trattoria was made the same year by Raffaele Chiosi at Vico Campane 7. What had been denied to Ruocco for two separate shops was however granted to Chiosi because there was a single shop, but also because he had asked for a trattoria and not a restaurateur.

RESTAURATEURS AND TRATTORIAS

At this point some clarification is required to underline that in the past the word "restaurateur" had a different meaning than at present. The restaurateur of today refers to the concept of a restaurant, which at that time was called a "trattoria" (this word today implies a family-run business). The restaurateur in Bourbon times on the other hand—at least according to the ordinances and licenses we have—could only sell "cold foods"; in other words, a limited variety of dishes, somewhat like sandwich shops today, though the owners could offer their customers bottled wine. Because they could be open even on holidays, many wine shops and taverns found it convenient to request a license to be a restaurateur or a bottled wine shop. This became so widespread that the Prefecture sent a circular in 1842 in which it underlined that "the Ordinance in force prescribes the sale only of cold foods and foreign (bottled) wines, excluding our own wines (in carafes)." The circular recommended the commissioners revoke the restaurateur and bottled wine shop licenses from everyone who was found selling "local wines by the glass."[8]

We can see the results by examining the dossier of Luigi Paccone, Strada Foria 17, who was denied a restaurateur license because he was "found to be running a wine shop and a tavern." Not the same for Giuseppe Mugnano (Strada Medina 60), who enjoyed a different outcome: the commissioner's report says that "the shop is a true restaurateur in that it has cold foods for sale [...] and the wine is contained in bottles and not in carafes. Among the wines he has Malvasia, the Moscato of Syracuse, the Bugezza, and Calabrian wine."[9] The case of Domenico Kappler is interesting: in December 1843 he asked for a license for a restaurateur "with the sale of diverse qualities of wines of Sicily and from abroad" at Via San Bartolomeo 51. The authorities responded that he could sell only "cold foods," otherwise he would have to apply for a trattoria license. Kappler did just that but then, ten days later, changed his mind and "giving up the application for a trattoria" asked "to be authorized to run a wine shop."[10]

It is notable that, apart from the citation from Dumas' *Il Corricolo*, the first time the word "restaurant" appears written like this (as in French), in the documents consulted is in the application of a certain Domenico Balboni. In 1847 Balboni, a Roman, asked to be permitted to run a restaurant in an apartment on the ground floor of Strada Chiaia 32. The distinction is important as the 1810 tax stamp law distinguished between "trattorias and restaurateur in apartments" and "taverns and restaurateur in a shop." In 1898 Alfonso Fiordelisi, an enthusiast of Neapolitan history, published an article entitled "Where our grandparents ate" in the magazine *Napoli Nobilissima*. Fiordelisi, talking about the first twenty years of the nineteenth century, made a clear distinction between the "popular" trattorias and the "noble" ones; the latter were often on the ground floor and served a clientele of a higher social level. Authors like Croce, Di Giacomo, Porcaro, and others who wrote about this industry in centuries past always talked about taverns, trattorias, osterias, and inns, but never about "restaurants." The use of the word "restaurant" is thus relatively recent and is pronounced in Naples as in French. Even down into the 1940s the bigshots of the Neapolitan food service sector said *"o restorant."*

The pizzeria business was most compatible with the tavern business. In 1843 Antonio Sepe, a wine shop keeper at Strada Santa Monica 24, requested a license to run a tavern. Once he received it, he asked for permission for "an oven to cook pizzas," which he was granted after the usual inspection by the police architect. There were other trattorias with pizzerias at Vico Baglivo Uries 6–7, Larghetto San Tommaso 6, and Vico Rotto San Carlo 16. For this last address Francesco Cutolo in 1854 asked for the licenses for a pizzeria and a trattoria "in the two upper rooms using the hearth in the lower room." Another combination business was at Vico Fico a San Biagio dei Librai 26, a long alley that connected two important streets. Today it is deserted but in the nineteenth century it must have enjoyed a different vitality, as it was the location of a number of trattorias, pizzerias, wine shops, and other businesses.

WATER AND PIZZAS: WELLS AND AQUEDUCTS

Another piece of information that the police architects provide us with is the presence of wells in the pizzerias, an important topic because it regards one of the basic ingredients in pizza, water. When people in the twentieth century talked about the "wholesomeness" and the success of Neapolitan pizza, they often said it was due to the softness of the water, and in particular the water from the Serino Aqueduct. The only thing they forgot was that the Serino Aqueduct reached Naples in 1885. Does that mean a century and a half of pizzas—made from hard work and sacrifice—should be thrown out?

It is of course impossible to compare today's pizza with that of yesteryear and we will never know if they were better or worse, lighter or harder to digest, softer or less tasty. The writer/journalist Mario Stefanile (who once tackled the question) could not give a definitive answer, though he concluded his essay by maintaining that his ancestors never would have known what they were missing in not being able to eat a pizza made with the water from the Serino. That said, when Stefanile wrote that, the globalization of the pizza was just beginning.[11] Following his line of reasoning, the thousands and thousands of pizzerias all over the world would have to hook up to the Serino Aqueduct in order to make a good product. In the meantime though, the water in Naples does not come just from the Serino but rather from a number of different sources, which means that many of the pizzas in Naples are not prepared using that water anymore.

Getting back to the wells, there are not too many described in the inspections. It is well-known that at that time there was no running water in houses or shops. Writers like Mastriani, Serao, and others often described how poor servants ran themselves ragged with the work of taking water to the houses where they worked. The shop boys had to do the same, although they did not have to climb four or five flights of stairs like the servants. Water was taken from the public fountains or from the wells that were to be found in the entrance halls of noble palaces, in the streets or in the piazzas. Both the fountains and the wells were fed by a series of tubes and subterranean conduits that kept the water at an easily reachable level with their pressure.

The wells were not supplied like today's (fed directly by an aquifer or a cistern), but rather from a complicated system of *"formali,"* a sort of collector placed in strategic positions in the city. These were able to supply both the city and the farmhouses in the periphery through a dense network of channels and pipes. This system was ancient, and many of the tunnels even went back to first century CE, having been used to replenish the supplies of the Roman fleet stationed at Misenum. It is clear that over time it was renovated a number of times and fed by water from several sources. In the mid-nineteenth century though, its water was not only considered insufficient for the ever-increasing needs of the population, but it was also seen as second-rate or even unhealthy. This was due to the age of the conduits and their proximity to an even older and more decrepit sewer system. Sometimes, especially when there were powerful storms, the sewers overflowed and contaminated the water supply.

At the time the city was supplied by two aqueducts: the first was called the Volla (or the Bolla), the second the Carmignano. Both brought water from the Apennines to the coast through many kilometers of conduits and open canals. Once they reached the city, the waters of the Bolla were distributed in the lower part of the city, while the Carmignano went to the middle reaches. The inhabitants of the city who lived on the surrounding hills had to make do with rainwater that was collected in cisterns. There were also urban wells, but these often gave brackish water. The exceptions were the wells at San Pietro Martire, at Santa Barbara and the well known as the "Acquaquiglia," near Santa Maria la Nova—all three wells were in the Porto neighborhood and were considered more or less good. Also good was the "sweet" water from the Santa Lucia well and the one at Leone a Mergellina; the latter was thought to be excellent, so much so that the royal apartments at

Chiatamone were connected to it. The Serino Aqueduct not only brought the city water that was more abundant and healthier but—along with the "Risanamento," begun at the same time—freed the city from the nightmare of future epidemics that had often decimated the city's population, especially the poorest and most numerous.

So only a few pizzerias had a well and the water was not always of good quality. Given this situation one might think that the pizzas in the nineteenth century were even dangerous and perhaps were even the cause of epidemics. Nothing of the sort was true. Today the pizza is considered a safe, healthy food, and it had the same reputation back then. We cannot forget that the pizza requires cooking that never lasts more than 60–90 seconds, but during that it is subjected to temperatures of 450–500°C (850–925°F), the temperature necessary for both fragrance and wholesomeness. It seems difficult to image that at these temperatures cholera vibrio or other similar bacteria could survive. If we then remember the antibodies our ancestors had, we have the whole picture.[12]

In reality, though, not everyone was in agreement about the healthy properties of pizza, and not just because of questions about the water quality. Achille Spatuzzi, a doctor and professor of hygiene at the University of Naples, wrote an essay in 1863 called "On the alimentation of the populace of Naples." After having observed that Neapolitans ate pizza "in abundance" and that there were numerous pizzerias, he added that "these pizzas are often made from dough that because of its long storage has undergone an acidic fermentation; often they are not well cooked and the fats used have gone bad."[13] This was echoed by another doctor, Errico De Renzi, who in a similar essay wrote that "oil is the condiment used by the populace [popolo minuto], lard is the condiment of the better-off [...]. Olive oil is pure fat and contains almost three quarters triolein and more than a quarter margarine." After deploring the fact that the populace ate too many fruits and vegetables, he maintained that "these have scant nutritional value but a low price" which evidently made them more accessible. Even the tomato, which the people used especially in the summer, had "inadequate nutritive power," according to De Renzi.[14]

As we can see the dietary criteria were quite different from today's. The poor tomato—earlier thought to be toxic, then an aphrodisiac—was then considered to have "inadequate nutritive power," along with fruits and other vegetables. All this is easy to understand when we consider that vitamins were only discovered in the first decades of the twentieth century. Perhaps it is easier to understand how the Neapolitan people survived their age-old misery and history's many adversities: the key might have been using olive oil instead of lard, eating lots of tomatoes, other vegetables, fruits, and—especially—enjoying pizza "in abundance." Without anyone realizing it, Naples had long ago discovered what everyone today thinks is the healthiest, most balanced food model: the "Mediterranean diet."

5

Uncertainty and continuity in hard times

STRUCTURAL DIFFICULTIES

As we have seen, one of the difficulties of living and working in Naples was real estate speculation. The fact that 400,000–500,000 people were forced to live in just a few square kilometers, and in an area of violence and oppression, also generated natural conflict as each person sought to find a space of his or her own. The economic gulf that separated social classes aggravated the situation: there were those who had too much on one side, and those who had nothing on the other. Such were the economic barriers and distance between the two groups that it was extremely unlikely—if not outright impossible—to rise from one class to the other. This was due first to the total closure on the part of the upper classes, but above all to the material impossibility of improvement given the enormous disparity in starting conditions. This impossibility created either total resignation or an acute sense of frustration that readily degenerated into violence.

If the propertied classes (both aristocratic and otherwise) were numerically limited, the middle class was also small and therefore had relatively little decision-making power. The vast majority of the population was made up of those who had nothing and who at best were able to live in "*bassi*" or "*fondaci.*" Almost all of these domiciles, as we have seen, had no running water or toilets; even in modest apartments there were only a few rooms with an amorphous mix of adults and children. The chronic lack of lodging kept rents high, even for the most miserable dwellings; rents were also high for shops. High rents for lodgings led to the phenomenon of "4th of May" mentioned earlier, whereas for shops it meant a high turnover in occupants. This was especially true for activities with a low value-added product and a high demand for labor, as was the case for both pizzerias and wine shops.

The fact that running a pizzeria required a certain "specialization" somewhat limited the phenomenon, so that we can find numerous pizzaioli in the records that were able to stay in the same shop for decades, even passing on their business to a wife or child. Just as numerous the pizzaioli who, while continuing in the trade, were forced to constantly change location. It is not clear whether this was because of the high rents, because it was not popular in that area, or simply because they had chosen a trade that demanded both passion and a spirit of sacrifice. The first hypothesis seems more likely, given contemporary reports and the assertions of historians, but perhaps just as important were the skill and the ability of the individual pizzaioli.

HEREDITY OF THE PROFESSION AND INTRAFAMILY CONTINUITY

One thing is certain: in some cases in shops that were long-time pizzerias there was a rotating door of owners, while in others there was continuity not of a single pizzaiolo, but even down through generations of the same family. Two of the most notable cases of long-running pizzerias were Sant'Anna di Palazzo and the one in Via dei Banchi Nuovi. The pizzeria of Sant'Anna di Palazzo was run by Pietro Calicchio even before 1829 (the date when a document records a fire prevention inspection) and most likely dates back to the first years of the century, given that Calicchio was born in 1780.[1] When he died in 1853, the business passed to his son Ferdinando, who was in the trade until 1883. That year he sold the pizzeria to Raffaele Esposito, the inspired pizzaiolo who supposedly baptized the old tomato, mozzarella, and basil pizza the "Margherita." Thus the same pizzeria was in business for at least seventy years.

The pizzeria in Via dei Banchi Nuovi (also called Largo San Demetrio) was run by the same family for over seventy years (from 1852 until 1924). Michele Mattozzi left it to his son Luigi, and his son Vincenzo spent his whole life there. Ferdinando Calicchio left the business in 1883 but his pizzeria survived with other owners. The situation for the Mattozzi's was the reverse: the pizzeria in Via dei Banchi Nuovi was sold after Vincenzo's death in 1924, but the business and profession were continued by his numerous brothers, sons, and nephews in other parts of the city, and the Mattozzis are still in pizza today. Another transgenerational pizzeria was the one at Strada di Porto 9, where Nicola Ottaiano (who had opened it there in 1845) left it in 1878 to his daughter Angela Maria. She in turn died ten years later and the pizzeria passed to her husband, Luigi Malato, and then to their son Giovanni who ultimately sold it to a certain Errico Lombardi. These examples are not rare, and there were many individual pizzaioli who ran their business for years in the same shop.

We have already discussed the Calicchios and the Ottaianos, but both apparently had relatives who were also pizzaioli. In the records we find an Antonio Calicchio (another son of Pietro Calicchio) who ran a pizzeria at Vico Campane 7; Leopoldo Calicchio opened a pizzeria first at Vico Bagliavo Uries (in 1844) and then in Vico Campane (1845–6). The Ottaianos were even more numerous. We can find two in the 1807 list, but others appear in the records for the whole nineteenth century. Mirto Alfonso, an orphan adopted by Nicola Ottaiano, can be added to that list as well; he ran various pizzerias between 1861 and 1877. The Paparcone family was also quite numerous: in addition to the two on the 1807 list, we can find another four family members in the records until the 1860s, most of them in pizzerias in the Montecalvario neighborhood. One of these was the patriarch Pasquale, who had had problems with the property owners above the pizzeria at the Salita Sette Dolori; in 1863, at eighty-one years old, Pasquale was still running a pizzeria in Pignasecca Street. The year before he was mentioned in the archives for something irrelevant to our topic but which we will examine here as it is characteristic of a place and time.

In October 1862 the Reale Stabilimento di Santa Maria Vertecoeli, one of the many institutions authorized by the Bourbon monarchy to collect offerings to be distributed to the poor, told the police chief "because of the necessity of getting back from the hands of the brothers (indicated in the appended list) the collection plate monies," that his authority was needed to make the "brothers" give back the money that they had been refusing to return. In the appended statement we find the name of Pasquale Paparcone, pizzaiolo, Strada Pignasecca 48. Naturally we cannot be sure how the affair ended, but it does not interest us in any event.[2]

Another unusual situation involved Luigi and Gaetano Ceso, father and son, and fifty-nine and thirty years old respectively.[3] In 1876 they asked for licenses for two pizzerias, the father at Via Santissimi Giovanni e Paolo 142 (a suburban area), and the son at Via Lavinaio 160, a street that even today is overflowing with people, full of shops and merchandise for sale. Luigi, the father, before even receiving the license, had already requested permission to move to a shop at Vico 5th Duchesca 15; after less than a year there he asked to move again, this time to Via Magnocavallo 21. He received permission to move the business on June 20, 1877, but he apparently did not like the new location because in August 1878, just over a year later, he requested permission to move his shop yet again, this time to the already-existing pizzeria at Strada Barrettari 74. One would think that in this location—proven by more than seventy years of business—he would finally have been content, but that's not how it went. On 10 June 1879, he yet again requested permission to move, now to Borgo Loreto 48. He probably lasted less than a year there because at this address in 1880 we find a certain Gennaro Longo. In four years Luigi had been in five pizzerias without finding the right one.

His son Gaetano had the opposite experience, perhaps because he was younger and more capable. He seems to have been able to build his customer base in Via Lavinaio, as he renewed his license for a number of years. But the magic spell suddenly ended, whether it was the highhandedness of the father, or perhaps the son had taken work in another pizzeria. Whatever it was, on September 4, 1880 the elder Cesa sent a request to the police chief in which he asked "that attached license of my son be put under my name." This time now-elderly Luigi lasted longer, perhaps because the business his son had started was more solid. But in 1894, at seventy-seven years old, he died. That year Gaetano sent a new request for a license, one which was given to him and was regularly renewed until 1900. After that we cannot be sure what happened, but this time the pizzeria had lasted twenty-four years in one place.

The opposite happened in a pizzeria at Vico Chiavettieri al Pendino 92, where Salvatore Mangiarulo turned over his business to Raffaele Pastore in 1846, only to almost immediately buy it back. In 1873 we can find Mangiarulo in a list of shopkeepers who had not renewed their licenses, though he is once again approved in subsequent years. Evidently either a warning or a fine had put him back on the right (bureaucratic) track. In 1883 Mangiarulo died and his twenty-three-year-old son, Gennaro, took over from him. Gennaro did not last long, as three years later he turned over the business to Luigi Fusco. This time, unlike with Luigi and Gaetano Ceso, the father had run the pizzeria for forty years, while the son had not even been able to do it for three.

The Sarnellis also had a family business with a pizzeria. In 1847, Gennaro Sarnelli asked for a license to reopen an old pizzeria at Selleria al Pendino 35, one which had been closed for ten years. It must have been a relatively successful business as around thirty years later (1876) we find his son Vincenzo in the same shop. Later, in 1883, a younger son Luigi opened another pizzeria at Vico Roselle alla Conceria 4. In the end Vincenzo transferred his pizzeria to that address, as we find him cited twice in a commercial guide to Naples (*Guida Commerciale Lo Gatto*, 1886 and 1888) and twice in police documents (1894 and 1896), though nothing thereafter.

We can underline a few other important names like Chiosi, Ferraro, Buonomo, Pastore, and the Corcione brothers, and for these and a number of others the reader can consult the sources at the end of the book. We lose all trace of these families in the twentieth century, except two or three as we will see. The intermarrying of the families of pizzaioli would merit its own chapter, even its own book. As much as we can tell from the records suggests that the phenomenon was quite pronounced. For those three or four families for which more thorough research has been done, these intermarriages seem quite common. Raffaele Esposito married Maria Giovanna Brandi, the daughter of the pizzaiola Ottajano. Antonio and Errico Lombardi married a Pepillo and a Scialò, both of whom belonged to families of pizzaioli. Vincenzo Basile and Angela Pedata (another married couple) also both had a pizzeria. Vincenzo Mattozzi married Concetta Scafaro, daughter of a pizzaiolo. Pasquale Brandi married Anna Pagliarulo, Pietro's daughter. Luigi Pace got married to Carmina De Felice, who was herself a pizzaiola. Even those they are just a few, they are sufficient to bear out the hypothesis of intermarriage.[4]

INDIVIDUAL PERSISTENCE

There are also many cases of pizzaioli who despite being capable (something we can deduce from many years in the same shop) did not pass their pizzerias on to family, or at least not to someone with the same last name.[a] For example, we meet Teresa Santelia in the archives for the first time in 1822 for a regular fire inspection, which provides us with a description of the rooms that her pizzeria occupied at Via Tribunali 35. She reappears in 1841 (again in a list of inspections done to prevent fires). It was a run that lasted twenty years at least, though we cannot be certain because there are no records before 1822 nor after 1841 that mention her.

---

[a] This happened, for example, with adopted children like Alfonso Mirto but also with husbands and daughters like in the Malato family. Wives that continued with pizzerias after being widowed also applied with a different last name, as in Italy women do not take their husbands' last names.

A certain Antonio Piccirillo ran a pizzeria for quite a long time at Vico Lungo Tre Regine 48–9. He started there at twenty-three years old in 1843 and left the shop at fifty-six years old in 1876, but only to move to the nearby Vico Tre Re, where he continued his business in a shop that was "completely new to this use." We can note on his penal certificate, issued by the trial court of Montecalvario, that he is listed as "of the profession of pizzivendolo [sic]." This was during the Savoy era, and the Piedmontese bureaucracy had brought with it not only new rules that were certainly necessary, but they also brought new bureaucrats who (given the misspelling of pizzaiolo) were unfamiliar with the local culture.

Speaking of bureaucracy and local culture, we can examine the case of a certain Alfonso Miranda, who took over a pizzeria and wine shop in Via Gennaro Serra 21 from Raffaele Esposito, who had just moved his pizzeria to the Salita Sant'Anna di Palazzo. In April 1886, Miranda requested permission to turn his shop from a "pizzeria and wine shop" to a "pizzeria and [bottled] wine shop," a formula which we have seen during the Bourbon period enjoyed a different set of rules. In a shop that sold wine in bottles, one could also (if one had the license) allow customers to stay and play cards after they had eaten.

The neighborhood commissioner (now called an "inspector") did not hesitate to exhibit the old habit of the police commissioners of showing himself to be particularly favorable to the pizzaioli's requests. Along with Miranda's request for permission to host "legal games," the commissioner added in his report in the dossier that "the business run by the same [Miranda] is not other than a pizzeria frequented by the right sort of person, where never has there been cause for an 'inconvenience.'" To the question later forwarded by the chief of police of whether the wine was kept "in barrels or in bottles," the inspector replied that "in the pizzeria of Alfonso Miranda wine is consumed almost exclusively by those who go there to eat, as happens in these businesses which are a specialty of Naples." Having to respond in the end to the question at hand, he declared that in the pizzeria they have both wine in bottles and "in barrels," which of course led to the immediate rejection of the license application. But, as we can see from the table attached to the dossier, the inspector had already granted permission on his own.[5]

However, leaving aside the bureaucratic problems, it is important to note that Miranda must have been quite a good pizzaiolo if he lasted almost twenty years. Another successful pizzaiolo was Ruoppo (or Ruoppolo) Girolamo, who in 1850 opened a pizzeria at Vico Pergola a Sant'Antonio Abate 18 and returned the license for it in May 1884, thirty-four years later. Giuseppe De Marco started a pizzeria in 1859 at Borgo Sant'Antonio Abate 205, moved to nearby Via Foria 222 (just then beginning to fill with buildings and people) where he ran the business until 1883.[6] We can add a woman to this list: Angela Rosa Aprea ran a pizzeria at Porta San Gennaro for twenty-four years, from 1863 to 1887. Since she was already fifty-eight years old in 1863, perhaps she entrusted the management of the pizzeria to another pizzaiolo.

Antonio La Vecchia on the other hand began in 1858, at thirty-two years old, in the old pizzeria and trattoria of Largo della Carità. He probably would have worked for a long time had death not taken him at only fifty-three years old. He left the

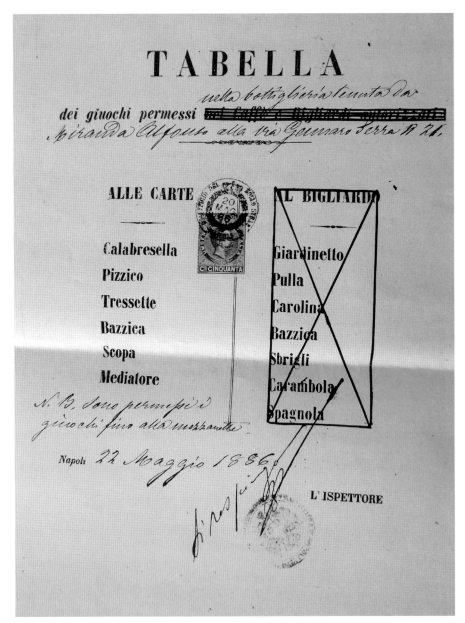

Figure 5.1: Table of Permitted Games. Naples, 1886.
This is a list of the card games permitted to be played by customers, who could therefore
remain in bottled wine shops after having eaten.
Courtesy of the Italian State Archives of Naples (Questura – Archivio Generale I Serie –
Fascio 1378 n.241 Publication authorization n. 33/2014).

business to his family, probably to his widow Carolina Monaco, who ran it until the end of the century.[7] Antonio Aragone reopened the old pizzeria at Supportico Nasti 30 in 1863, which he left in 1876 to move to Strada Piazzetta di Porto. We can find him again in Strada Corsea in 1900, after both of his previous locations had been demolished as part of the "Risanamento." Finally, Filomena Corso, who ran the pizzeria at Via Speranzella 150–1 from 1876 until 1899, and who must have had other pizzaioli who rented the shop given the other names licensed at that address.

GIVING UP

The list of successful pizzaioli could go on, but rather than continue, we refer the reader to the sources at the end of the book. There is one aspect of the specialized and strenuous work of a pizzaiolo: giving up and leaving the trade. There are two types of quitting. The first is leaving or turning over a pizzeria to another person, after a more or less limited time—for this case it is enough to simply consult the sources in this volume. But there is another type of quitting, when a pizzaiolo stays in the same shop but gives up running a pizzeria, transforming it into a similar category: a tavern, a wine shop, or something else. We will look at some examples now.

On January 19, 1841 the request of a certain Luigi Dramand was sent to the Prefecture from the commissioner of San Ferdinando's office. Dramand, "a French baker" who "had rented a shop from the Marquis of Pietramelara D. Vincenzo Di Palma in Vico Sergente Maggiore 53 where before there was a pizzaiolo" asked that the oven be used exclusively "to cook bread for use in his warehouse." It could seem to be an exception because it has to do with a French baker, but there is no lack of even more pertinent cases.

In January 1847 a certain Giuseppe D'Arrigo obtained a license for a wine shop and a pizzeria at Strada Magnocavallo 27, but already in July of the same year he asked to transform his license for a pizzeria and wine shop into one to "sell cold foods and wines domestic and foreign." From pizzeria and wine shop he moved on to being a "seller of bottled wine and restaurateur." Indeed, along with this request he also asked for permission to hang a sign bearing the inscription "Il Ristoratore Siciliano." Perhaps here as well the rejection was motivated by ethnic and cultural reasons. In 1876 Antonio Caldarelli changed his pizzeria and wine shop (at Piazza Tribunali 76) into just a wine shop. Perhaps he liked this work better, as he continued with this sort of license even later at other locations.

Giuseppe Franchini also had a wine shop and pizzeria at Via Salvator Rosa 311. When he moved to Via San Nicola dei Caserti, he dropped the license for the pizzeria because the new location was "too narrow." In his next two moves (to Santa Maria Apparente and to Sant'Anna a Capuana), he only applied for licenses for the wine shop. All these moves were in one calendar year, in April, July, and December of 1888.[8] Vincenzo Carrino changed his pizzeria at Corso Garibaldi 13 into a café and a bottled wine shop while Giovanna Estremo, in moving her pizzeria and wine shop at Strada Corsea to Corso Vittorio Emanuele 412, also kept only the license for the wine shop.

Now it is time to draw some conclusions from all of this data. Of the many pizzerias we have read about in these records across a century, how many disappeared, how many are still around today and (most importantly) what was their distribution in the city?

6

The distribution of pizzerias across the city

POLITICAL AND URBAN SHAKE-UPS

Starting from the 1807 list of pizzerias and maintaining the original division of the city into neighborhoods, we can now try to determine what the distribution of pizzerias was in the urban space during the nineteenth century. For the sake of an easier comparison, we can divide the history into two periods. The first is from 1807 (for which we have the first list of pizzerias) until 1860 (the end of the Bourbons and the loss of Naples' role as a capital, and with it regional importance). The second is from 1860 until the turn of the century. The end of the nineteenth century saw the rebuilding of the city in full fervor, and resulted in the demolition of a number of century-old pizzerias.

While the phenomenon of the persistence of a certain activity in the same shop for decades or even centuries was apparent in other trades as well, for nineteenth-century pizzerias it was practically the rule. This is a result of the fact that a pizzeria was not at the time a kind of trade that was easy to move from one place to another like almost any other—not as much because of favorable locations or the capacity of the shop's space but rather for problems relative to the physical plant. An oven is not something that can be disassembled and taken along like a piece of furniture. This was not only because of the cost (expensive today as then) but rather the infrastructure: the hood and the chimney, which had to reach the roof of the building. We have already seen the complaints that the owners of space in buildings with pizzerias, and all the resulting hassles. To these we can add the difficulty of finding adequate shop space, both large enough and, above all, with vaulted brick ceilings rather than the wooden beams that were often, as we have seen, a problem.

All these details meant that a pizzeria, apart from an able pizzaiolo, had a number of prerequisites: a good commercial location, a suitable chimney, neighbors who were approving or at least tolerant, and adequate space capable of hosting dozens of customers. This sort of shop attracted not only people who wanted to taste pizza but also for pizzaioli themselves. For this reason we find that pizzerias, even when they change pizzaioli (sometimes more than once a year), stay pizzerias for the whole century. Many of these pizzerias—like many taverns that were always in the same place—were already "historic" by the end of the nineteenth century. There would have been many more today with this adjective had the "Risanamento" not been necessary. As part of this massive urban "renewal" plan, whole neighborhoods were gutted and dozens of streets vanished from the map. The life of the city was turned completely upside-down and, though many problems were resolved, many others became (paradoxically) much more acute.

The problem of housing for the least fortunate part of the population became (if it were even possible), even more dramatic. The poor wretches who had been driven from their habitations—from the *bassi* and the *fondaci*—with the promise of being moved to less noxious places and into houses that were more comfortable, were bitterly disappointed. For the vast majority of those people the whole project became a nasty joke. Yet again real estate speculation took over and rents that were absolutely beyond of the budget of those who had been moved, were demanded for the houses meant for them.

A perverse phenomenon developed: many of the people who had lost their homes but could not move into the new lodgings had to go and live in the few buildings that were left untouched, with relatives or friends. The already precarious living conditions in the buildings that had escaped the wrecking ball did not get better, but instead actually became more crowded.[1] The living conditions in general in Naples did, however, improve: with the opening of the broad new streets, the majority of the decrepit sewer system—the primary cause of the cholera epidemics—had to be rebuilt. In addition, the new Serino Aqueduct became operational at the same time, and so many of the old conduits also had to be renovated. The result was that with this two-headed project, both the hygiene-sanitation problem and the lack of good water were both simultaneously solved.

It is difficult to peer into the souls of these humble shopkeepers and understand if in that moment of upsetting events, they were hopeful or disappointed, full of faith in the future—or desperation. The city had certainly not stood out up until then for its booming economic conditions, nor had it enjoyed a healthy environment, other than the climate and the beautiful surroundings. Certainly the loss of the status of capital of the former kingdom, and then the subsequent gutting of the city center had to have caused both great distress and great expectations for people who lived in daily contact with dirty streets, stale air in alleyways, and the highhandedness of the police.

The life of a pizzaiolo must not have changed much though, judging from the moves, the transfers of a pizzeria from one pizzaiolo to another and the return of the former to his old pizzeria later. It appears to have been a supportive community of tradesmen and women who knew each other and who, even though they were not organized in a guild, certainly felt that spirit in the best possible way.[2] We can discern this clearly from the archives, first and foremost from the intermarriage discussed before, but also consulting the police documents: only very rarely can we find disputes or criminal acts done by pizzaioli. The fact that Salvatore Sangiorgio would act as a guarantor for the young Palmentieri, or Aniello Buonomo doing the same for the wife of one of his waiters (on the pain of himself going to jail), or the prompt restitution of the offerings to the church that had been entrusted to Pasquale Paparcone: all of these are evidence of a meek and benevolent character. It suggests people used to plugging away from morning until night, intent only on preparing the best product they could and making it as tasty as possible.

THE BOURBON PERIOD

In the first period under examination—the years between 1807 and 1860—the total number of pizzerias recorded in the archives comes to about 120. If we subtract from this total the ten to fifteen addresses that in 1860 were no longer operating (for various reasons) we come out with between 105 and 110 shops. Among those that disappeared between 1807 and 1860 were almost certainly the two in Via Toledo, the most important street in the city, a place where the authorities sought to maintain a certain "decorum." Here, beginning in the first decades of the nineteenth century, trades that were seen as "not very decent" were no longer allowed to operate. These included activities which increased the filth in the streets (e.g. butchers, fruit, and vegetable vendors) or those that produced disagreeable odors or customers who were too plebeian, like wine shops and taverns and—by extension and association—pizzerias. These shops were moved to the numerous side alleys. In other neighborhoods of the city a number of pizzerias on the 1807 list no longer existed in 1860 at the same addresses for reasons that are we do not know, but can perhaps intuit.

An analysis of the make-up of the neighborhoods reveals the following situation. On the first list (Table 2.1) both the Chiaia and San Carlo Arena neighborhoods were absent. In all the years between that list and 1860, there was only one pizzeria in each. The first was the one in Vico San Pasquale a Chiaia, which we noted above in the section on wine: an example that reminds us that even at mid-century, that area had few shops. The other pizzeria was in Via Foria, where the numbering of the street had not yet been completed in 1855. In the document in which the applicant requests a license from the Prefect, the address is given as "in front of Saint Mary of the Angels [Church], [the] house [belonging to] Vittoria." This is probably the pizzeria registered in later years at number 222. The delay is because those two neighborhoods were still only sparsely inhabited and therefore not suitable for a business that, as we have said, required a large turnover to be profitable. Not surprisingly both pizzerias were centrally located: the first in the heart of the Chiaia neighborhood where it could draw on a large zone for customers, and the second in the low part of Via Foria, near the busy alleys in the Avvocata area of Borgo Sant'Antonio.

There were, however, notable increases in number of pizzerias in the three neighborhoods of the administrative center: San Ferdinando, Montecalvario, and San Giuseppe. Here the number went from seven to fifteen, from five to sixteen and from six to twelve, respectively. This strong increase was definitely due to the fact that the three neighborhoods, in addition to having a very high population density, all had as their epicenters Via Toledo, which was (as we have seen) a reason for growth. In addition, after the return of Ferdinando I from Sicily, the area of

San Giacomo degli Spagnoli was renovated (between 1815 and 1825). All the old buildings were demolished and an enormous complex, the Palazzo San Giacomo, was built, destined to become the home of various ministries and government offices.

After the unhappy experience with a constitution in 1848, and the ill-advised repression that followed it, Ferdinando II had initiated a major urban renewal project. The plan was to open a grand boulevard (Corso Maria Teresa, the present-day Corso Vittorio Emanuele) to create an outlet from the higher part of the Quartieri Spagnoli neighborhood, from the Magnocavallo neighborhood, and from all of the other densely populated streets and alleys that were above Via Toledo. In addition, it would directly connect the Infrascata area with the Mergellina area, creating an artery that was later called Naples' first beltway. Via Toledo was also completely rebuilt with new sewers and sidewalks; the repaving also corrected the incline of the street itself, which many anecdotes connected to inevitable flooding on rainy days.[3]

Looking at the entire area we can see that the San Ferdinando neighborhood—with its historic pizzerias at Sant'Anna di Palazzo (indisputably the most important of the era), Vico Campane, and Vico Rotto San Carlo (formerly Vico Chianche)—saw the opening of another two pizzerias in Vico Campane, as well five more in alleys off Via Toledo. A second neighborhood, Montecalvario, had a tripling in the number of pizzerias. These were located in a maze of side streets that make up the majority of the Quartieri Spagnoli and the densely built up area that was centered on Strada Pignasecca. This was then, and is still now, the beating heart of a wide variety of commercial activities whose products were primarily food; in the middle of the century it was one of the most densely populated areas. Of all of these nineteenth-century pizzerias only a few of the ones in Via Pignasecca, and the one in Largo della Carità (about which we will return soon) survived.

The San Giuseppe neighborhood had the advantage not only of the construction of the new palace that housed the ministries at San Giacomo, but also the transfer of the central postal offices to Palazzo Gravina in Via Monteoliveto. With the loss of the two pizzerias in Via Toledo, the opening of these new ones were evidently the result of these new buildings, given that the neighborhood remained the same for all other aspects. It was completely redesigned and rebuilt only in the 1930s and 1940s. For other neighborhoods the increase in pizzerias was somewhat varied. In the Avvocata area their number went up to five, three of which were in the Infrascata area (the present-day Via Salvator Rosa). This was an ancient zone of country trattorias that, with the opening of Corso Maria Teresa, became part of the city's territory; this meant an increasing population because of all the new building. The Stella and Vicaria neighborhoods also doubled their numbers of pizzerias, going from four to nine in the former case and four to eight in the latter. All of this happened again because of an increase in the number of residents, especially in the areas near the Salita Santa Teresa and in the area just outside of the Porta Capuana. The pizzerias in the San Lorenzo neighborhood tripled their number (from four to twelve) as pizzerias had great success especially in Via Tribunali (always full of people),[4] but also Vico Purgatorio, Vico Fico, Vico Maiorani, and others.

In the three neighborhoods that were the most densely populated (but also the most decrepit)—Mercato, Pendino, and Porto—the increases in numbers were more limited, taking into account some closings that had occurred since 1807. There, pizzerias went from ten to fifteen, seven to twelve and from six to ten, respectively; this was apparently due to a certain market saturation. Another possible cause for the relatively small increase in the number of pizzerias is the fact that these three neighborhoods had been the most affected by the cholera epidemic of 1833–4. One new development was the opening of three pizzerias in Strada Reggia di Portici around 1850. This marked the first, timid beginning of the expansion of pizzerias beyond the city walls.

AFTER UNIFICATION

At the end of the century (after unification in 1860) the number of pizzerias operating in Naples did not change much. If we assume that the count of 120 in the census of 1871 is accurate, the ten to fifteen that disappeared in the Bourbon period were replaced in the first year after unification. The number would probably have grown even more—given the population increase in the new neighborhoods—had it not been for all of the demolition done during the gutting of the city, politely referred to as the "Risanamento." The result was that at the turn of the twentieth century there was a negligible change in numbers—what changed quite a bit was the distribution across the city.

The boom in this post-unification period was in the Chiaia neighborhood where the pizzerias went from one to fourteen. With the construction of the new Principe Amedeo ward, this neighborhood built up the high-class reputation it had acquired in the preceding period with the opening of important hotels along the Riviera di Chiaia. This fame belonged to an even earlier period, as some of the royal apart-ments and certain important embassies were located there. All along Via Piedigrotta and the beginning of Corso Vittorio Emanuele the density of housing blocks had increased. The area continued, however, to play host to enclaves of marginalized people made up of groups of the lumpenproletariat. These pockets of underprivi-leged people went back to previous centuries, when the zone had been inhabited almost exclusively by families of fishers who had lost their social identity with the passage of time. Even today the alleyways of the Riviera are full of *bassi*, one of the fundamental causes of the persistence of degradation in Naples; also known for its *bassi* is the higher ground above Via dei Mille, where narrow, densely-populated alleyways, just a few meters apart, underline the pronounced social and economic divides in the city.

The disproportionate growth in pizzerias in this neighborhood can then be explained not only with the rise of the number of residents, but also because pizza was now enjoyed by all social classes. In addition, because of its beauty the area became an attraction for the Neapolitans themselves; in that period, with the new means of public transport, it was easily reached from all the other parts of the city.

It was quite a different story for the San Ferdinando neighborhood: in the area in front of the Teatro San Carlo, it saw the demolition of a number of buildings as well as the loss of several streets with the construction of the Galleria Umberto I. As we have seen before, it lost the pizzerias in Vico Campane and Vico Rotto San Carlo, but a number of other pizzerias took the places of those recorded in the documents—from fifteen pizzerias it went to nine in the post-unification period. Of all the pizzerias, only the one at Salita Sant'Anna di Palazzo remains; all the others have been turned into restaurants. The Montecalvario and San Giuseppe neighborhoods moved in opposite directions: in the former the number went up, in the latter, down. In the Quartieri Spagnoli neighborhood, on the other hand, there were twenty-two (up from sixteen); the San Giuseppe area saw a slight decline, from twelve to nine. San Giuseppe was also the site of radical urban renewal during the twentieth century, which left only the pizzeria in Via Port'Alba.

For the other neighborhoods the results were varied: in certain cases the number of pizzerias went up, in others down. In San Carlo Arena there was an increase in housing possibilities with the completion of Via Foria, and there were four pizzerias at the end of the nineteenth century. In the three neighborhoods that were the principal sites of the "Risanamento"—Mercato, Pendino, and Porto—there was a general decline in numbers. The latter two neighborhoods had the largest number of demolitions and by the century's end they only had a few pizzerias.

The Risanamento had the opposite effect on the Vicaria neighborhood, where the building of Nuovo Corso Garibaldi and the adjacent Vasto ward saw the construction of many more housing blocks than had been demolished: here eight pizzerias became fourteen. With the expansion of the city into the new Vomero neighborhood, pizzerias moved outward. In 1890 Luigi Mattozzi, by this time a veteran and therefore undaunted (about whom we will discuss in a later chapter), opened the first pizzeria in Via Bernini in a building so new that it did not yet have a street number.[5]

As for the twentieth century, what was said above is valid: many pizzerias disappeared and others were opened, so their number stayed almost the same until the outbreak of the Second World War, after which there was a large expansion. But what are today known as the "pizzerie storiche" (the historic/oldest pizzerias)—apart from the ones at Sant'Anna di Palazzo, Largo Carità, Port'Alba, and a few other nineteenth century pizzerias—were all opened in the years between the two world wars, when pizza was still an exclusively Neapolitan product.

EVERYDAY WORK IN THE PIZZERIA

Getting back to nineteenth-century Naples, the number of pizzerias (about one hundred, give or take) stayed constant despite periodic ups and downs. Also, the method of preparation of pizzas remained more or less the same as well. As long as pizza was still exclusively Neapolitan (i.e. until the Second World War), things did not change much. Pizzerias opened at seven in the morning and closed at midnight. There was no afternoon period of closure, nor days off—not even Sunday, when indeed there was even more work to be done. In the Bourbon period, the only holidays were Easter and Christmas. Under the Savoys, Easter Monday, the Feast of the Assumption of Mary (August 15), and the Feast of Saint Stephen (December 26) were holidays, though pizzerias were open for a half day on Easter and Christmas.

Table 6.1: Pizzerie in Naples, listed by neighborhood (*)

Quartiere	1807	1860	1900
Chiaia	–	1	14
S.Ferdinando	7**	15	9
Montecalvario	5**	16	22
S.Giuseppe	6**	12	9
Avvocata	1	5	5
Stella	4	9	9
S.Carlo Arena	–	1	4
Vicaria	4	8	14
S.Lorenzo	4	12	10
Mercato	10	15	12
Pendino	7	12	6
Porto	6	10	6
Vomero	–	–	1
	54	116	121***

* These totals are of course subject to revision whenever new documents are found.

** The three "historic" pizzerias (which will be discussed in the next chapter) have to be added to the numbers given here. The total in the statistics found by Galasso in the Bibliotheque Nationale was sixty-eight, but we do not know which ones were in which neighborhoods.

*** We have to subtract from this total all of the pizzerias that were located in the streets demolished during the "Risanamento."

Except for rare cases, the license for the pizzeria was in the name of the pizzaiolo. When he did not have family helping him, he did the long hours himself, interrupted only by breaks to lie down on a bed if his house was nearby or if he lived in the shop. If that was not the case, he slept a bit on a chair, resting his head on top of an arm, on a table in the back of the shop. The employees had it even worse: they had no sort of protection at all, neither healthcare or a pension plan. The only defense they had were a few days at home that were conceded here and there, especially if they did not have a family to provide for (though obviously this "holiday" was without pay). One other benefit was a sort of severance pay that they received when they left a job; and the result was that they often changed jobs to get a few days rest and relaxation. Old age did not worry them as only infrequently did they even reach it—and in any event, if they did grow old, their children would take care of them. In the absence of children, there was always begging or hospice in a charitable institution. This state of affairs lasted almost unchanged until the breakout of the Second World War, despite the fact that at the beginning of the 1930s a type of social security was launched.

The same continuity existed with regards to the making of pizzas: pizzaioli naturally did not need any sort of schooling to teach the trade, as it was learned on the job. As they were a small group and all specialized, pizzaioli followed unwritten

Figure 6.1: Receipt for the payment of the municipal tax. Naples, 1878.
The tax on businesses had to be paid annually to the Municipality of Naples.
Courtesy of the Italian State Archives of Naples (Questura – Archivio Generale I Serie –
Fascio 1889 n.652 Publication authorization n. 33/2014).

rules and norms from which they hardly ever deviated. Today the method of preparation of pizzas and their ingredients have only changed as much as modernization
and progress have induced. Examining various aspects of pizza preparation, we
will now attempt to underline the differences while trying to recapture some of the
jargon used both then and now in Naples.

Very different from restaurants, which have two completely separate areas—the
kitchen and the rooms where people eat—a pizzeria has everything together: the
working and eating were almost always in the same place. The preparation and the
actual cooking of the pizzas happened in front of the customer's eyes: she/he could
then watch all the phases, from the spreading of the dough to the toppings used,
putting it in the oven (whitish, lifeless, no odor) to the removal and the presentation
on a plate, still steaming, a joy with its aroma and colors. All this in just a few
minutes: we can say that in addition to the "Mediterranean diet," with pizza fast
food was invented as well.

In the 1800s as well as earlier in the 1700s (but in the early twentieth century
as well) the pizzaiolo began work at dawn. In reality the preparation of the dough
was begun the day before. At the time natural yeast was used instead of brewer's
yeast, by adding a bit of the dough from the day before. This piece was called

the "criscito" (today called the "yeast mother") and was set aside to be added to the next day's dough. The ability of the pizzaiolo was measured in part by his or her ability to use the correct amount for the quantity of dough for the next day. There was no official recipe to follow: everything was based on the ability and the experience of the pizzaiolo. We can see that the times have changed as the rising time is quite different: in the nineteenth century the dough was made the night before, allowed to rise for twelve hours, then divided into smaller loaves (*panetti*) the next day, when the shop was opened and the oven lit.

The whole process was as follows: around five o'clock in the evening the pizzaiolo measured out the salt and the "*criscito*" (the dough to make the new dough rise). He put a small amount of tepid water into a special chest for making bread, and began to dissolve the salt and *criscito*, mixing the three ingredients together. The salt was coarse and had been previously ground finer with a bottle used as a rolling pin.

Once the right mix had been obtained, he added enough water for the amount of dough needed for the next day. He then added flour, handful after handful, mixing slowly. The flour was taken not from a sack but rather from the wooden chest, large enough to hold a hundred kilos of flour. The mixing began in one corner of the chest but the dough never took up more than a third of the space. At this point an assistant took over—if he were an expert at the mixing, he might have done the whole process—and began the actual hard work of making the dough, the kneading (as there were of course no electric mixers then). He would fold and refold the mass, burying his hands and lower arms in it. His hands had to go in as fists but come out open-palmed. As soon as the desired consistency was reached, he covered the dough with a moist towel and left it to rise. Contrary to what is often believed, the *criscito* led to a rising that was much slower than with brewer's yeast. Its effect was also much "sweeter," as the dough lasted until the next night without acidifying.

While the dough rose, the evening's work began and sales of pizza went on until midnight. The next morning when the shop opened, the pizzaiolo and his assistants began their work lighting scraps of wood in the oven to start a fire, cutting up garlic cloves or pieces of cheese (mozzarella or *fiordilatte*) in strips or slices, or making the little round loaves from the previous night's dough. If it were a small shop, it would have been the pizzaiolo doing everything, one thing after another. Cutting off the loaves was not much different than today, though the names were different. The little loaves were called *batocchi*, and the cases in which they were placed were *martolelle*. The pieces of cheese were put into a glazed earthenware bowl called a *scafarea*.

The counter was similar to today's: even if we do not have any illustrations, there are detailed descriptions given by some of the writers we have cited. It was a marble countertop with one or two crystal shelves on which the various little bowls with the ingredient were placed: garlic, oregano, salt, basil, grated pecorino cheese, rendered pig's fat (*sugna*), anchovies, mushrooms, or other things. In other, larger bowls there would have been tomatoes (already crushed), pieces of cheese and (when available) other small fish. The countertop was complete with a particular kind of oil receptacle with a long spout, the *agliara*, still in use today.

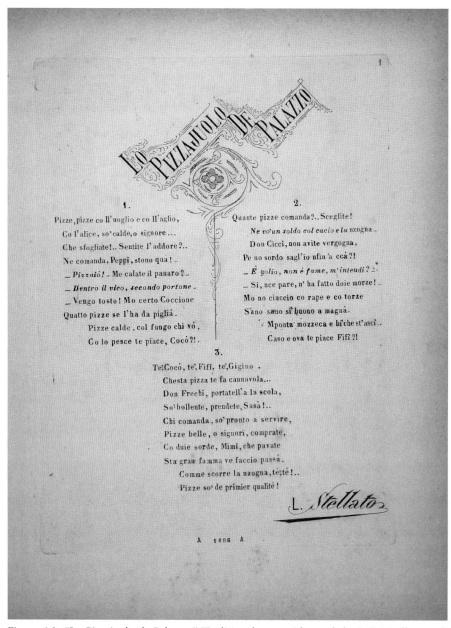

Figure 6.2: "Lo Pizzajuolo de Palazzo." Traditional song with words by Luigi Stellato and music by Francesco Finamore. Naples, c. 1860.
This comes from the collection *Marechiaro: Canti popolari in chiave di sol*. In the text the ingredients for the typical nineteenth-century pizza are given: *uoglio* (oil), *aglio* (garlic), *alici* (anchovies), *fungo* (mushrooms), *cacio* (cheese), *nzogna* (lard) *e ova* (egg). Courtesy of the Biblioteca Nazionale di Napoli, MiBACT (L.P. Canz. Nap. A.16/34).

While these preparations were taking place inside the pizzeria, outside the streets were starting to wake up. The first hawkers' voices could be heard, along with the rumble of the wheels on the pavement of any number of wagon and carts, the vehicles that delivered to the shops. The first domestic servants and workers headed to their jobs, the porters towards the market or the port and then the artisans to their shops. Of all these people, none (perhaps some rare exception) had had breakfast at home. All had to make it to the midday meal, each tried to reconcile the stomach's needs with what was in the pocket of their pants. The stomachs' rumblings were abundant, the pockets' contents less so. The temptations of the hawkers were also numerous and they assaulted the senses of the poor workers with their colors and their aromas.

The journalist Matilde Serao, in her book *Il Ventre di Napoli* (The Belly of Naples), has left us with a long list of foods that Neapolitans could buy with one or two *soldi*: a slice of pizza, a little paper cone of fried fish, ten boiled chestnuts, a portion of zucchini or eggplant marinated in vinegar and put on a piece of bread brought from home, a piece of boiled octopus, and many other similar snacks, as well as all kinds of fruits (pears, figs, apricots, and melons). Everything was for sale from the never-ending ranks of vendors (hawkers and those with stands) who filled all the streets and alleys of the city. This gamut of foods was bought and eaten on the spot, in the street, by the majority of the population that had only a *soldo* or two. Serao tells us that "as soon as he has three *soldi* [...] any good Neapolitan does not go anymore to buy pre-cooked foods, but rather eats at home, on the threshold of the *basso*, or on an old chair."

We have said several times that the Neapolitan pizzeria as a Neapolitan phenomenon (before it went global), lasted about 200 years until the Second World War. But it was not only the pizzeria as exclusively Neapolitan disappeared with the end of that period: many of the characteristics of "old Naples" lasted until then, despite the various transformations that had occurred. It is hard to believe but still in the 1920s goats (even cows) were milked right in front of the customer, house by house, with the goats and cows down below the buildings. Getting back to pizza, until the end of the 1930s pizzas were sold in slices at the entrance to the pizzeria. One quarter of a pizza cost three *soldi*, whereas a whole pizza was twelve *soldi* (sixty cents of a lira). The pizzaiolo that Mastriani mentions sold it walking around for two *grana*, the one Emanuele Rocco talks about for three *grana*, though this was a pizza with just garlic and oil that had to feed a father, a mother and a little girl.

But let us return to our story. While the city woke up, in the pizzeria everything was now ready and the first pizzas began to be prepared and cooked. Some were given to the hawkers, while others were sold, in slices or whole, on the "stand" at the pizzeria's entrance. Even at eight in the morning there were people who were having hunger pangs. These first pizzas were quite simple and very inexpensive, although there were also people who came in and ordered a pizza like he or she wanted it, at a higher price. The most common types today represent two basic kinds, the Marinara and the Margherita, to which each person added ingredients. In reality these "classics" are more like templates: from the descriptions from contemporaries, we know that in the nineteenth century there were pizzas made in many different ways.

Especially very early in pizza's history, the "bianca" (white) pizza—with just some lard and cheese, or with oil, oregano, and garlic. Its versatility made it a container for many different toppings. In days when fishing was good it was easy to find pizzerias with small fish put on top of the Marinara. At other times the most abundant topping was mushrooms,[a] various molluscs, mussels, Venus clams (*Chamelea gallina*), anchovies, Neapolitan pepperoni, or other things. It was always a local product, whether San Marzano tomatoes cultivated near Nola or cherry tomatoes from near Vesuvius (that lasted into the winter), cheeses from Agerola or other places in Campania, or fish from the gulf. This was also a reason for the slow spread of pizza: only recently are these products able to be found anywhere, and not always as good as the originals.

We have discussed tomatoes, cheese, and products from the garden and the sea but we have not talked about the most fundamental ingredient of pizza: flour. Before there was one type of flour that was used for everything, and it was up to the pizzaioli to find other types to mix together. Today the situation is much different: the milling industry has created specialized mixes of different types of wheat to make different kinds of flour for bread, for pizza, for pastries, and so on.

The Neapolitan mills are numerous, but the one most specialized in making different flours is the Molino Caputo. It was founded by Carmine Caputo in 1924 in Capua, then moved to Naples in 1939 by his son, Antimo. His sons and grandsons, the current managers, have created a high quality product with a slow milling that does not damage the starches and proteins, made with domestic grains and without any additives. It is a flour, that in addition to having a large share of the Italian market, has also gone international and today is in over fifty countries.

---

[a] Often these were *Armillaria mellea*, called "honey fungus" in English and *chiodini* ("nails," for their shape) in Italian.

7

Historic pizzerias

There are only thee or four pizzerias that are referred to as "storiche" (historic) in Naples—in other words, the ones that go back to the beginning of the nineteenth century or even before and are still open today. If we add the few that are still around that were opened in the course of the 1800s, we would have a maximum of ten. This is because, as we have seen in detail, between the end of the nineteenth and the middle of the twentieth centuries the topography of the city was radically modified. The alteration was the result not only of the great transformations wrought on the urban fabric itself, but also because of the various social and economic changes that played out in those decades. The innumerable pizzerias today in Naples were almost all opened in the twentieth century and many of these replaced the older pizzerias not only because of the level of quality that they had attained, but also because they had achieved a certain level of fame. These two elements—together with the fact that they were opened seventy, eighty or even ninety years ago—have made them "historic" Neapolitan pizzerias in the fullest sense. But for now our discussion will stay anchored in the nineteenth century.

The pizzerias of the twentieth century are often listed in gastronomic guide-books, as well as in articles, and more recently on many websites. However, all of these articles (no matter how widely they are publicized) turn out to be lacking in historical accuracy. Part of this is due to their reliance on the tradition of nineteenth-century literature which, as we have seen, does not stand out for its correct reconstruction of the facts. Another problem is that the articles often rely on the memories of the pizzaioli themselves who, given that they're interested parties, often draw on their fictional oral tradition. This oral tradition is especially rich in exaggerating the origins and ancestries of the pizzerias. As a result, it would be much better if the gastronomic guides stuck to evaluating pizzerias according to their culinary standards—leaving out the pizzerias' history, which is often (for the reasons given above) inexact or "confused."

We can give one example that can stand in for many others, drawn from a recent guide of a famous series. In his review of Pizzeria Mattozzi in Piazza della Carità the author, after having correctly observed that it is one of the oldest pizzerias in Naples, adds this gem: "Opened in 1890 by Gennaro Mattozzi, at the beginning of the 1900s it was the first pizzeria to offer restaurant fare as well." In just one line, three errors are squeezed in. As we shall see in the following pages, the founding date, the name of the pizzaiolo and the fact that it was the first pizzeria to offer restaurant fare are all wrong.

THE OLDEST PIZZERIAS

Among the oldest pizzerias that are still around, the only one that has enjoyed fame for two centuries in a row is the one at the Salita Sant'Anna di Palazzo. Tradition claims that it was opened in the middle of the eighteenth century. According to this version of history it would have been one of the first pizzerias in the city, though it became famous only in the first decades of the nineteenth century under the management of the famous Pietro Calicchio. Another old pizzeria is the one in Via Port'Alba, which it has been suggested was founded in 1738.[1] However, pending an actual document about or referring to its founding, we have to admit that we have many reservations about this date. Indicating a date without citing a precise documentary source slides back into that folkloristic tradition from which we had already distanced ourselves in the introduction. A third pizzeria that is both very old and famous is the one at the Largo della Carità.

Excluding the pizzeria at Sant'Anna di Palazzo—for which there is a precise reference of the historian Raffaele De Cesare, who indirectly links its opening day to the mid-eighteenth century—we can assume that the founding dates for the other two are exaggerations, and occurred because of the notoriety of the two pizzerias in the twentieth century. Their fame made them eager to ennoble themselves further by backdating their founding. Also, the names of some of the families that raised the prestige of Neapolitan pizza in the twentieth century are attached to both pizzerias.

The fact that none of these three pizzerias are cited in the list from 1807 would seem to confirm the hypothesis of backdating, if it were not for the fact that the traditional story is seemingly (if paradoxically) supported by this absence. As we have already seen, the list included only pizzaioli "not subject to [taxation] by the City Council nor by the craft guilds"; in addition, that 1807 list sent to the Minister of Finance has fifty-five pizzerias, whereas in the French statistics published by Giuseppe Galasso the number sixty-eight is given. These two particulars therefore lead us to suspend judgment and accept—with some reservation, and in any event pending the discovery of a document that clarifies the situation—the traditional story that holds that these three pizzerias are quite old.

The reason for the longevity of these three pizzerias is that, in addition to having been run for long periods by able pizzaioli, all three were located in streets that for over 200 years never lost their "strategic" position. There were certainly other pizzaioli who were capable and other "illustrious" pizzerias but, unfortunately for them, they had the misfortune to work in streets and in shops that were demolished to make room for new streets and new buildings—or they simply lost their previous importance and their attractive force.

If we look at the locations of these three pizzerias on a map, we see that they are in fact laid out along a longitudinal axis, Via Toledo, the most important street in Naples since the sixteenth century. It starts at the Royal Palace and the Piazza del

Plebiscito; it then leads through an important district full of shops and with a lot of pedestrians (and back then carriages); and after crossing the Largo della Carità arrives in Piazza Dante. Here, at the end of the hemicycle dedicated to Carlo di Borbone, the majestic arch of Port'Alba rises. From here it continues in a street, short but full of traffic, that goes towards Via Tribunali—today as then always crawling with people at all hours of the day and night. The three pizzerias were (and still are) located along this axis: one at the beginning, the second in the middle and the third at the end of this street.

PORT'ALBA AND LARGO DELLA CARITÀ

Even though they have this extraordinary longevity in common, the three pizzerias each had their own characteristics. The Port'Alba pizzeria was more plebian, frequented by students and by the mass of people who passed by in front of it and ate their pizza while standing, folded "a libretto."[a] We can be sure that bourgeois families went there as well; they sat upstairs and ate, in addition to pizza, various dishes prepared by the cooks of a shop that was already in those days both a pizzeria and a trattoria. The archives of the police contain abundant documentation about the dual nature. After a simple mention in 1837 (for an inspection of the chimney made by the agents of the commissariat of the San Giuseppe neighborhood), a document from 1842 states that "a certain Domenico Esposito requests that the licenses for the trattoria and pizzaria [sic] at Strada Porta Sciuscella 18[b] be put in his name, with a sign 'Trattoria e Pizzaria da Monzù Testa.'" As proof of purchase Esposito turned in two older licenses to the commissioner. These had been issued to his predecessor in the shop, Giuseppe Pacella.

We cannot be sure how long Pacella had run that pizzeria because at that time the licenses were valid for a year; at the end of each year the shopkeeper turned in the old license and, having paid the fee, received a new one valid for the next year. Without the previous document it is therefore difficult to deduce how long the shopkeeper (in this case, the pizzaiolo) or the shop (the pizzeria) had been there. Only after unification in 1860 was the new license introduced, now issued by the police organ, the Questura, rather than the Prefecture.[c] It was a document on which a stamp was made each year on the reverse side, showing renewals. We do know that after only two months, Esposito, who had had a pizzeria at Via Materdei 2 the year before, requested permission to move it to Via Nuova Capodimonte 93. We do not know the reason for the move but, as we have seen, it was not a rare occurrence. Later in Via Porta Sciuscella (now called Strada Port-Alba)[2] we find a certain Giuseppe Gargiulo, who in 1855 was sixty-five years old. He had perhaps taken the

---

[a] In Naples this means folding the pizza in half and then in half again, "like a libretto." One also hears "a portafoglio" (like a wallet) for the same sort of folding. See the picture of Bill Clinton eating pizza in this volume.

[b] "Strada Porta Sciuscella" is the old name for the street that was later called "Via Port'Alba."

[c] Under the Bourbons, the Prefecture had police jurisdiction over the city of Naples. After 1860, the new Questura (police) had jurisdiction in the city of Naples, while the Prefettura had jurisdiction over the provinces, an administrative division introduced by the Piedmontese government.

pizzeria after Esposito left in 1842. Gargiulo later requested permission to move his business to Largo delle Pigne 17 (today Piazza Cavour), to a shop he had rented from another shopkeeper.

These transfers of licenses and the links between pizzaioli confirm what we had asserted earlier: that is that we are talking about a small community in which everyone knew each other and were friends, if not actually related. This made possible these moves and license-swaps, though we cannot know what the contracts were like, what their agreements were or what guarantees they offered each other. It also confirms that a pre-existing pizzeria was preferable to one that had to be created *ex novo*. Moreover in 1889 (when the Risanamento was about to begin), the president of the "Society of Mutual Aid Among Bakers" sent a letter to the daily *Il Roma*. He hoped that the authorities in charge of the construction (and demolition) would take into consideration "the sad fate of shopkeepers that run bakeries, both managers and their boys [*garzoni*] who, with the renewal works, will be without a home or work and therefore poor" because "it is not easy to find a shop for their trade, nor do landlords want to allow an oven on their property."[3] We have already seen that pizzaioli had the same problem.

In 1855 Domenico Sorrentino (thirty-seven years old) took over from Gargiulo; Sorrentino apparently lasted quite a bit longer than Gargiulo as we have to wait until 1880 to find a new pizzaiolo, Raffaele Urciuolo. Urciuolo in turn ceded the pizzeria to Giuseppe Ferrante, whence it passed to Francesco Trotti, and then in 1884 to Francesco Buongarzone, who finally turned it over to Guglielmo Ferraro.

Francesco Ambrosio finally put an end to this revolving door when he rented the pizzeria in 1892. He and his family brought the pizzeria to the apogee of its splendor during the twentieth century. It is this notoriety that Ambrosio (and later his son and grandson) achieved—hosting famous locals in their pizzeria for a meal— that probably led them to backdate the pizzeria's founding.

It is a similar ending point, though with a different route, for the pizzeria at the Largo della Carità. It was located in a strategic spot at the middle of Via Toledo, a location that allowed it to stay open even after the ban on pizzerias in that street; this exception obviously allowed it greater stability. It was not mentioned in police documents until 1858, although we know of its existence thanks to the narration of Francesco De Sanctis (cited above). De Sanctis remembered how in 1833 as a young student from the provinces, he and his friends from the Basilio Puoti School often went in the evenings to eat pizza "in certain rooms upstairs at Largo della Carità."

The 1858 document that mentions this pizzeria (also a trattoria) records a cession of the license from the old pizzaiolo Salvatore Sangiorgio to the thirty-two-year-old Antonio La Vecchia. This was not a regular license transfer but rather the result of Sangiorgio's death, and the apparent impossibility of his widow carrying on the business. By fatal coincidence, La Vecchia himself died young—he was fifty-four years old and in the prime of his career after twenty-two years of managing his pizzeria. In the commercial guide to Naples from 1880 (*Guida Commerciale Bonner*), the entry reads "Antonio La Vecchia, Successors of" and in the 1881 edition of the same guide "Antonio La Vecchia, Widow of." In an 1883 document

Figure 7.1: Pizzeria Gennaro Mattozzi, Largo Carità. Naples 1940.
A group of pizzaioli and customers in front of a pizzeria. Ernesto Mattozzi is seated in
the middle, in the dark suit.
Courtesy of Donatella Mattozzi.

the owner of the pizzeria is given as Carolina Monaco; evidently La Vecchia's wife
had asserted her role formally.[4]

In 1900 Alfonso Pavone took charge of the pizzeria, running it until 1915.[5] This
was the year that Gennaro Mattozzi became the pizzaiolo after the license was ceded
to him by Pavone. Gennaro, together with his numerous brothers, had continued
and built upon their family tradition of running pizzerias. With this new acquisition
the Mattozzi brothers (who already had other pizzerias) became so famous that in
the post-war period their name became almost synonymous with pizza, as we will
see below. Under Gennaro's management the pizzeria that already had a century of
tradition behind it achieved fame that it still enjoys today. Even now the pizzeria,
despite being run by managers not in the Mattozzi family, still bears (sixty years
after its sale) the sign "Pizzeria-Ristorante Mattozzi." The Mattozzis still practice
their 160-year-old family tradition in other pizzerias around Naples.

SANT'ANNA DI PALAZZO

Tradition accords illustrious customers to the pizzerias of Port'Alba and Largo
della Carità, and they certainly had them, though in the twentieth century. In
the nineteenth century, however, they were less important than another historic

pizzeria, the one at Sant'Anna di Palazzo (about which we have already heard).
The difference is that the last pizzeria is located near the Royal Palace, the benefits
of which are easy to imagine. The most important detail about this pizzeria in its
two centuries of documented existence (leaving out the as-yet unknown earlier
pizzaioli), is that it had only three pizzaioli in the nineteenth century and three
more in the twentieth. This tells us much about the stability of the business and the
ability of the managers.

The first documented pizzaiolo was Pietro Calicchio, who was born in 1780 and
must have started in the first decade of the nineteenth century. He became so famous
that, as Raffaele De Cesare wrote around 1890, the Salita di Sant'Anna di Palazzo
was known as "the street of Pietro the pizzaiuolo." Calicchio spent his entire life
in that pizzeria and evidently had brought his product to a high level of quality,
knowing that he was serving a public that was as demanding as it was prestigious.
We have already heard about the fire in Calicchio's pizzeria and how the matter was
immediately resolved by the authorities. The fire had also been the indirect cause of
the death of three young employees of the butcher next to Calicchio: they had gone
down into "the contiguous cellar to retrieve a side of beef that was there in reserve"
and asphyxiated on account of the extremely dense smoke produced by "the fire
that had developed in material of slow combustion in the storage pit below."[6] To
slow the spread of the fire, all of the air holes for the storage pits had been plugged
up; this had led to such a concentration of smoke that it had filled the other cellar
rooms, among them the one where the three unlucky boys were later found. As is
clear from the document cited, despite the deaths of the three boys, the authorities
deemed it important to reopen the pizzeria.

Pietro Calicchio died in 1853. At first his sons took over, then the one son
Ferdinando by himself. An 1857 document notes that Ferdinando "turned the wine
shop at number 30 over to a certain Pasquale Curtazzo,"[7] apparently in observance of
the law that prohibited having two trades (even if they were similar) in two separate
shops. In 1863 we find Ferdinando again registered as the owner of the pizzeria
at number 1 and the wine shop at number 30, which he had apparently bought
back; after the unification of Italy the old law about not having two trades in two
shops had been annulled. Important to note is that numbers 1 and 30 were directly
opposite one another, and this detail—insignificant in a normal sized street—was
very important in an alleyway not wider than four or five meters. It suggests that
father and son had already been working closely, given the proximity of both shops
and types of work. Today the pizzeria is made up of the former shops at numbers 1,
2 and 3 as well as the space directly opposite, more than likely the former wine shop.

The third famous nineteenth-century pizzaiolo (who worked for many years in
the twentieth century as well) was Raffaele Esposito. With journalistic exaggeration
that one finds only in Naples, the creation of the "Pizza Margherita" is attributed to
him. The Margherita is a pizza with mozzarella, tomato sauce, and basil—in other
words one that has the colors of the Italian flag. Thinking that Esposito invented the
Pizza Margherita is at best a half-truth, given the statements of the writers quoted at
the beginning of this book, which show that a pizza with these three ingredients had
been around since the early years of the nineteenth century.[8] Esposito's genius lies

not in "creating" this type of pizza but rather—according to various versions of the story—calling it "Margherita" in homage to the Queen of Italy, present in Naples for the inauguration of the Risanamento construction.

The queen arrived in Naples on the evening of May 21, 1889 (this much is confirmed by the city's newspapers) and took up residence at the palace of Capodimonte. In one of the subsequent days she expressed the desire to try the famous Neapolitan dish, and her attendants immediately made it possible by inviting to court the most famous pizzaiolo of the city. Some versions of the story even have Esposito's wife, Giovanna Brandi, going with him to Capodimonte. Esposito prepared three pizzas: the first with olive oil, cheese, and basil, the second with anchovies[d] and the third with tomatoes, mozzarella and basil. The queen expressed appreciation for the third made with the now-famous ingredients and the pizzaiolo then and there baptized his pizza "the Margherita." We can ignore the picturesque elements of this story, but a document (still on display today in the pizzeria) from the royal household seems to prove it. It is important to note, however, that the text reads "the three kinds of pizza were found to be excellent," not just one. One thing is certain: Raffaele Esposito could say that he had prepared this originally plebian dish for the queen of Italy.[9]

But who was Raffaele Esposito? We do not know if he was really a fervent supporter on the new Savoy monarchy, although it is clear that he must have had a lot of ambition and an acute sense of marketing. In 1877 he had a license for the old pizzeria in Vico Rotto San Carlo 16, which just before his arrival had been turned into a café and which Esposito reconverted into a pizzeria. In 1877 he also married Maria Giovanna Brandi, the daughter of Luigia Ottaiani, who herself ran a pizzeria at Strada di Porto 125 (near her family's pizzeria).[10] Raffaele and Maria moved to Via Gennaro Serra 21, where we find them in the first months of 1883. In April of the same year the flanking movement towards the much-desired pizzeria of Sant'Anna di Palazzo worked: Ferdinando Calicchio ceded the shop to Esposito and went back to running the old wine shop at number 30.

As soon as he had taken possession of his new shop, Esposito sent two requests to the authorities; both reveal his management panache and his ambition to reinforce the pre-exisiting fame and prestige of the pizzeria. In the first, after having stated that he ran "a pizzeria with the sale of wine" at Salita Sant'Anna di Palazzo 2, he added that "for a very long time already, even when there were other prior shopkeepers, the upstairs room at street number 1 was space to eat said pizzas; now he [Esposito] begs leave of his most illuminated mayor to add the room at street number 1 as a space to eat. In the event they are necessary, he adds a copy of the rental contract, his license and the receipt for the taxes paid for the transfer." Esposito had probably renovated, connecting the shops at numbers 1 and 2. The

---

[d]Many versions of this story written in Italian give the second pizza topped with cecenielli rather than acciughe. The former are technically fried anchovy and sardine (newly hatched fish), and the most literal English translation is "whitebait." The fact that the words for fish are often not specific to a particular species, and the fact that this story is not based on any document that mentions the fish by name (and is very likely an invention anyway) makes a longer discussion of the correct name unnecessary.

mystery remains, however, as to why from the very first documents, the pizzeria is identified with the street number 1, despite the fact that (as we can see from the request) it was at number 2.

Even more revealing of Esposito's creative spirit is the second request, which also shows his "managerial" capabilities. Immediately on taking over the pizzeria, he requested permission to put up a sign with "Pizzeria of the Queen of Italy" on it. Even if in those days the names "Roma" and "Italia" were a cliché on business signs; the fact that Esposito's sign referred to the queen tells us much about his dreams and his plans. As we can see, the name of the tricolor pizza—the white of the mozzarella, the red of the tomato, and the green of the basil—was in Esposito's head long before 1889. Perhaps the queen's "taste" was more a result of his maneuvering than of the sovereign's curiosity. We cannot be sure for that time, but today this sort of marketing is quite common, and not just in Naples. In an interview published as a small book, one of the latest owners of that pizzeria, Vincenzo Pagnani, confessed that when American president Bill Clinton (in Naples for the G7 summit in 1994) ate pizza in Via Tribunali, he felt bad that the president had not "honored" the "pizzeria where the Margherita was born." His complaints were partially successful as a few days later, while the president was in meetings, Pagnani had the satisfaction of having Clinton's daughter Chelsea and her grandmother in his pizzeria.[11]

Esposito died in 1917 and the pizzeria was then run first by his widow Maria Giovanna Brandi and then, after 1925, by Pietro Pagliarulo. In 1932 Giovanni Brandi (the widow's nephew) inherited it, though he turned it over to his brother Pasquale, who had married Pagliarulo's daughter. It was Pasquale Brandi who, despite ups and downs, remade the glorious tradition of the pizzeria. He underlined its prestige by attracting famous visitors so that, whereas in the 1800s it had been famous as "the pizzeria of Pietro il pizzaiuolo," in the 1900s it became known as "Pizzeria Brandi at Sant'Anna di Palazzo." Today it still holds sway in Naples. Pasquale's sons followed different career paths, so the pizzeria was bought after his death by one his older employees, Vincenzo Pagnani. Well-versed in the shop's tradition, he showed his ability in the pizzeria's management. After his recent death the business passed to his sons, the current owners of the pizzeria.

OTHER NINETEENTH-CENTURY PIZZERIAS

It is difficult to trace the stories of the other nineteenth-century pizzerias that are still active, of which in any event there are only a handful. They certainly had, and continue to have, able managers, but their importance for this present research derives above all from their location in the city. Also important is their continuity—which is exceptional given the city, despite certain aspects, has undergone innumerable transformations. We can make a quick list: the oldest are those in Via Tribunali 35 (mentioned already several times, recorded in the police archives for the first time in 1922), and the two at Via Porta San Gennaro 2 and Via Pignaseccca 28, first licensed in 1841 and 1842, respectively. Today they are run by families who became pizzaioli in the interwar period: the Sorbillos, the Capassos, and the Fiorenzanos.

The pizzeria at Via Gennaro Serra 20–1 is another very old one, though slightly more recent than the others. Its reopening goes back to 1877 and its address reminds us that in Naples' center the place and street names in some cases have been the same since the eighteenth century. Indeed, before the construction of the church of San Francesco di Paola (after Ferdinando I's return from Sicily), this street began at the Largo di Palazzo, today the Piazza del Plebiscito. To make room for the church, a number of buildings on this street were demolished, up to number 19. After this radical transformation, no one worried about updating the street numbers: even today the numbering does not begin with number 1 but rather with number 20.

In the 1807 list there is a pizzeria registered at Via Speranzella 115; however, this pizzeria is not mentioned in the documents for the rest of the nineteenth century. More than likely it became a wine shop, or a tavern, or it was one of the pizzerias listed in Via Conte di Mola. It reappears in the 1932 *Guida Stellacci*, although at number 113, licensed to a certain Pasqualina Magliocca. The hypothesis that this pizzeria is the same one from 1807 is supported by the fact that the pizzeria, located almost at the corner, has two entrances: one is on Via Speranzella and the other on Via Conte di Mola (the latter street, before the building of the Teatro Augusteo, reached Via Toledo).

In 1935 one of the Mattozzi brothers, Salvatore, took over this pizzeria, which he ran proudly until 1967. That year he turned it over to one of his employees (as we have seen, this was common), who then passed it on to other owners. The pizzeria is still open today.

The pizzeria in Via Bernini goes back to 1890, the first one in the new Vomero neighborhood—now full of buildings, people, and naturally pizzerias. Founded by that era's unofficial dean of pizza, Luigi Mattozzi, this pizzeria too has a proud tradition. In 1916 it was turned over to Salvatore Grasso, with the name "Pizzeria Gorizia," and it is still run today by his heirs.

Figure 7.2: Pizzeria Gorizia. Naples, c. 1920.
The famous actress Leda Gys during filming of a movie. In those years Naples was the
capital of silent movies. In the Vomero neighborhood alone 200 movies were filmed.
At the entrance of the pizzeria is Salvatore Grasso with his son Salvatore.
Courtesy of Salvatore Grasso.

8

A family affair

PROBLEMS WITH DOCUMENTATION

If for the objectives of this present research the history of pizzerias is important, just as important is the history of the pizzaioli and their families, especially when we find several generations who all work in the trade. While for the history of a shop it is enough to say (even on the basis of a few primary source documents) that for a certain period the pizzeria enjoyed a certain success, or that it was run quite well by one pizzaiolo or another. It is quite another job to attempt to describe the daily life of people who lived long ago, who experienced both pain and pleasure, and about which we want to know a bit more—their habits, their behaviors, their customs—than what cold documents tell us.

Attempting to do this brings us into conflict with the enormous difficulty presented by having people in front of us who, apart from their trade and the temporary presence in a pizzeria, have left very little trace of themselves (e.g. diaries, or letters) because of their social position. There are two ways to get past this lack of documentation and to try to rescue their history: the first is to trace out a collective history, created from a choral representation of their trade and their affairs. This was what the earlier chapters of this book attempted to do. The second way is to try to reconstruct a history of individuals through their families. Naturally this is possible only when there is continuity in the business and also an acceptable quantity of concrete facts. We cannot trust only the lore provided by their descendants, based as it is exclusively on memories handed down from their ancestors: these are always fragmentary and very often subject to "mythologization," and therefore unreliable.[1]

The nineteenth-century families—just like the individual pizzaioli—seem to be "without history" except for some mentions in the archives. For each of them it would be necessary to cross-check dates, numbers, kinship, and other facts, and even then the results are of uncertain quality and utility, given that we are talking about families that have long since left the trade. We need, therefore, to make a selection—the present sample is from searching for families that were already in the trade in the nineteenth century but are also still involved in pizzerias today. If, as we have seen, there are only a dozen or so pizzerias that were founded in the nineteenth century and are still open today, the number of families that ran pizzerias in the 1800s and

still do so today is even smaller. Many of the renowned pizzaioli families have disappeared, like the Ottaianos, the Calicchios, the Cesas, the Ambrosios, the Brandis, and
many others that left their mark on the history of pizzerias in the 1800s. There are
just three families that are still around today and have pizzerias: the Mattozzis, the
Lombardis, and the Paces.

For all three families we have the same situation as with the three historic
pizzerias: despite going back to the nineteenth century, for two of them (the Paces
and the Lombardis) there is a lack of reliable documentation of their pizzerias. Nor
is it simple to reconstruct kinship, as their last names are common and therefore
in the marriage registers for each year we find pages of entries for their last names.
Because of this it is difficult not only to reconstruct the family relationships but also,
given the gaps in the archives about the pizzaioli, to confirm their continuity in the
trade which, from the documents consulted, sometimes seems intermittent. The
situation is different for the third family, the Mattozzis, as their last name is unique
in Naples in the sense that all family members can be traced back to one ancestor.[2]
The family's first pizzeria is documented in 1852 and of the third generation
(seventeen children), all nine sons were pizzaioli. Seven of the nine were owners of
one or more pizzerias, following the example of their prolific father who opened
five documented pizzerias.

THE LOMBARDIS: A VOYAGE BETWEEN NAPLES AND NEW YORK

Of the three families, the Lombardis have the most linear, simple history, but also
the one that is the most mysterious and almost unknown to the current pizzeria
owners. They have a memory of a certain Errico Lombardi who, not knowing how
to make ends meet, decided one fine day in 1902 or thereabouts, that the only
solution was to emigrate to the far-off Americas. He was not alone in thinking this.
As he made ready to leave for the port, he gave his eight-year-old son Luigi a perfo-
rated spoon and a metal rod—tools to take fried pizzas out of boiling oil—with
which to provide for the family that he, Errico, was abandoning.

We do not know in which country he made landfall, or what he did once he
arrived. His descendants recount that he arrived, then left again; changed direction
and then came back, without ever giving up his trade. It seems he was a traveling
pizzaiolo who, given his relatively unstable character, could never put his economic
troubles behind him definitively. After his final return to Italy (perhaps after the
outbreak of the First World War) he opened a pizzeria with his son (now an adult)
in Via Tribunali, in front of the Church of the Pietrasanta. He ran this only for a
brief time, as his son had opened his own pizzeria in the Strada Trinità Maggiore,
today Via Benedetto Croce. Though Errico no longer had a pizzeria of his own, he
continued in the trade, working sometimes for his son but also for other pizzerias,
leading a vagabond sort of life as he always had.

These are family stories, but now we come to the documented history. In
March 1896 we find in the police commissioner's archives a pizzeria at Strada di

Porto 161 whose license belongs to Errico Lombardi (son of Tommaso, a manual laborer), thirty-four years old. The next month, on April 15, Errico requested permission to move from number 161 to number 9. This was the old pizzeria of the Ottaianos which had been passed down to Giovanni Malato from his mother Angela Maria. We do not know what sort of luck this very active pizzeria had under his management, but we must remember that shortly thereafter the Strada di Porto was demolished and numerous businesses had to move or simply close. This was perhaps the reason that pushed a desperate Errico to look towards the sea.

By chance we find in the records a brother of Errico, Antonio, who in 1892, already ran a pizzeria at Via Genova 23. In reality the license for the pizzeria was held by Concetta Pepillo, twenty-three years old, "married to Antonio Lombardi, son of Tommaso."[3] Consulting the marriage registers we see that the two had married on January 16, 1892 and that while Antonio was resident in Via Genova 23 (the pizzeria), his wife was resident at Via Antonio Villari 68. Evidently they ran the pizzeria together and probably already had for several years, as the marriage certificate states that about two years prior they had had a baby. The little boy was named after his late grandfather, Tommaso, and they now made him legitimate by "renaming" him.[4] Further traces of this family have been lost and the current descendants did not even know of their existence. The pizzeria was subsequently run by Vincenzo Fiorillo, who appears in the archives in 1904 and ran the shop for many years. Did the Lombardis emigrate? Perhaps. In that case the research would have to continue on the other side of the Atlantic, where perhaps they had something to do with the founding of Lombardi's Pizza in New York.

Getting back to Errico, we can see that in 1887, at twenty-five years old, he married the eighteen-year-old Concetta Scialò; she too was from a family of pizzaioli. He was therefore about forty years old when he began his peregrinations. Between one voyage and another, they brought four children into the world, three boys and a girl. In 1917, only forty-eight years old, Concetta died. Errico finally lost his wanderlust and opened a pizzeria in Via Tribunali, but he did not last too long in that spot with his unsettled character. Helped by his son Luigi he continued working in one pizzeria or another, as the family history had held. He died in 1938. His son Luigi was his polar opposite, untiring and frugal as the father was undisciplined and spendthrift. It seems that the family history was right here as well: his youth had taught him that you cannot get anything without sacrifice.

Apparently in the pizzaiolo community he was laughed at because to save a few cents, he would go personally to buy all the products necessary for the pizzeria, rather than have them delivered to his shop. He even went to find wood shavings: he would rent a handcart and go to sawmills to fill it for a few cents or even for free. Today shavings are no longer used for pizza ovens: they are not considered healthy as they are a mix of wood and have fragments of formica, plastic, paint and other materials that would poison the air in the oven. This said, a "shovel of shavings" gave the pizza a fragrance that cannot be specified and now cannot be reproduced. Shavings produced a burst of heat and cooked the pizza in a way that left the commentators of the past without words. They all stated, with a certain

Figure 8.1: Pizzeria Luigi Lombardi. Naples, 1947.
A group of pizzaioli in front of the pizzeria in Via Foria; the first from the right is Enrico Lombardi.
Courtesy of Enrico Maria Lombardi.

naïveté, that the pizzas came out of the oven "more burnt than cooked" without understanding that this was the norm for Neapolitan pizza.[5]

Luigi had two brothers, Antonio and Pasquale, who had two different professions. The former was in the fruit and vegetables business while the latter became an antiquarian book dealer. This trade was passed down to Pasquale's nephew Luigi (Antonio's son), who today still runs an antiquarian bookshop in Via Costantinopoli. They say that Luigi worked hard and with his sacrifices was able to put away some savings that he needed when misfortune struck. We have already seen that since the 1920s he had had his pizzeria in front of the Basilica of Santa Chiara. Directly in front of this monument was a five-floor building, an example of a bad Neapolitan habit of building houses right on top of various architectural treasures. In any event, it was here that Lombardi and his family lived.

One black day, though—August 4, 1943—a furious bombing by the American air force almost completely destroyed both the basilica and the building in front of it. In one direct hit, poor Luigi lost both his house and his pizzeria. Soon thereafter, though, was the armistice with the Allies (September 8, 1943), the "Four days of Naples,"[a] and the subsequent liberation of Naples and arrival of Allied troops on October 1. Life slowly returned back to normal and it was decided to save the first floor of the building, where the shops were. The old businesses began reopening, the pizzeria among them. The events had taught hardworking Luigi a lesson: to cover his back he bought a second pizzeria at Via Foria 12, though at first (the pizzeria at Santa Chiara now reopened) he rented it out.

At the end of the 1950s a discussion started in Naples about restoring the old portal (now underneath the apartment building) of the basilica. Luigi saw that in a few years he might once again be without his pizzeria and began to look for a new location. He had the good luck to find it a few meters away, at Via Benedetto Croce 59; he moved there in 1963 and his old pizzeria was subsequently demolished. Always precocious, he had married the nineteen-year-old Giovannina Tucci in 1915, when he was only eighteen years old. They had a number of children, three of whom (the sons) followed in their father's footsteps. The oldest, Enrico, took over the pizzeria in Via Foria, leaving it later to his two sons Luigi and Ferdinando. They still run it today with their two young sons, Enrico Maria and Carlo Alberto. When Luigi died in 1979, his other two sons, Luigi junior and Alfonso, inherited the pizzeria in Via Benedetto Croce. The latter died in 1996, while the former still runs the pizzeria, although his children all have other jobs.

THE MYSTERY OF THE PACE FAMILY: 1800S OR 1900S?

Somewhat more complicated is the story of the Pace family, which goes back to two distinct families that probably have the same origin (the evidence for which is still lacking). This hypothesis of a common origin is supported by the fact that both families

---

[a] September 27 to 30, 1943, a popular revolt in Naples against the German army.

were in the pizzaiolo trade and both also had a series of reoccurring first names that were the same in both families. Worth noting is that the first family (now out of the pizzeria business) appears in the archives back to the nineteenth century, whereas the second family (still active) is easier to document in the twentieth century than the one prior. The first pizzaiolo family tradition starts with Luigi Pace (son of Lorenzo), born in 1838 and in the archives a second time in January 1876 in connection to "a pizzeria with consumption of wine" at Vico Fico al Purgatorio 36. His father is given as a "carriage carpenter," so Luigi seems to have started in a completely new business.[6] In the same document there is a note of the inspector (the new name, after unification, for what had been called the neighborhood police "commissioner") of the San Lorenzo neighborhood. The inspector states that Pace "had closed the business, [but] that he had not returned the license" and that the new renter was another pizzaiolo.[7]

We find Pace again a few years later at Via Foria 104, where he ran a pizzeria and a trattoria until 1896. That year he requested permission to move to Via Banchi Nuovi 16–17 "with an upstairs room as [a] domicile." It was the pizzeria of his contemporary Luigi Mattozzi who (as we will see below) was busy with other pizzerias. He probably had offered the management of the pizzeria in this difficult time to Pace; the bonds of solidarity were perhaps stronger then.[8] Pace had a life that was constantly in movement, as seems to have been the norm. He was married the first time to Carmina De Felice (she too was a pizzaiola), with whom he had a number of children. Only one, Raffaele, followed in his father footsteps.

Widowed, he remarried Fiorentina D'Orazio when he was fifty-two years old. She too was a widow and a pizzaiola. Only two years later she died and left Pace alone again. A few months later Pace married for the third time, in 1893. Four years later it was his turn to die. He was only fifty-nine years old, his son Raffaele (now thirty-three years old) reported to the police. Raffaele had become a pizzaiolo as we find him for the first time in a commercial guide (*Grande Guida Lo Gatto*) in 1888 at the pizzeria in Via Foria 104. It was the year before his father's death, so apparently he was working with his father. Later we find him at Strada Pignasecca 34, mentioned in the 1915 *Annuario Detken* guide and then in the 1925 *Guida Stellacci*. In 1930 he died at the age of sixty-five, and only two years later his young son Vincenzo (then thirty-six years old, also a pizzaiolo) died as well. With Vincenzo's this branch of the Pace pizzaiolo tradition died out.

The story of the second family (still active in the pizzeria business) is quite different. It begins with Ferdinando Pace, born in 1850, who died at forty-six years in 1896—just a year before his (possible) relative Luigi. The death certificate states that he was a pizzaiolo and that his father was named Giovanni and was a baker; it also gives his mother as Marianna De Rosa, whose residence was at Vico Castrucci ai Miracoli 3. This was the same address of the person who reported the death, Raffaele Pace, himself a thirty-year-old pizzaiolo. It is tempting to think that it was Raffaele who reported the death of Luigi Pace the next year; our doubt is resolved by the fact that Luigi's son was a bit older than Raffaele and lived in Via Portamedina (i.e. near where his father had been a pizzaiolo). We lose sight of Raffaele (Ferdinando's son), though his great-grandson thinks that he too left for America, as did many of his generation.

Getting back to Ferdinando and his background, we find a small mystery about his birth. His death certificate from 1896 records his age as forty-six, from which we can calculate that he was born in 1850. This date is confirmed by his son Carmine's birth certificate from 1876, in which Ferdinando is given as twenty-six years old. Looking at the birth registrations for that year, we find a Ferdinando Pace, son of Giovanni (a wine shop keeper) and Marianna Izzo. All of the details correspond except for the last name of the mother, though it could simply be an error in transcription. Continuing in the same registers we find, in 1852, a Vincenzo Pace with the same parents; then again in 1853 a Maria Pace with the same parents. In these two documents the father Giovanni states first that he is a cured sausage vendor and then a pizzaiolo. The plot thickens because it seems improbable that the mother's last name was written incorrectly three times.

This mystery is resolved when we discover the marriage certificate of the two parents, Giovanni Pace and Marianna Izzo. Giovanni, according to this document, was the son of Lorenzo Pace (a carpenter) and Rosa Scalera (twenty-three years old). We are talking about the brother of Luigi from the first Pace family, who had married Marianna Izzo (daughter of Domenico, a macaroni vendor).[9] The problem is that Ferdinando (the son of Marianna De Rosa) is impossible to find in the registers of the babies born between 1846 and 1855—his certificate has gone missing, like who knows how many others—nor do we find him in the requests for licenses for pizzerias in the police archives. It is possible that he worked for other people and that the pizzerias of the second Pace family started around the turn of the century. This could be the reason that some pizza historians have said "the Pace family is a more recent one but not for this any less aristocratic in the world of Neapolitan pizza."[10] One of the numerous sons of Ferdinando, Carmine, opened several important pizzerias in the course of the twentieth century, at first by himself and later with his sons.

Carmine married Rosa Cuomo, with whom he had several children. Some of them died while still quite young, as was common for that time. What is surprising is that among those that died one was called "Ferdinando" and two "Raffaele"; the first was for his grandfather while the other two were probably in memory of the brother, Raffaele, either dead or far away. It is with Carmine, in any event, that the family's take-off begins. He married Cuomo when he was twenty-one years old (she was eighteen), in 1897, one year after his father's death. He had around ten children (common at the time) but also—together with his wife—an entrepreneurial spirit. We can find him again at Via Tribunali 292 where he ran for an old pizzeria for a number of years. Thereafter, in 1917, he took over an already well-known pizzeria from Francesco Ambrosio (busy with his reopened pizzeria in Via Port'Alba). This shop, at Piazza Cavour 22, brought Pace to the highest levels of efficiency and fame.

Riding the success of the pizzeria in Piazza Cavour—where the pizzeria was functioning at full speed and at capacity because of the density of residents, the presence of various schools, and the considerable foot traffic—he opened a pizzeria–ristorante with his now adult children. This was in Via Santa Brigida, just around the corner from the heavily-trafficked Via Toledo, and was followed by a restaurant at Borgo Marinari. The Santa Brigida location was initially more of a pizzeria than a restaurant; the other location, opened in 1936, was near two old, famous restaurants "Zi" Teresa" and "La Bersagliera." Given the presence of these two competitors, the new Pace location was more restaurant than pizzeria. After the Second World War Pace opened a third location in the upper part of the Vomero neighborhood, in a street that filled up with apartment buildings and stores in the 1950s, Via Bernardo Cavallino. The restaurant was called "Il Cavallino d'oro."

Carmine's children—Ciro, Vincenzo, Carmine, and Nunzia—got along well enough that, although each had their own family, they ran these businesses if not quite in common, at least in groups of twos and threes, sometimes interchangeably. Of these three locations the oldest and the most famous is the one in Via Santa Brigida. Today it is run by three cousins, Carmine (Ciro's son), Carmine Stentardo (Nunzia's son), and Vincenzo's son Antonio. In addition to taking care of the restaurant, Antonio also dedicates a lot of this time to the union. He is president of the pizzeria union and one of the most active promoters of the association created to defend the genuineness of Neapolitan pizza.

THE SAGA OF THE MATTOZZIS

The oldest and most numerous family of pizzaioli that is still active in the sector are the Mattozzis. Over the last 160 years they have given the pizza world more than twenty pizzaioli, all closely related to each other—fathers, sons, brothers, nephews—and opened at least twenty-four pizzerias (all well-documented). For this they merit the title "dynasty," and that is exactly how more than one journalist has defined them. This word—so far from the modesty and humility that characterize pizzaioli—finds justification in the fact that from the very beginning the trade has always been passed down from father to son. The generations from the end of the nineteenth century until the 1960s, all eleven male members of the family (nine brothers, a father, and a nephew) each ran by themselves or together one or more pizzerias. The history of this family as pizzaioli began in 1852, but the documents about their origins go back to the last decade of the eighteenth century.

The patriarch of the family was Emiddio Mattozzi, probably an emigrant from the Ciociaria region near Rome, where the last name "Mattozzi" is more common. Emiddio was a public servant[11] who in the 1790s married a woman from Salerno, Orsola Cantarella. They had at least two children, a boy and a girl. The boy, Michele, was born in September 1798 and in 1824 married the eighteen-year-old Fortunata Cioffi. She lived in Vico Equense at the time of their marriage, and had eight children.

Michele was a brazier, an artisan who works with brass. He must have been good at it if he had three boys who all went to school. Luigi, who became a pizzaiolo; Giuseppe, who was a priest; and Antonio, a music teacher. Naturally the one we are interested in is Luigi, the oldest of the three. He was born in 1833 in the Porto neighborhood, at Rampa San Giovanni Maggiore 11. Just nineteen years old in 1852—but in a period in which, as we have seen, the pizzeria business was undergoing a marked expansion—Luigi convinced his father to ask permission "to reopen the old bakery to cook *focacce* at Largo San Demetrio 17." This widening in the street, eventually called Piazzetta Teodoro Monticelli, followed the numbering of the Strada Banchi Nuovi, according to the Neapolitan tradition.

In reality we cannot be sure whether Michele the brazier decided on his own to start a new business, or whether it was the dynamic Luigi to convince him to lend his son his name in order to obtain the license that the youth could not have got (as he was, under Neapolitan law then, still a minor). Given the regulations of the time, which required the presence in the actual shop of the holder of the license, we can imagine that at least at the beginning the father and son worked together. We only know for sure that the very next year it was Luigi asking on his own for a license in his name "to put a sign above his shop with the words: 'Rooms for Dinner.'" This detail leads us to believe that the true engine in that situation was Luigi, and it also tells us that the pizzeria had rooms upstairs, something a later document confirms.

The license was not immediately issued, as the response from the Prefecture was that "Michele and not Luigi Matuzzi [*sic*] has a license for the oven for pizzas at Largo San Demetrio."[12] In any event, sign or not, the business must have gone quite well: despite ups and downs, it allowed Luigi to marry twice, bring seventeen children into the world, buy property and even open other pizzerias. His first wife, Fiolmena De Simone, was just fifteen when they got married. His wife's dowry was described with meticulous detail in a marital contract signed in front of a notary.[13] Their house was at the end of the present-day Corso Garibaldi. In 1875, just thirty-two years old, Filomena died while giving birth to their fifth child, a son. The infant did not live long: after less than a year, he died as well. It must have been a difficult year even for the indomitable Luigi. Five children (including a newborn) and a pizzeria that held him prisoner for fifteen or sixteen hours a day must have made life that much harder. But he was not the kind of man to let himself lose heart. In the space of just a few months he went from being a widow to being a newlywed. Only five months after his wife's death he took Luigia Germano (not even twenty years old) to the altar. She was a seamstress from Sant'Arpino, where her family owned property. It is important to remember that the bridegroom was forty-two years old; this must not have weighed on him too much as he brought twelve children into the world with his new wife. The first few years must not have been very happy for the bride, though. In addition to having to take care of five children who were not hers (of which the youngest died just three month after the wedding, during her first pregnancy), she also had to bear the pain of watching her first-born child die at nine months. But life is sometimes stronger than death. Despite all of his personal calamities, Luigi and Luigia found their balance and had eleven more children, of which only two did not live beyond infancy. But Luigi was not just prolific in procreation, but also for pizzerias. In 1881 we find him at Strada Banchi Nuovi and also at Strada Chiaia 166,[14] a shop ceded to him by a certain Giosuè Arpaja, who had converted a pastry shop into a pizzeria.

In 1883 he opened a third pizzeria at Vico Sedil Capuano 27, this time putting it in the name of his wife Luigia.[15] At this point he had had ten children, of which five with his first wife and as many with his second wife, though only seven of the children were alive. Perhaps he was just using his wife's name. One thing is certain:

Figure 8.2: Luigi Mattozzi, portrait by Lionello Balestrieri. Naples, c. 1880.
With his pizzeria at the Largo San Demetrio ai Banchi Nuovi, Luigi became (in 1852) the
first Mattozzi to become a pizzaiolo.
Courtesy of Donatella Mattozzi.

after just two years the pizzeria was turned over to another pizzaiolo. In 1884 the umpteenth cholera epidemic broke out, one which killed over 7,000 people. Among the improvised ordinances issued by the authorities was a decree that closed all of the wine shops. By mistake a notification of closure was sent to Mattozzi as well: not being a wine shop and feeling unjustly punished, he sent an appeal to the police commissioner.[16] This was sent on October 15. The epidemic, which has begun in the middle of August, had reached its acme and would end in the next month. We have no idea how long the pizzeria was closed as on Mattozzi's appeal was written in the margin only "keep this in mind for the next ordinances." It is certain only that the unlucky pizzaiolo reopened his shop and began his usual work, but the epidemic had provided him with yet another regret. Another block was about to fall on his head just a few years after, as we will see.

The epidemic of 1884, the last in a long series of epidemics, brought the age-old problems of Naples to the attention of a national audience and forced the central authorities to intervene forcibly. After a visit of Prime Minister Agostino Depretis and King Umberto I himself, it was decided that the city needed a radical public works program that would resolve in one fell swoop the problems of the sewer, the water supply, and the unhealthy *bassi* in the overpopulated neighborhoods.[b] A "gutting" was proposed for the lower part of the city, the most decrepit, and a plan was developed. This plan foresaw the demolition of scores of buildings and the construction, in their place, or two long boulevards, the present-day Corso Umberto I and Corso Garibaldi. The latter would go through the area where the Mattozzi's house stood, and as a result all of the apartment buildings there would be torn down. With the decision of August 13, 1889, the Prefect of Naples decreed the expropriation and the subsequent sale to the Society for the Risanamento of Naples of the houses that belonged to Luigi Mattozzi.[17] He was offered the sum of £14,400. We do not know where he moved with his large family, though two of his children had already married early.

Given the children that were growing up and new ones being born, it seems natural that Mattozzi was looking for new opportunities. We should not be surprised to find him in the Vomero neighborhood, which in 1890 was still under construction. There was no street numbering system yet, just buildings marked with letters and the names of their owners; it was here that Mattozzi opened the first pizzeria in what would become Naples' second major urban center after the historic district.[18] The great pizzaiolo had a strange habit, though: each time that he went to the city offices to record the birth of a new child, he almost always gave a younger age than the real one, and he always gave the address of his pizzeria in Via Banchi Nuovi as his residence. In addition to a custom of the times, apparently the pizzeria was indeed considered his actual residence if in six separate birth certificates (of the twelve found) he gave his domicile as Via Banchi Nuovi.

In two of the birth records (of Salvatore in 1892 and Maria in 1894), the residences given are Strada Pantaleone 21 and Via Genova 23, the addresses of two other pizzerias. Given Luigi's habit of giving the address of his shop as his

---

[b] In Italian, "risanamento" means both "renewal" and "cure."

residence, and assuming that he did not actually live in the pizzeria (as other documents exclude that possibility), we could presume that industrious Luigi had some interest in the other two pizzerias as well, even if at the moment there are no known documents that confirm this. Probably each time he opened a new pizzeria, not being able to be everywhere all the time, he turned it over to be managed by some pizzaiolo he trusted. An example could be Luigi Pace, whom we mentioned earlier, or perhaps Mattozzi's now-adult children.

In 1898 his second wife, just forty-two years old, died, leaving Mattozzi with children that were still small. Luigi was now sixty-five years old and had thirteen living children and two unmarried sisters. The first, Margherita, lived by herself at the Salita Arenella, an old resort location that even today is very pleasant. She must have had a job or some sort of business (or in any event some savings), because after her death her two siblings bought a new house in Vico Fornelle a Santissimi Giovanni e Paolo. Luigi himself died in 1908, not having ever left his profession. In the purchase agreement for the new house, his residence was given as Via Foria 146, the address of yet another pizzeria, registered to his name in a guide to the city in 1904 (*Guida Commerciale Prestreau*).

Prior to this, in the last decade of the nineteenth century, the four oldest children had become adults, had all married and had looked for their own place and economic independence. The oldest son Vincenzo had taken over from his father in the pizzeria in Via Banchi Nuovi, where (following his father's custom) he declared his residence in the birth certificates for six of his ten children (all those born between 1892 and 1905). True to his trade and family tradition, he stayed in that pizzeria until his death in 1924. After him the pizzeria was rented and we find the license made out to a certain Anna Passaro[19] who ran it for a number of years, after which it was closed definitively. The pizzeria in Via Banchi Nuovi was one of many run by the numerous Mattozzi brothers. While his father was at the Vomero location, the second son (also called Luigi) asked for a license in 1891 for "a pizzeria and sale of wine by the glass" at Vico Carrozzieri a Toledo 12, and then in Via Foria.

The last of the four children from Luigi Sr.'s first marriage, Gennaro, did not have children despite being married twice, though to make up for it he was the most dynamic of the family. Like his father, he opened a number of pizzerias that he then entrusted to his stepbrothers, all of whom had a deferential respect for him. His first pizzeria was at Via Tribunali 202. It was a perfect spot, situated at the end of a much-trafficked street, practically in front of that bustling intersection that the courthouse then was. Mattozzi appears on the records for that address in 1900, when he was twenty-eight years old. Two years later he added two bassi and four rooms at Fondaco Paparelle, and the next year another *basso* and five apartments in Vico Zite al Lavinaio.

In 1908 the family had two funerals. In January, Francesco, one of the brothers born during Luigi's second marriage, died at just twenty-six years old. In October Luigi himself, the patriarch, died. The situation as far as the management of the pizzerias was as follows: the three brothers from the first marriage (Vincenzo, Luigi, and Gennaro) each had their own pizzeria in (respectively) Via Banchi Nuovi, Via Foria, and Via Tribunali. The five brothers from the second marriage—Eugenio, Ernesto, Giuseppe, Alfonso, and Salvatore—were distributed in these pizzerias.

Gennaro, however, was not the type to rest on his laurels. In Via Depretis, one of the principal new arteries to come out of the Risanamento, many buildings were still under construction.[20] Just like his father had done in the Vomero neighborhood, Gennaro opened a pizzeria there in two rooms that had just been completed, at numbers 85–7.[c] It was 1911 and he entrusted it (as we saw above) temporarily to Pietro Pagliarulo, who then moved on to Sant'Anna di Palazzo. The next year he put his brother Vincenzo in the pizzeria in Via Tribunali and went to run the new one in Via Depretis personally, later actually buying (not renting) the two shops. In the meantime the two younger brothers, Alfonso and Salvatore, had reached the age for military service.

These were four difficult years: though there was less business because of the war, there were still four pizzerias to run. The situation returned to normal at the end of the war. The pizzeria where Luigi junior had been in Via Foria changed hands, but we do not know what happened to Luigi. Vincenzo continued to run the two in Via Tribunali and Via Banchi Nuovi, helped by his stepbrother Eugenio and his adult children. Gennaro made a new acquisition: the old pizzeria and trattoria at Largo della Carità. It was a step ahead for the family, because it was a pizzeria with a long tradition. Gennaro knew how to make it even more prestigious and brought the Mattozzi name to place it in the pizzeria business.

The pizzeria in Via Depretis was then given to the four youngest brothers, though this arrangement did not last long. In 1920, the youngest brother, Salvatore, married and went to live in Via Tribunali 203, in the building next to the pizzeria run by Vincenzo. The two, together with the other three brothers (Ernesto, Giuseppe, and Alfonso), bought the whole thing: the pizzeria at number 202 and the four apartments above it (at number 203). The first floor had access to the pizzeria and became an upstairs room, while Salvatore, his two sisters, and their families lived in the second, third, and fourth floors. A few years later, after the death of Eugenio (the oldest of the children from the second marriage) in 1923, Vincenzo himself died. By 1924 only five brothers and four sisters remained of the once-numerous family.

At this point the management of the pizzerias was once again shifted around. The one in Via Banchi Nuovi was turned over to other people, while Gennaro continued to run the one at Largo della Carità. In the meantime he had opened yet another pizzeria, nearby at Via Speranzella 70.[21] Salvatore had taken over the pizzeria in Via Tribunali and the other three brothers stayed in the pizzeria in Via Depretis. In the 1930s life seemed to have returned to normal. The international economic crisis had only had a small effect on the city's economy, which had always been in crisis in a certain way. In addition, a pizzeria needed only a few materials: flour, tomatoes, dairy products, garlic, and oregano. All of these were inexpensive products available locally.

The five Mattozzi brothers continued in their same locations, but once again something did not go quite right. While Gennaro's pizzeria at Largo della Carità and Salvatore's in Via Tribunali went quite well, the Via Depretis location was in the red,

---

[c] It is a photograph of this pizzeria that is on the cover of the this book.

and not because business was not good or there were not many pizzas being sold. The problem was that the three brothers at that location had very different characters. Alfonso, the youngest, was the most involved in the work, perhaps because he had the most children. Ernesto, the oldest was the least involved but the most likely to spend money, again perhaps because of his family situation (he was married but had no children). The third, Giuseppe, had the vices and virtues of the other two: he worked hard like Alfonso, but was a spendthrift like Ernesto. Even if he was a bachelor he had a family: he had fathered four children, all of whom died young. All were listed as "of an unknown mother" but all recognized as legitimate by him.

All three brothers shared the till and naturally, as each dipped into it without any sort of rigorous accounting, problems developed, ending with an ever-increasing debt. We have to remember too that the three brothers owned the real estate in Via Tribunali in common with a fourth brother. This meant that although the debt was much less than the value of the property, any one brother's debt involved all four other owners. There were a number of mortgages—all with "sale forbidden" on them—that begin in the 1920s and continued in the 1930s. Each one followed the paying off of the previous mortgage, perhaps a payment made with the help of the other two brothers, Gennaro and Salvatore. This situation would perhaps have worked itself out, had the guillotine not been about to fall on the brothers' heads: eminent domain again. The High Commission on Public Works had decided that, as part of the opening of a new street (today Via De Gasperi) which ran into Via Depretis diagonally, the building where the pizzeria was located would be demolished. It was taken over by the Commission; today, in the place where the two streets meet, there is a triangular building where the finance police are located. As if the event was meant to be preserved for posterity, yet again the street numbers were not updated. Today the numbering on the seaward side of Via Depretis has a gap of thirty numbers, going directly from 75 to 105. The pizzeria was at 85–7.

The situation deteriorated quickly now. The shop and apartments in Via Tribunali had to be sold as they were, as was said at the time, "undivided property." Salvatore had the greatest losses, principally because he was not responsible for the debt of the other brothers and also because in addition to leaving the pizzeria, he had to leave his house. One again the sale of the pizzeria happened within the community of pizzaioli: the buyer was Salvatore Grasso, who already ran the pizzeria at Via Bernini 29, today still in the hands of his family. But the Mattozzis were not the kind of people to stand around with their hands in their pockets; within a few years all of them had new pizzerias. Salvatore took over the one in Via Speranzella 113, Giuseppe opened a new one in Via Duomo 349. Ernesto and Alfonso opened a pizzeria–restaurant in Via Marchese Campodisola in front of the stock exchange (still owned by their descendants today). They were years of intense work for the brothers, though they were able to bring their business up to the level it had enjoyed in earlier decades. The five Mattozzi pizzerias (Vincenzo junior had one as well) all enjoyed excellent reputations.

Each one was in a different area, and had its own characteristics. The one at Largo della Carità remained the most prestigious, counting on the city's best clientele (which it divided with Pizzeria Brandi). In the evenings it was open late,

Figure 8.3: Pizzeria Mattozzi, Via Depretis. Naples, c. 1920.
The Mattozzi brothers, with other pizzaioli. The first from the right is Alfonso, and the fourth from the right (behind the counter) is Salvatore. The pizzeria, at number 85–7, would be demolished a few years later during the widening of the street.
Courtesy of Alfonso Mattozzi.

hosting the clients from the Teatro Nuovo, the movie theater Sala Roma, and students from the nearby university. The one in Via Speranzella, on the other hand, was a typical neighborhood pizzeria: by day it had employees of the city, of the various banks from Via Toledo, or of the shops in the area. In the evenings it was the families of the middle class, then more numerous in the Quartieri Spagnoli neighborhood. The pizzeria in Via Duomo (at the corner of Via Marina) was in front of one of the various gates to the port, then very busy. The location in Via Marchese Campodisola (also a restaurant) had, like the Carità location, an excellent clientele that came from the nearby stock exchange, from the university and from all of the numerous offices in the area. The last pizzeria, at Porta Capuana, was much more plebian and was well known to the working class. It is important to recall that this was just before the Second World War and pizza was still a Neapolitan specialty, known only in Naples. The number of pizzerias was small, and with all of the privations of war, the bombings and the resulting misery that number tended to get smaller rather than larger. The ones that survived are today the nucleus of Neapolitan pizzerias.

At the end of the war life got back on course, but in a different climate: more liberal, more active, and more dynamic. Naples headed towards democracy, political struggle, and elections. As soon as the *joie di vivre* returned to daily life, pizza—traditionally one of the most popular and inexpensive ways to enjoy life in Naples—regained its centrality to Neapolitan gastronomy. The Mattozzis with their five pizzerias, also regained their position. And something happened that, despite having nothing to do with pizza, made their name synonymous with pizza. What happened? The centuries-old problem of housing in Naples had been made even more dramatic with the bombardments and the destruction caused by the war. A politician named Capozzi tried to take advantage of this situation, which was then fundamental for so many Neapolitans. He became a candidate in one of the first elections held in 1946 and 1948, and had the brilliant idea of a typical demagogue, "a house for everyone." He coined a slogan that went: "Want a house? Vote for Capozzi!" His idea was brilliant but did not rest on solid foundations; the slogan had a rhythm that left you waiting because it was too short. The two things together—the impracticality of the plan and the overly-brief slogan—excited the imagination and the irony that have always been right at home in Naples.

Among the students at the Istituto Pontano a Cariati was a young Ugo Gregoretti, who later became a famous director and screenwriter. One day after school he and his friends decided to go get a pizza and, walking down the Strada Conte di Mola, they went into the Pizzeria Mattozzi in Via Speranzella. Like all boys, they were joking around, and looking at the wall in front of them they saw Capozzi's slogan. It is not clear if it was Gregoretti's idea or one of his friends (the director very modestly asserts that they all made it up together, though given his personality, it was probably him) they hit upon something. Playing with the similarity of the two last names, they everything together and came up with "Want a house? Vote Capozzi! Want a pizza? Vote Mattozzi!" The slogan spread quickly, by word of mouth and in graffiti on walls, and was soon on everyone's lips. Any Neapolitan born before that time will remember it today. The fame of Mattozzis, naturally, only grew with this new (and entirely free) form of advertising. It lasted for quite a long time, also because the five pizzerias were well distributed over the city's center. It had been a century since the first Mattozzi pizzeria had been opened and the five remaining brothers, grandsons of the founder of the "dynasty," were all by then quite old. It was the moment to pass the baton, but the five Mattozzis only two had sons. It was only Alfonso who kept up the family business, still run with pride today.

Alfonso died in 1955, leaving the pizzeria in Via Marchese Campodisola to his two sons, Eugenio and Luigi (just seventeen years old). They had already been working with their father and continued the business with their uncle Ernesto, the brother and partner of their father. Gennaro died in 1958 without leaving any direct heirs. After the war the more than seventy-year-old man had turned over the prestigious pizzeria at Largo della Carità to Raffaele Brandi, the brother of the Brandis of Sant'Anna di Palazzo; Brandi had married one of Gennaro's nieces. It was exceptional, as before he had run a restaurant in Bagnoli, one that had been destroyed by the only bombardment that neighborhood had seen in the war. Under his management the restaurant returned to its old glory; it would have lasted had he not died prematurely. In 1961 two of the employees at the stock exchange location took the pizzeria over.

Giuseppe left his pizzeria in Via Duomo to his adopted daughter, Carmela Delle Curti, who in turn entrusted the management of the pizzeria to her son, and later to Alfonso's nephew. The shop was later demolished with the widening of Via Marina. Of Salvatore's five sons four chose other professions and only one, Vittorio, continued as a pizzaiolo, though in another pizzeria. This was due to the slow post-war decline of the Quartieri Spagnoli neighborhood. He took over a milk store in Corso Garibaldi and turned it into a pizzeria of high quality. Both the father and the son eventually turned their pizzerias over to other people, the former in 1967 and the latter at the end of the 1990s.

Five years after Alfonso's death, his brother Ernesto died. They had been together since opening the Via Depretis location and had then run the stock exchange location for over twenty years. These sad events risked creating the same ruinous situation as in Via Depretis; as we have seen, Alfonso's two sons had taken over after his death, running the pizzeria with their uncle. The business was run by both brothers but the license and the rental contracts were only in Ernesto's name. There were no documents or contracts that showed that the business was shared between them. This naïve decision lacked foresight: put together with his lack of shrewdness and inability with money meant that once again there was a huge debt. On their uncle's death they risked losing everything, with no proof of being the legitimate heirs of the two partners (Ernesto and Alfonso).

They received an eviction notice because of the arrears in the rent from the company that owned the pizzeria, and the two brothers had no right to inherit the license which various authorities threatened to revoke. The pizzeria stayed closed and they ran the risk of repeating the same experience that their uncles had in the 1930s in Via Depretis. What was worse, the revenue lost while the pizzeria remained closed only added itself to the unpaid debts. The two brothers struggled through this situation. Luigi looked for another way out, and started to manage other people's pizzerias, only later opening a few of his own. He opened one first in Via dei Cimbri, then a restaurant in Via Posillipo, and finally a pizzeria–restaurant in Via Filangieri, which he runs today with his three sons.

Eugenio on the other hand was the older of the two and perhaps more capable. He fought relentlessly to regain the old pizzeria. He hired lawyers and mediators, involved acquaintances and finally was able to get it back and pay off the debts. Wanting to break with the past and give the shop a new image, he gave the new (old) location the name "Ristorante Europeo." Several decades have passed and Eugenio has brought the pizzeria-restaurant "L'Europeo di Mattozzi" to a level fitting with his family's past. Once again the Mattozzi tradition of passing a pizza down from father to son has been repeated: after Eugenio's recent death, his son Alfonso (with the help of his daughter Luigia) hosts a clientele of the highest level. He has received a number of awards and enjoys an excellent reputation in many international guidebooks.

The Mattozzis, after over 160 years of uninterrupted business, are now at the fifth and sixth consecutive generation of pizzaioli and restaurateurs. Luigi and his three sons (Eugenio, Alfonso, and Giuseppe) run the pizzeria-restaurant in Via Filangieri; Alfonso and his daughter Luigia run the "Europeo" in Via Marchese

Campodisola in front of the stock exchange; Nunzia (Alfonso's sister) runs a restaurant in Via Pietro Colletta and Fabiana (Alfonso's other daughter) has taken over an old trattoria in Strada della Pignasecca, together with her husband. Another Mattozzi pizzeria is at Via Nuova Marina 71–2 (an old Mattozzi location). The sign has another last name, Festa, because Antonio Festa married on of the Mattozzi daughters. The pizzeria at Largo della Carità, despite still having the name "Pizzeria e Ristorante Mattozzi," is today run by Paolo Surace, who is not related to the family at all.

Yesterday's pizza, today's pizza

Making a balance sheet for the phenomenon of pizzerias is quite difficult in that it is something that is in continuous evolution. It began in Naples where the hundred or so nineteenth-century pizzerias multiplied to such an extent that the city limits no longer held them. They spilled out into the surrounding towns, then the rest of Italy, then Europe, the Americas and further. The phenomenon known as the pizzeria is in expansion all over the world. Proof of this can be found the recent news of an Italian pizzeria in Mumbai, India. The pizzeria, Francesco's, is experimenting with drones for home delivery of pizza, yet another example of how diverse the pizzeria is today. But our story is of the evolution of the Neapolitan pizzerias that, for almost two centuries, remained tied to the history of the city of Naples—this is the path we will continue to follow though simultaneously keeping in mind the new directions pizzerias have taken.

FROM ANTIQUITY TO THE EIGHTEENTH CENTURY

Born around the middle of the eighteenth century, pizzerias (whether they were just workshops or actual places to eat food) continued to bubble and ferment in Naples, just like the dough they made, for more than two centuries. We are discussing here specifically about pizzerias and not pizzas, because, as we have seen in the previous pages, it was only in pizzerias that Neapolitan pizzas were made. This bears repeating: pizzas were not made in convents (as the Abbot Galiani said), nor in other kinds of bakeries (as Basile held), nor in the ancient world. Often books refer to "pizzas" made in the ovens at Pompeii, in the Greco–Roman excavations in Naples or (most recently) at the dig at Rione Terra di Pozzuoli. In these ancient ovens, *piceae* or *pittae* or *bizze* were produced, but certainly not Neapolitan pizzas as we know them today, but rather a simple flatbread that any country woman or nun or baker would have known how to make.

As we said before, flatbreads made with crushed grains have always been a part of civilizations. Some historians assert that already in the thirteenth century the imperial cooks in China prepared *ping tse*, a flatbread made from rice flour, topped with spices and other ingredients. Earlier Herodotus, a Greek historian from the fifth century BCE, wrote that the Babylonians prepared flatbreads made with fish flour and cooked in an oven. Even earlier, in pharaonic Egypt, it was customary to eat flatbreads made with flour and aromatic herbs. There is no lack of references to flatbreads in all the classical literatures of various civilizations, as well as in medieval and modern writing. What is clear, though, is that what was being referred to was something quite different from Neapolitan pizza. After the Second World War, which brought contingents to Italy from all over the world with the Anglo-American armies, the true globalization of pizza and pizzerias began. Pizzerias, initially only 100 or so in number, became 1,000, then 10,000, then 100,000 and continue to spread over the whole globe. As often happens when a product of uncertain (and distant) origin reaches a global degree of diffusion (and universal approbation), the claims about ownership begin to be heard.

There have been so many assertions about the origin of pizza that a group of American scholars (whether in the spirit of research or in jest, we cannot be sure) organized a "trial" to settle this delicate question. In May 1991 George T. Choppelas, a judge in San Francisco's city court, opened a debate in which various possibilities were defended, from a Chinese origin to a Mediterranean birthplace. The court examined various accounts from the literatures already mentioned above but arrived at the conclusion that Italy was the birthplace of pizza. In the "sentence" issued by the judge and his jury of scholars, the paternity of pizza was legally established—though they decided that pizza went back 3,000 years and that the name was from Latin *picea*.

GENUINE NEAPOLITAN PIZZA

Saying Italy is a half-truth, thus not quite right. As the documents used for this present research show, the true birthplace of pizza is Naples—it is not a coincidence that pizza is accompanied by the adjective "Neapolitan." This is to distinguish it from the many different kinds of flatbreads made all over the world, but also to protect the genuinity and the originality of the ingredients. Indeed, it is the wide spread of pizzas and the dish's versatility in being able to bear the most varied ingredients—on that disc of dough chocolate has been spread, or even spaghetti or beans—that has made Neapolitan pizzaioli form an association. They even have a statute, to defend the authenticity of their product.

Indeed, several different associations with different names are all pursuing the same goal: to protect the name and defend the product while spreading it to other countries. These include countries whose food tastes and gastronomic traditions are the furthest from theirs, like Japan (where pizza is very popular), China, Korea, and other countries in the Far East. The leader of these initiatives was (and still is) Antonio Pace who together with other pizzeria managers, founded the association "Vera pizza napoletana" in the late 1980s.[a] Ten years later another organization—

---

[a] "Vera pizza napoletana" and "Verace pizza napoletana" are only very subtly different, with much semantic overlap. The former could be rendered "Real Neapolitan Pizza" while the latter could be "Genuine Neapolitan Pizza." The former association was transformed into the latter.

the "Associazione Pizzaiuoli Napoletani"—was created by Sergio Miccù. Though they work together, the two organizations have different (though convergent) objectives. The first association tends to be more involved with the protection of the originality of the product: the traditional Neapolitan pizza, its ingredients, its preparation, and its spread in the original form. The second association, on the other hand, unites all of the producers of pizza: the people who prepare the dough and make pizzas, the pizzeria owners, and workers. The goal is to obtain recognition and increase the professionalization of this category of worker that was so badly treated in the past. We can remember that in the eighteenth century the pizzaioli did not even have their own guild, and in the nineteenth century they were in any event on the last rung of the social ladder. Today they seem to have finally achieved some professional dignity. The association's work has already produced results: in 2010 the European Union granted "Neapolitan pizza" the Traditional Specialities Guaranteed (TSG) denomination.[b] The two associations have also organized schools for pizzaioli, and have promoted a number of initiatives that the poor nineteenth-century pizzaioli would have trouble understanding. Their work back then was only the daily grind, hard and not appreciated, nor paid very well at all.

What are the claims made by these two associations and what were the recipes, the ingredients and the tools that the pizzaioli of the nineteenth century used? It is well known that pizza is one of the first dishes to figure on the list of those that are part of the so-called "Mediterranean diet." The pizza's base ingredients—soft wheat flour, tomatoes, extra virgin olive oil, dairy products, herbs like basil, garlic, and oregano— provide the body with the right quantity of calories, vitamins, antioxidants, and other beneficial substances. Mixed together in just the right proportions, they offer a degree of digestibility difficult to find in other foods. In asking for the Traditional Specialities Guaranteed denomination, the Association had to give specific characteristics both of the final products and of the ingredients, not to mention the method of preparation and production. The *disciplinare*, the rules that govern making what the Association considers the genuine Neapolitan pizza, give the simple recipe below.

INGREDIENTS AND PREPARATION

In the *disciplinare*, it is asserted that traditional Neapolitan pizza is only one of two variants, the "Pizza napoletana Marinara" and the "Pizza napoletana Margherita." The ingredients are as follows: soft wheat flour (called "type 00" in Italy) with a small addition of type 0 flour, spring water, brewer's yeast, peeled tomatoes (puréed) or cherry tomatoes, sea salt, and extra virgin olive oil. Other ingredients, depending on which pizza is being made, are garlic and oregano (for the Marinara), or mozzarella and basil for the the Margherita.[c]

After listing the required ingredients, the *disciplinare* moves on to a description of the method of preparation of pizzas. It begins with the dough, which is made

---

[b] The Associations are now lobbying UNESCO to add "the art of the pizza" to its list of Intangible Cultural Heritage.
[c] For the regular Margherita, another cheese called *fiordilatte* can be used instead of mozzarella.

with flour, water, salt, and yeast. Contrary to what is often thought, the fundamental ingredient (to which the others are added in proportions according to mass)
is water, not flour. Water is put in the mixer first, then 5 percent salt and 18–20
percent flour, by mass. Mixing begins by hand and yeast (0.3 percent by mass) is
added to the dough. As soon as it is certain that there are no lumps of flour or
yeast in the dough, the electric motor is turned on and flour is added, handful by
handful, until the perfect consistency is reached (called "punto di pasta" in Italian).
At this point the electric dough kneader finishes the work (another twenty minutes),
kneading until the dough has become a compact mass.

The entire operation consists of ten minutes of mixing and another twenty of
kneading. The quantities used, for each liter of water, are 50–5g of sale, 3g of
yeast, and about 1,800g of flour. The final dough has to have a soft, compact feel,
not sticky. The second phase (rising) now begins. The dough is removed from the
kneader and is left on a wooden table for around two hours, covered with a moist
towel to prevent a crust from forming. After this, the dough is divided into the
individual loaves. This is done by breaking off pieces of dough with a large trowel-
like tool, then rounding the pieces by hand. The loaf-balls should have an average
weight of 200g (from 180 to 250g, depending on the kind of pizzeria and the
clientele). These balls are then put in a wooden (or sometimes plastic) case whose
sides are no higher than 10 cms, and allowed to rise for another four to six hours.
After this second rising, pizzas can be made. With the trowel, the pizzaiolo/a takes
one of the rounded loaves from the case and puts it on the pizzeria counter. With
rapid handwork, the loaf is made flat, transforming it into a thin disc ready to hold
toppings. For the Marinara, the tomato sauce is poured on and spread to cover
almost the whole surface, leaving only a small border without sauce. A sprinkle of
salt, some oregano and a clove of garlic cut finely are added. A thin spiral of olive
oil from a watering can-shaped container completes the preparation.

For the Margherita, the dough, tomato and oil are added in the same way;
instead of the oregano and garlic, mozzarella or fiordilatte cheese pieces are put
on the pizza, along with a few basil leaves. Another characteristic of the traditional
product is how it is cooked: it should only be made in a wood-fired oven, baked
at a temperature of 450–500°C (850–930°F) for between 60–90 seconds. A final
suggestion of the *disciplinare*, meant to ensure the deliciousness of the dish, is
that the pizza be eaten just after it comes out of the oven, still steaming with its
characteristic perfume, with its vivid colors and its inimitable taste. Taking a pizza
somewhere else away from the pizzeria assures the loss of this traditional taste. This
is of course an old complaint, often leveled at the old pizza hawkers (we can think
of what Valeriani and Serao wrote) and now aimed at the American pizza chains
like Domino's (and others) that have made their colossal fortunes on pizza delivery.
President Pace and his colleagues have done well to define the precise characteristics of a product that claims to be "Neapolitan pizza"; the same can be said of
the pizzaioli's association and their training for people who decide to practice this
profession.

Naturally this is valid only for those who want to follow the old Neapolitan
tradition. The work and mission of the Association has been codifying the old trade

Figure 9.1: An old-fashioned agliara from the collection of "La Casa della Pizza" (The House of Pizza), a project directed by Gino Sorbillo to promote Neapolitan pizza. The agliara, the container for oil, is made of copper with tin on the inside. It has a long, narrow spout and is still commonly used in pizzerias.
Photo by Donatella Mattozzi.

and reinventing tradition, then trying to export it beyond Italy's borders. Thanks to an intense campaign of propaganda and proselytizing it is been able to reach all the continents. Through the founding of local delegations the Association has been able to get innumerable pizzaioli to join and follow their code and the disciplinare. From just a few at the beginning of this campaign, there are around 100 members in the US and Canada, about seventy in Japan (many Japanese piazzioli come to Naples to learn the trade), ten in Australia and some others elsewhere.

THE TWENTIETH CENTURY IN NAPLES ...

The turn of the century from the nineteenth to the twentieth did not bring with it major changes in the history of pizzerias. To the contrary, apart from some address changes, both pizzerias and pizzas were largely the same as before. Roberto Minervini (cited above) indeed wrote in 1956 that "the first half of this century did not bring with it new variants in preparation (now fixed) of pizza, [though] new ingredients, as desired, were added." The process of evolution of both pizzerias and pizzas was already mature in the nineteenth century. There were, however, significant changes in the urban design and the administration of the city. The "Risanamento," begun in 1889 with the gutting of several neighborhoods and the construction of new buildings, continued until after the Second World War. Even if we can read in a guide of the day (*Guida Commerciale Lo Gatto*, 1890) that "the demolition of the existing buildings requires the transfer of 45,000 inhabitants. 15,000 will remain in the same area, whereas another 30,000 will move to the new neighborhoods of Arenaccia, Sant'Eframo, Ottocalli, Miradois, Materdei, Amedeo, Vomero and Arenella." In the end, very few people actually moved. The new houses cost too much and some of the 30,000 who were supposed to move ended up staying and making the buildings that remained even more crowded.

The situation was different for pizzerias. Given the normal equation of higher population density meaning more pizzerias, the number of pizzerias destroyed in the demolitions (of densely-populated areas) was significant. The streets that were torn apart (Vico Campane, Strada Porto, and the alleyways that made room for Corso Umberto I and Corso Garibaldi) were some of those with the most people. The pizzerias that remained were still affected by the transition, and the pizzerias in the new neighborhoods had a hard time reaching a level where they were working at capacity. Of the neighborhoods mentioned in the guide above, only the Arenaccia–Vasto (behind Corso Garibaldi) and the Vomero–Arenalla neighborhoods saw new pizzerias open. According to the commercial guides of the period, the Italian State Archives of Naples, and the archive of the Chamber of Commerce, the number of pizzerias that opened in the new neighborhoods was slightly smaller than the number that had been torn down. The map of their distribution across the urban space changed a great deal.

The administrative changes also played a role. On January 20, 1910 law number 121 was passed, modifying the responsibilities of the Chambers of Commerce. These regional institutions now were responsible (among other things) for keeping a register of all of the information regarding businesses for all economic activity. In Naples all this information was written down in around seventy volumes, kept in the archive of the local Chamber of Commerce. Unfortunately, for one reason or another, about ten volumes (approximately fifteen percent of the registrations) are missing. Luckily this information can be taken from the various commercial guides (like those cited repeatedly in this volume), which were published every year from 1900 until 1915. These guides were supposed to be a census of all of the artisanal, commercial and professional businesses which were operating in the relevant territory and under obligation to register themselves. In reality, though, many people did not register, and there were even pranksters: at entry number 943 of volume 18, for May 27, 1911, we can read "Benedetto Annoscia, Via Napoli, Pozzuoli, business of nothing, never begun." Amusingly, even these registrations were faithfully transcribed into the registers. On January 4, 1925 a new law was passed that instituted a new kind of registry. Perhaps because the government had noticed that the previous law had often been ignored, the new law repeated the obligation to register any business; it also "invited" those who had already registered themselves to repeat the process. From 1911 to 1924 only twenty-four pizzaioli with twenty-nine total pizzerias registered themselves, whereas in the commercial guides we find fifty-seven of them, more than double those officially registered. To those fifty-seven we can add an unknown number of other ones, as certain pizzaioli had not paid the fee for the guide and therefore were not listed. After 1925 (and the new law) another eighteen pizzaioli declared that they had begun their business prior to that date. We do not know how many, on the other hand, had left the trade. The First World War had led to great suffering in Italy and had made the crisis even worse, triggering social divisions and conflicts that ultimately led to the rise of Fascism.

Returning to the discussion of pizzerias, a variety of sources confirm what we had stated earlier: there was a small drop in the number of pizzas, then the number remained stationary for a long time, growing only in the 1930s. In the 1920s, though, we see a something new in the documentary record: bankruptcy, or in any event bankruptcy proceedings. This reminds us of the difficulties that shopkeepers in Naples faced. We have already said that the "new" historic pizzaiolo families that are still active today in general began with pizzerias in the years between the two world wars (1918–40). Despite the fact that these pizzerias (and even those who began after 1940) reenergized the sector and are today among the most important, all of them (apart from some rare exceptions) had problems with debt and bankruptcy, ending in most cases with agreements with creditors. We can now return to the history of these twentieth-century pizzerias and the dates they were opened. These are according to the archives consulted in Naples, and often are not in agreement with the dates claimed by the current generation of pizzaioli families, who (relying on oral history) backdate their own foundation. There is occasionally an error in a document, but often it is the pizzaioli who garnish their memories with the same fantasy they use to prepare pizzas. Just as often it is over zealous journalists who are happy to recount in their articles—stories about local color that everyone likes—or guidebook writers who (on a Lenten fast from real history) eat up every tale that is told to them.

Skipping the Ambrosios, Esposito-Brandis, Lombardis, Mattozzis, and Paces (about whom so much has already been said), several other families merit mention: Alfonso and Pasquale Di Napoli (father and son) opened a pizzeria in 1912 in Via Alessandro Poerio 52. They left it to their descendants, who rent out that pizzeria but run others. In 1916 the "Pizzeria Gorizia" was inaugurated in the Vomero neighborhood, at Via Bernini 29. The license holder was Salvatore Grasso, who later took over the pizzeria at Via Tribunali 202 from the Mattozzis (in 1936). Grasso left the Vomero location to his son Salvatore, who left it in turn to his son (also called Salvatore), who is the current owner. On January 1, 1919 Giovanni Capasso from Atella (an old provincial city in Campania) opened a pizzeria at Via Porta San Gennaro 2, today run by his descendants. Other descendants own a pizzeria at Via Giulio Cesare 156–8, though because of a clerical error their name is Cafasso.

According to the records,[d] in 1925 another now-famous pizzeria was opened, "Da Michele," by Michele Condurro at Egiziaca a Forcella 16, though it later moved to its current location in Via Cesare Sersale 1. It has become so famous that

---

[d]The current owners backdate the founding, though perhaps Condurro too had ignored the 1910 law.

Figure 9.2: Pizzeria Da Michele. Naples, c. 1930.
The Condurro family in front of the pizzeria, along with other pizzaioli. In the center
top is Michele. At this side are his brothers Antonio and Salvatore. Below are his sons
Mimì and Luigi. Luigi, born in 1922, still works at the pizzeria every day from 10 a.m.
until noon, "to keep himself in shape."
Courtesy of Sergio Condurro.

it was recently chosen as a location for the film *Eat Pray Love* with the beautiful
Julia Roberts. In 1932 Ciro Leone opened a fried food shop at Via San Cosmo 54;
in 1959 he moved to Via Pietro Colletta and this time opened a pizzeria. In 1936
Salvatore di Matteo (a scion of a family that had since the nineteenth-century been
vendors of fried food) opened a pizzeria at Via Tribunali 94. It is now run by his
grandson. It was here that in 1994, during the G7 meetings, President Bill Clinton
wanted to taste Neapolitan pizza.

Another pizzeria that is always full of people is the one that belongs to Gino
Sorbillo, a young but capable pizzaiolo, often invited to take part in televised shows.
In 1995 he left his shop in Via Tribunali 35 (a pizzeria already open in 1822) where
his grandfather had opened a pizzeria in 1936, and moved a few meters away to
number 32, where he has had unprecedented success.

There are many other examples we could cite—between the beginning of the
twentieth century and the end of the Second World War almost 300 pizzaioli and
as many pizzerias were registered—but we will limit ourselves to mentioning just
three cases of bottled wine shops that were turned into pizzerias. In 1923 Umberto

Figure 9.3: Bill Clinton in the Pizzeria Di Matteo. Naples, 1994.
In July 1994 the international G7 summit took place in Naples. During a break from the proceedings, Bill Clinton allowed himself a walk through the historic center and up Via Tribunali. He was offered a pizza by the Pizzeria Di Matteo. The day after, the photo of the president eating his pizza folded "a libretto" was on the front cover of all the newspapers.
Courtesy of Salvatore Di Matteo.

di Porzio opened a bottled wine shop at Via Alabardieri 30–31; he turned it into a pizzeria in 1937 and added restaurant service in 1953. In the mid-1930s, Attilio Bachetti turned a bottled wine shop at Via Pignasecca 17 into a pizzeria, currently run by his grandson Attilio. Another bottled wine shop transformed into a pizzeria is the one at Via Materdei 27, which Antonio Starita made exceptional. His sons now runs it, as he opened a pizzeria in New York and is constantly going back and forth. It is interesting to note that already in 1841 there was a pizzeria in Via Materdei (still open today), at number 2.

We have listed only men—what about women? As in the nineteenth century, women were of course involved in pizzerias, though they were fewer in number. As in the previous century, their job was principally making fried pizzas. In addition to the women who made pizzas in their "bassi" with the "oggi a otto" payment system, there were also women who actually had their own pizzerias. We will mention only three examples, but all important ones: the first is Esterina Sorbillo.

After the death of her father, Esterina (the oldest of twenty-one children) continued the family tradition in the old pizzeria at Via Tribunali 35, though she made only fried pizzas. Esterina died in 2010 and her nephew Gino decided to

Figure 9.4: Menu from Pizzeria Da Attilio. Naples, 1944.
A historic menu, dated January 31, 1944, from the pizzeria of Attilio Bachetti, opened in
1938 at Via Pignasecca 17. This was preserved by his grandson Attilio, who still runs the
business in the same pizzeria.
Courtesy of Attilio Bachetti.

reopen the old pizzeria at number 35, while he continued to make pizzas at number
32. The other example is that of the three Apetino sisters, Giuseppina, Immacolata,
and Carmela. They worked in a working-class neighborhood of Forcella, at Via
Giudecca Vecchia 36, in a pizzeria called "De' Figliole" (in dialect this means "The
Gals" [Pizzeria]) where they made exclusively fried pizzas. Finally, "The Daughters
of Iorio" are three young women who run an eponymous pizzeria in the Porto
neighborhood is a pizzeria-trattoria in the classic Neapolitan style. It is at Via Conte
Olivares 73, and was begun by their father in the 1940s.

In the towns in Naples' hinterland the first pizzeria was registered in Portici in
1910, a second in Torre Annunziata in 1921, a third in Castellammare di Staba
in 1922 and the slowly in Frattamaggiore, in Caivano, and other little suburbs so
that today they have a number of pizzerias equal to Naples itself. We can also find
excellent fare here, for example in the pizzeria Fornito in Frattamaggiore, opened
in 1927, or the Salvo brothers' pizzeria in San Giorgio a Cremano.

There Salvatore and Francesco continue the family tradition, begun by their
grandfather Salvatore in 1962. They are scrupulous about the ingredients and
able to describe them in minute detail whenever some customer asks about where

Figure 9.5: Esterina Sorbillo. Naples, c. 1970.
Esterina Sorbillo, the oldest child of Luigi Sorbillo, with a tray of fried pizzas in her
pizzeria in Via Tribunali 35.
Courtesy of Gino Sorbillo.

they are from. Another prestigious pizzaiolo is Franco Pepe in Caiazzo who, in
addition to a meticulous attention to detail, continues the tradition of preparing and
kneading his dough by hand, "like my father did it," as he says. We cannot finish
this brief overview without mentioning one other young protagonist of the history
of the pizzeria, Enzo Coccia. He was brought up in a pizzaiolo family and was one
of the first to return to traditional pizza making with a meticulous attention to the
quality of the ingredients (and their place or origin and seasonality), and careful
preparation of the dough. This has made him the only pizzeria in Naples to merit a
place in the famous Michelin guides.

... AND BEYOND[e]

There are plenty of anthropological studies that explain to a global audience who
a certain producer makes a certain food product, how it is eaten, and how it is
integrated into the daily life of the population that eats it. Even though most of this
present study could fall into the category of ethnography, of a producer and place
of production unknown to most people (the pizzaiolo and the Neapolitan pizzeria),

---

[e] This section was largely written by the editor, with revisions and additions by the author.

Figure 9.6: Salvatore Salvo. Naples, c. 1950.
Salvatore (behind the counter) belonged to a family of prolific Neapolitan pizzaioli,
the Salvos. In this photograph we can see the difference in the dimensions of earlier
pizzerias, which were much smaller than todays. There is also an indication of the price
of the times, 30 lire for both fried and baked pizza.
Courtesy of Umberto and Salvatore Salvo.

Figure 9.7: Pizzeria Pepe. Caiazzo (near Caserta), c. 1950.
Francesco Pepe in his pizzeria. At his side one of his workers prepares a pizza on a wooden *màrtola*, where each day's dough is prepared by hand.
Courtesy of Franco Pepe.

pizza today is known all over the world. From Napes to Tokyo, from Montevideo to Ottawa, everyone eats pizza now.

One of the fundamental themes of this book is the difficulty that Neapolitan pizzaioli had in establishing themselves and surviving, but also expanding into new areas. How can we explain that at the last Pizzafest that took place in Naples in September 2014, in the "Pizza Classica" category, in the competition to designate the Best Pizzaiolo, a foreigner (and indeed, a woman) Mayo Ota from Japan, won?[1] And that four years before that another Japanese citizen had won? How did this trade manage to carve out a spot for itself in the gastronomic marketplace all over the world, and in such a short time? Even though we have to break out of the chronological scope of this study (the nineteenth century) the surprising success of both contemporary pizzerias and pizzaioli obliges us to trace out, however briefly, the trajectory of this take-off.

Some historians of pizza like Benincasa and Stefanile (cited above)—as well as the author of this volume and at least one American commentator, Ed Levine (cited below)—believe that the beginning of pizza's internationalization has its roots in the Anglo–American occupation of Italy during the Second World War. The food historian Harvey Levenstein does not agree, at least for the US. Levenstein holds that it was the arrival of mass media, more than the direct experience of GIs in

Italy, that helped the spread of new tastes among Americans.[2] More appropriate then is an attempt to date the popularization of the dish, rather than the date of its arrival. Perhaps another trend that made pizzas and pizzerias more common was the creation of new culinary–cultural spaces by the automobile. As Eric Schlosser explains in *Fast Food Nation*, the genius of the McDonald brothers (the founders of the eponymous chain), was not in selling hamburgers—many entrepreneurs did this in 1950s-era America—but rather selling hamburgers to people in cars.[3] The McDonald brothers, sick of washing or replacing silverware, had the ingenious idea of selling only foods that could be eaten by hand, while driving. It is easy to understand how pizza, already street food in Naples (folded in half, "a libretto," or sliced), packaged in a box that could even be a common plate for the whole family, easily spread in such an automobile-centric market.

The United States is certainly not the only country where pizza arrived in the post-war era, but the success it had in the American market (at that time the largest in the world), certainly gave a big push to the global spread of both the product and the trade. Carol Helstosky, discussing the spread of pizza delivery, underlines that home appliances also contributed to the popularity of pizza in the US. Frozen pizzas could be easily reheated whenever there was not time to cook a dinner.[4] But long before pizzas were frozen they were already being taken home: American chains were born in the 1950s, among them Pizza Hut, founded in Wichita, Kansas, in 1958. The American influence (that is to say, of the large chains), however, while it elevated the position of the pizza, lowered the position of the pizzaiolo. At the same time that the spread of chains led to more mass-production, it also demanded differentiation. Donna Gabaccia notes that when Pizza Hut moved out of the American Midwest eastward, it had to change the style to compete with Italian-American pizza, already well known to East Coast Americans.[5]

The genius of Ray Croc—who bought the franchising rights from the McDonald brothers, and who is the true "founder" of the Golden Arches—was bringing Henry Ford into the restaurant. The artisan (the pizzaiolo) cost to much and Croc introduced the assembly line with a series of automatic movements to be performed by the teenagers who worked for him. "Follow instructions! Listen for the buzzers! Look when the lights begin to blink!" This logic was followed by the CEOs of the pizzerias as well. The pizzaiolo went from being an artisan-owner (albeit of a tiny shop) in the alleyways of Naples to an automaton at Pizza Hut. Even though the workers at Pizza Hut, Domino's, Papa John's, and Little Caesar's are not really pizzaioli, the chains did generate an interest in pizza that sparked the imagination of many entrepreneurs the world over. The US hegemony during the Cold War was also a driving factor in the spread of representations of the pizzeria—in television series, magazines, books, and other types of pop culture—as the perfect place for young people.

These representations were seen and imitated everywhere. Many enterprising people realized that a food like pizza could be successful in their country, too. Even Maya Ota thought so, and with her many young Japanese people, using the skill of the Japanese of assimilating foreign technologies and even improving on them, they opened innumerable pizzerias in their country. Japan is now the third-largest producer of pizza after Italy and the United States. Franco La Cecla, in his interesting book on the pizza, talks about ethnic restaurants and reminds us that when the pizzeria was introduced for the first time in a foreign country it was considered an "ethnic restaurant." Ethnic restaurants, according to La Cecla, represent a kind of compromise between authentically foreign food and the cuisine of the country they are in: the clients want to take a culinary trip, but they do not want to go too far.[6] But is it still like this? Maybe in some country where pizza has just arrived, going into a pizzeria still means taking an exciting journey, but pizza today is considered a universal food. Even if the associations in Naples hold that the only "true" Neapolitan pizzas are the Marinara and the Margherita, we know that pizza is inherently flexible. These two types represent the basic Neapolitan pizzas but already in the nineteenth century many ingredients were put on pizzas depending on the taste and requests of the customer.

This is the secret of pizza's global popularity: it is a container for everything in the local cuisine. In Hawaii they put pineapple on top, whereas in Buffalo, it is Buffalo Wings.[f] In Berlin you find sausage, and something else in Hanoi. After Kim Jong-Un, maybe the North Koreans will put kimchi on top. This flexibility—seen in Naples as a "corruption"—has given a chance to many small businesspeople to open their own business and adapt this doughy disc the most diverse imaginable local conditions.[7] But its success is also due to the notable increase in the "culinary capital" of Italian food in general.[8] Perhaps the two things reinforce each other: once the Italian restaurants in New York were considered quite plebian, but today Italian cuisine has passed French cuisine and moved into the culinary pole position. It is not a coincidence that one of the most famous chefs in the world, Mario Batali, decided to open ... a pizzeria.[g]

We're now in the third century of Neapolitan pizza and its particular taste, together with its nutritional value and its "flexibility" as far as garnishing, have made it one of the most widespread foods in the world. Pizza, already a universal food, passed down through millennia of experience with flatbreads, was reborn in Naples. Made more beautiful and even tastier, it had its cradle in Naples' pizzerias, its nurses in the hundreds of pizzaioli that raised it, one after another, for over two centuries. It then became an adult and began to travel ever further, adapting itself to the traditions it encountered. All we can hope is that its now innumerable grandchildren do not move too far away from the style and the taste of their ancestors.

---

[f] In reality, it is difficult to say where "Hawaiian Pizza" was invented. It could have been Rochester, NY, as easily as Honolulu.

[g] After the success of his pizzeria in New York, "Otto," Batali opened a pizzeria in Boston (Babbo Pizzeria), where in 1905 one of the first pizzerias in the US had been opened.

SOURCES—NEAPOLITAN PIZZERIAS IN THE 1800S (BOURBON PERIOD)

The Italian State Archives in Naples safeguards all of the documents that, in the course of the centuries (from the fourteenth to the twentieth), all the institutions, authorities, guilds, monasteries, noble families, and other bodies deposited in the archives of the Kingdom of Naples and the Kingdom of Italy. They were brought together in the Archives after unification in 1860. There are millions of documents that the expert personnel have gradually selected and classified according to topic, institution of origin, period, or year. The files are put into large folders numbered and ordered depending on their contents. The contents of each folder is called a "*fascio*," abbreviated with an "f" (e.g. f.2203).

The documents that follow below are from the Ministry of Finance, the Prefecture of Police (in its various articulations over the years) and the General Archive of the Police (*Questura*) of Naples after 1860. They are subdivided by the number of the folder in which they are located. The last section of sources is not a list of archival documents but rather pizzerias cited in the various commercial guides that were published between 1880 and 1900.

PIZZERIAS IN THE NINETEENTH CENTURY— BOURBON PERIOD

Italian State Archives of Naples—Ministry of Finance

1807

Name	Address	Neighborhood
Di Mase Vincenzo	Str. Campane, 7	San Ferdinando
Pecoranio Antonio	Vico Chianche, 16	San Ferdinando
Riccardo Andrea	Str. Carminello, 8	San Ferdinando
Quagliariello Agostino	Str. di Chiaia, 20	San Ferdinando
Quagliariello Agostino	Str. S.Pantaleone, 1	San Ferdinando
Izzo Gennaro	Vico lungo Trinità degli Spagnoli, 17	San Ferdinando
Sirij Luigi	Str. Speranzella, 115	San Ferdinando
Lenoci Domenico	Vico S.Sepolcro, 23	Montecalvario
Paparcone Domenico	Str. Pignasecca, 24	Montecalvario
Ottaviano Gaetano	Vico Barretta, 28	Montecalvario
Izzo Michele	Salita Montecalvario	Montecalvario
Bozza Domenico	Vico lungo S.Matteo, 47	Montecalvario
Brusciante Filippo	Vico I Gravina, 4	San Giuseppe
Di Mase Gioacchino	Str. Toledo, 24	San Giuseppe
Ramaglia Gioacchino	Str. Toledo, 100	San Giuseppe
Novembre Giuseppe	Largo S.Tommaso, 4	San Giuseppe
Piacente Nicola	Vico Carrozzieri a Toledo, 12	San Giuseppe

Fedele Orsola	Str. Corsea, 92	San Giuseppe
Franceschetti Alessandro	Str. S.Efremo Nuovo, 80	Avvocata
Spadaro Vincenzo	Str. Misericordiella, 8	Stella
Profilia Scuotto	Str. Stella, 72	Stella
Mellone Alessio	Str. Imbrecciata alla Sanità	Stella
Apresta Raffaele	Cavone di S.Vincenzo	Stella
Paparcone Carmine	Str. Porta Capuana, 5	Vicaria
Saporito Saverio	Borgo S.Antonio Abate	Vicaria
Di Massa Nicola	Parrocchia Tutti i Santi	Vicaria
Gioia Raffaele	Str. Porta Capuana, 10	Vicaria
Romito Maria Rosa	Str. Gesù delle Monache, 12	San Lorenzo
idem	Str. Porta S.Gennaro, 27	San Lorenzo
Casato Antonio	Str. Purgatorio, 48	San Lorenzo
Benevenia Arcangelo	Vico Purgatorio, 3	San Lorenzo
Rosolia Michelangelo	Str. Barrettari, 74	Mercato
Taglialatela Elisabetta	Str. Barrettari, 25	Mercato
Marramarra Vincenzo	Str. Annunciata, 1	Mercato
Gargiulo Gaetano	Str. Lavinaio, 60	Mercato
Persico Domenico	Borgo di Loreto, 112	Mercato
Massa Pietro	Str. Madonna delle Grazie al Lavinaio, 20	Mercato
Ruggiero Antonio	Borgo Loreto, 203	Mercato
De Caro Domenico	Str. Conciaria, 1	Mercato
Zambrano Catiello	Vico Salajoli all'Orto del Conte	Mercato
Di Giacomo Angela	Borgo Loreto, 225	Mercato
Di Giacomo Angela	Borgo Loreto, 225	Mercato
Vecchione Felice	Vico Pozzari	Pendino
Capuozzo Rosa	Fontana de' Serpi, 12	Pendino
Di Pietro Paolo	Loggia di Genova	Pendino
Ottajano Paolo	Str. Pendino	Pendino
Ottajano Gaetano	Str. Vicaria Vecchia, 16	Pendino
Soreca Lucia	Str. Vicaria Vecchia	Pendino
Pendino Elisabetta	Str. Nuova Marina	Pendino
Nardelli Berardino	Strada di Porto, 20	Porto
Fusco Gennaro	Str. Ecce Homo, 4	Porto
Esposito Salvatore	Vico Monaco, 4	Porto
Guadino Vincenzo	Str. Nasti, 25	Porto
Fierro Giosuè	Str. Porta di Massa, 2	Porto
Aprea Antonio	Strada di Porto, 125	Porto

ITALIAN STATE ARCHIVES OF NAPLES—POLICE PREFECTURE—3° DEPARTMENT

1821

| Salvati Pasquale | Pizza oven—copper utensils without tin or worn down | | f.1454 |

1822

:......... Rosa	L.go S.Paolo, 72	copper	f.1455
Barone Gioacchino	Str. Barrettari, 74	fire inspection	f.1455
Cuomo Raffaele	Str. Barrettari, 26–7	fire inspection	f.1455
Santelia Teresa	Str. Tribunali, 35	fire inspection	f.1455

1823

Order to request a license for those businesses at risk of fire.

1829

Calicchio Pietro	Salita S.Anna di Palazzo 1 (following fire prevention norms)	f.1463

1837

Vico 1° Gravina, 4	f.1481/I
Vico Baglivo uries, 8	
Vico Carceri S.Felice, 26	
Loggia di Genova, 67 (baker and seller of fried foods)	
Largo S.Tommaso, 5	
Str. Sciuscella, 18	
Str. Toledo, 12	

ITALIAN STATE ARCHIVES OF NAPLES—POLICE PREFECTURE—2° DEPARTMENT

1840

Calabrese Sabato	Str. Orticello, 96 (quite old)	f.411
Esposito Domenico	Str. Materdei, 2	f.411
Mezzanotte Raffaele	S. Maria Antesaecula	f.411
Ruocco Gennaro	Vico Campane, 7 and 65—The request for #65 was rejected, though one issued to his brother Antonio	f.411
Sangiorgio Salvatore	Str. nuova Capodimonte—Case Di Fiore—pizza, cooked foods, and sign	f.411
Calicchio Ferdinando	Calata S.Anna di Palazzo, 30—wine shop	f.411

1841

Buonocore Anna	Str. Lavinaio, 61	f.459–el.
Chiosi Antonio	Vico Campane, 69	f.459–el.
Calicchio Antonio	Vico Campane, 7	f.459–el.
De Simone Pasquale	Str. Lavinaio, 83	f.459–el.
Dramand Luigi	Vico Sergente Maggiore, 53—French pastry chef, converts pizzeria into pastry shop	f.443 f.443
Esposito Domenico	Str. Materdei, 2	f.459–el
Ferraro Angelo	Str. S.Pietro Martire, 2	f.459–el
Ferraro Antonio	Str. Porta di Massa, 6	f.459–el
Ferraro Gaetano	Vico Monaco, 4	f.459–el
Greco Angelo	Vico Bonafficiasta vecchia, 3	f.443
Ottaiano Gaetano	Str. Tribunali, 266	f.449–el.
Ottaiano Nicola	Str. Porto, 18	f.449–el.
Ottaiano Vincenzo	Str. Vicaria Vecchia, 26	f.449–el.
Pacella Giuseppe	Porta Sciuscella, 18—two licenses, one for a pizzeria and the other for a trattoria	f.470 f.470
Palumbo Domenico	Supportico Nasti, 30	f.449–el.
Paparcone (Pasquale)	Str. Sette Dolori, 20	f.466/I
Piccolo Baldassarre	Str. Speranzella, 150	f.471
Santelia Teresa	Str. Tribunali, 36	f.449–el.
Spadari Giuseppe	Porta S.Gennaro, 2	f.449–el.
Valerio Francesco	Vico Carminello a Toledo, 8	f.449–el.
Zittollo Antonio	Vico lungo Gelso, 49	f.449–el.

1842

Barone Nicola	Str. Pignasecca, 48—pizzeria and cooked foods	f.471
Bianco Giovanni	Larghetto Trinità degli Spagnoli, 17—complaint about danger of fire	f.484
Cenname Raffele	Vico Tre Regine, 49	f.497
Chiosi Raffaele	Vico Campane, 7—pizzeria, trattoria and bottled wine shop	f.471
Corrado Giuseppe	Vico Lungo Montecalvario, 42	f.471
Esposito Domenico	Porta Sciuscella (Port'Alba), 18—sign "Trattoria e Pizzaria da Monzù Testa"	f.470
Formerly of Pacella Giuseppe	Str. Nuova Capodimonte, 93 (da Materdei, 2) formerly of Mazzella Giuseppe	f.471
Esposito Domenico	Supportico Nasti, 38—died 1846 (see f.708/I del 1850)	f.471
Esposito Stella	Str. Speranzella, 150—fomerly Piccolo Baldassarre—license for awning	f.471
Palmentieri Raffaele	Complaint made about him in 1844	f.549
Sangiorgio Salvatore	Str. Nuova Capodimonte, 6–7	f.498/I

1843

Buonomo Aniello	Vico Baglivo Uries, 7—guarantor for Anna Maglioccola (accused of prostitution, wife of his employee Antonio Esposito)	f.512
Chiosi Antonio	Vico Campane, 69—closes in 1844 because of civil suit	f.525/II
	Vico Campane, 7—in the complaint about a risk of fire Antonio Chiosi is listed as the shopkeeper and Ruocco Gennaro as the license-holder	f.502/I
Esposito Giobattta	Str. Pendino, 86 (at the corner of Vico Neve al Pendino 4?)	f.497
Ferraro Gaetano	Vico Monaco, 4	f.525/II
Ippolito Tommaso	Str. Nuova Capodimonte, 6–7—four licenses: pizzeria, cooked food, awning and sign "Tommaso Ippolito"—formerly of Sangiorgio Salvatore	f.498/II
Piccirillo Antonio	Vico Tre Regine, 49—formerly of Cenname Raffaele	f.497
Ruocco Gennaro	Vico Campane, 7 (see Chiosi Antonio)	f.525/II
Sepe Antonio	Str. S.Monica, 24—in June wine shop and tavern, in October a license for a pizzeria was added	f.497
Tanga Giuseppe	Str. Sanità, 63	f.526
Tutino Filippo	Vico Baglivo Uries, 7 (n.7 pizzeria and n.6 trattoria)	f.526

1844

Balia Nicola	Str. Sanità, 63—formerly of Tanga Giuseppe	f.526
Calicchio Leopoldo	Vico Baglivo Uries, 6–7—formerly of Tutino Filippo	f.526
Chiosi Raffaele	Vico Nunzio, 3	f.525/I
Di Perna Bernardo	Vico Campane, 7—in place of Raffaele Chiosi	f.525/II
Donadio Stefano	Str. Nuova Capodimonte, 93—license to "cook pizzas and bake bread"—formerly of Esposito Domenico	f.526
Esposito Giobatta	Str. Pendino, 86—requests permission to fry pastries to "secure the subsistence of his family"	f.525/I
Ferraro Antonio	Porta di Massa, 6	f.559/II
Ferraro Raffaele	Vico Campane, 69—in the place of Chiosi Antonio, "expelled for a civil suit"	f.525/II
Ottaiano Vincenzo	Vico Monaco, 4—formerly of Ferraro Gaetano	f.525/II
Rippa Domenico	Largo Chiodaroli, 30	f.525/I
Romano Antonio	Vico Neve a Pendino, 4—formerly of Esposito Giobatta	f.525/I
Sepe Antonio	Str. S.Monica, 24—wineshop, tavern and pizzeria	f.620

1845

Buonomo Aniello	Str. Tribunali, 271 (but the license for n.214)	f.587/II
Buonomo Pasquale	Larghetto S.Tommaso, 6	f.587/II
Calicchio Leopoldo	Vico Campane, 7—buys the business of (Di) Perna Bernardo	f.558/I
Esposito Camillo	Larghetto S.Tommaso, 7	f.587/II
Giannoccoli Francesco	Vico Nunzio, 3—formerly of Chiosi Raffaele	f.559/I
Ottaiano Nicola	Str. Porto, 9—various renovations	f.559/II
Ottaiano Vincenzo	Str. Tribunali, 15—moving from Vico Monaco, 4	f.558/II
Palumbo Domenico	Largo S.Demetrio, 17 (there for a number of years)	f.587/II
Pastore Antonio	Porta di Massa, 6—formerly of Ferraro Antonio	f.559/II
Picoranio Antonio	Vico Baglivo Uries, 6–7 (pizzeria and trattoria) formerly of Calicchio Leopoldo (there is a pastry shop at Str. Chiaia, 166)	f.558/II

1846

Antico Antonio	Larghetto S.Tommaso, 6—taking the place of Buonomo Pasquale, "detained for criminal reasons"	f.587/II
Di Napoli Vitantonio	Str. Tribunali, 271—formerly of Buonomo Aniello	f.587/II
Esposito Giobatta	Largo S.Demetrio, 17—formerly of Palumbo Domenico	f.587/I I
Mangiarulo Salvatore	Vico Chiavettieri al Pendino, 92	f.620
Palmentieri Raffaele	Str. Speranzella, 150—license renewal	f.586
Paparcone Domenico	Vico Pallonetto S.Liborio, 18	f.620
Romano Antonio	P.za Mercato, 315	f.620
Russo Francesco	Vico Campane, 69—takes possession in April, then	f.587/I
	Larghetto S.Tommaso, 7—moves here in September	f.587/II

1847

Auriemma Raffaele	Str.Tribunali, 38—wine shop and tavern—pizzeria license added	f.620
Chiosi Raffaele	Vico Campane, 7—bought by Calicchio Leopoldo—remains there until 1856	f.621
D'Arrigo Giuseppe	Str. Magnocavallo, 27—in January asks to sell wine wholesale and by the glass, plus a pizzeria—in July gives back license for wine shop, requests permission to sell cold foods and bottled wine, with the sign "Ristorante Siciliano"	f.620
De Giorgio Alfonso	Vico Carceri S.Felice, 24	f.676/I
Esposito Pasqua	Loggia di Genova, 69—shop with a well	f.621
Pastore Antonio	Piazza Mercato, 315—formerly of Romano Antonio	f.620
Pastore Raffaele	Vico Chiavettieri al Pendino, 92—formerly of Mangiarulo Salvatore	f.620
Pepe Gaetano	Vico Pallonetto a S.Liborio, 18—from Paparcone Domenico (deceased)	f.620
Sarnelli Gennaro	Str. Selleria al Pendino, 35 (shop closed for ten years)	f.621
Sepe Antonio	Str. S.Monica, 24—license renewal (from 1843)	f.620
Varriale Nicoletta	Str. Infrascata, 122—"country" trattoria and pizzeria	f.620

1849

Calicchio Pietro	Salita S.Anna di Palazzo, 1—meeting of various public officials because of the fire in the basement	f.697
Di Napoli Vitantonio	Str. Tribunali, 34—(son of the late Salvatore), 36 years old, asks for a license for a trattoria but having a pizzeria at n.271 already, must put the trattoria in another name	f.676/I
Pastore Luigi	Vico Pozzari, 8	f.708/I
Piccirillo Antonio	Vico lungo Tre Regine, 48–9	f.708/I
Sangiorgio Salvatore	Vico Carceri S.Felice, 24—turned over by De Giorgio Alfonso	f.676/I

1850

Arpaia Giosuè	Str. Nasti, 30	f.747/II
Di Martino Carmine	Vico Pozzari, 8—(son of Gennaro), 28 years old—formerly of Pastore Luigi	f.708/I
Palumbo Giuseppe	Str. Nasti, 30—(son of the late Raffaele), 28 years old, turned over from Esposito Stella, probably died in 1846, the year in which the shop was closed	f.708/I
Ruoppo Girolamo	S.Antonio Abate, 18 (Vico Pergola)	f.708/I
Russo Francesco	Vico lungo Tre Regine 48–9 (son of the late Giuseppe), 51 years old— requests permission to move from Largo SanTommaso d'Aquino, 7	f.708/I

1851

Giannoccoli Francesco	Vico 1° Gravina, 4	f.782/I
Palomba Domenico	Str. Nasti, 30—(son of the late Giobatta), 46 years old—formerly of Arpaia Giosuè—"oven to cook Focaccia"	f.747/II
Paparcone Luigi	Vico Neve al Pendino, 29—(son of Pasquale), 28 years old, shope with a well, closed for the last two years	f.747/II

1852

Correale Raffaele	Vico 1° Gravina, 4—(son of Bernardo), 34 yeas old, young pizzaiuolo— formerly of Giannoccoli Francesco	f.782/I
De Marco Angelo	Str. Vicaria Vecchia, 19 (son of the late Giuseppe), from Airola, 37 years old, formerly a pastry shop	f.781/II
Giordano Camillo	Vico Verde alla Selleria, 4 (son of the late Pasquale), 32 years old, baker, requests permission to "cook pizzas in the afternoon hours"	f.781/II
Giustiniano Margherita	Vico S.Pasquale a Chiaia, 26—requests permission to sell wine at the table	f.781/I
Iovine Raffaele	Str. Trinità Maggiore, 4 (son of the late Antonio), 26 years old, baker, a former pastry shop	f.782/I
Liccardi Antonio	Str. Vicaria Vecchia, 8 (son of the late Biagio), 50 years old	f.781/II
Mattozzi Michele	Largo S.Demetrio, 17—(son of the late Emiddio), 54 years old, requests permission for "focaccia"	f.781/II
Palmentieri Carmine	di Raffaele, a, 16—pizza hawker arrested as he was believed to be a pimp, released on the guarantee of Sangiorgio Salvatore	f.811
Paparcone Luigi	Str. Magnocavallo, 27 (son of Pasquale), 26 years old	f.781/I
Pastore Luigi	Strada Reggia di Portici—houses belonging to Signor Perretti—pizzeria and bottled wine shop	f.781/II
Rossi Francesco	Loggia di Genova, 27 (son of the late Giuseppe), 53 years old, from Airola, shop formerly a pastry shop	f.781/II
Sangiorgio Salvatore	Vico Barletta allo Spirito Santo—guarantor for the young Palmentieri	f.811

1853

Liccardi Mariano	Str. Porta Nolana, 6 (son of Antonio), 30 years old, formerly a pastry shop	f.845/II
Mattozzi Luigi	Largo S.Demetrio, 17 (son of Michele), 24 years old (in reality 20), requests permission for sign "Rooms for Dinner"—denied because he was not on the license	f.844
Muriggio Francesco	Vico D'Afflitto, 38 (son the late Carlo), 37 years old	f.842

1854

Cutolo Francesco	Vico Rotto S.Carlo, 16 (son of the late Antonio), 30 years old, pizzeria and trattoria	f.872
Gargiulo Giuseppe	Port'Alba, 18 (son of the late Nicola), anni 65, pizzeria and trattoria	f.889/II
Sorano Vincenzo	Loggia di Genova, 67 (son of the late Giovanni), 50 years old, shop with wooden partition wall	f.871

1855

Di Matteo Carmine	Str. Lavinaio, 160—tavern—adds pizzeria—complaints	f.889/II
Gargiulo Giuseppe	Largo Pigne 17 (P.za Cavour)—(son of the late Natale), 65 years old, move of trattoria and pizzeria	
	From Via Port'Alba—sublet from Ruggiero Pasquale	f.889/I
Imparato Giovanni	Larghetto Spina Corona, 1 (son of Raffaele), 34 years old	f.889/II
Paparcone Luigi	Str. Foria di fronte S.M.degli Angeli, houses of Vittoria (di Pasquale), 28 years old	f.889/II
Parisi Francesco	Calata S.Sebastiano, 72 (son of the late Giuseppe), 30 years old, trattoria, adds pizzeria	f.889/II
Pastore Antonio	Strada Regia, Portici, case Naldi (son of the late Francesco), 52 years old	f.889/I
Sorrentino Domenico	Port'Alba, 18 (son of Felice), 37 years old, formerly of Gargiulo Giuseppe	f.889/II

1856

Cerullo Raffaele	Vico 1° Gravina, 4	f.956/II
Chiosi Raffaele	Vico Campane, 7—since 1846	f.956/I
Correale Raffaele	Carceri S.Felice, 25 (adopted son of De Rosa Bernardo), 36 years old	f.924/II
Di Matteo Giuseppe	Str. Soprammuro al Carmine, 58 (di Antonio), 37 years old, maker of *joummette* (sugar candies)—adds pizzeria	f.924/II
Ferraro Pasquale	Vico Rotto S.Carlo, 16 (son of Raffaele), 30 years old	f.956/II
Gargiulo Raffaele	Strada Regia, Portici, case Perretti (son of Michele), 21 years old	f.924/I
Piccirillo Antonio	Vico lungo Tre Regine, 48–9 (son of the late Gaetano), 38 years old	f.924/II

1857

Aiello Antonio	Vico Teani a S.Aniello dei Grassi	f.1023
Balestrieri Aniello	Vico Rotto S.Carlo, 15–16 formerly of Niglio-Cangiano	f.988
Caiazzo Angelina	Str. Cedronio, 13 (son of the late Alessio), 54 years old, widow, shop formerly of pastry chef Gaetano Pintauro	f.956/I
Ferraro Pasquale	Vico Campane, 7 (da Vico Rotto S.Carlo)—formerly of Chiosi Raffaele	f.956/I
Giannocca(oli) Francesco	Vico Nunzio, 3 (dal 1845)—fire started in the chimney	f.985/II
Niglio Giuseppe	Vico rotto.S.Carlo, 16 (son of the late Gennaro), 50 years old, goes into partnership with Cangiano Antonio who has the trattoria at n.15 (next door but connected)	f.956/I
Grilli Gaetano	Largo S.Tommaso, 6 (trattoria and pizzeria)	f.956/II
Panza Giuseppe	Str. Regia a s.Giov.a Teduccio, case Fumarola—(son of Giovanni), 35 years old, pizzeria, wine shop and tavern—formerly of Cuomo Vincenzo	f.957
Russo Francesco	Vico 1° Gravina, 4 (son of the late Giuseppe), 40 years old, formerly of Cerullo Raffaele	f.956/II
Sangiorgio Salvatore	Largo Carità, 3	f.989/I
Calicchio Ferdinando	Turns over the wine shop at Salita S.Anna di Palazzo n.30	

1858

Ajello Antonio	Vico Teani	f.1023
Alex Giovanni	Str. Infrascata, 213—in the request an oven "for cakes" is written, but the license reads "for pizzas"	f.989/II
Cangiano Francesco	Vico rotto S.Carlo 15–16 (son of Antonio), 37 years old, formerly of Ferraro Pasquale, who had taken it over in March from Balestrieri Aniello	f.989/I
Carpentieri Raffaele	Vico Nunzio, 3 (son of the late Pasquale), 33 years old, formerly of Giannoccoli Francesco	f.989/II
Correale Raffaele	Via Pellegrini, 27–8	f.1024/I
Ferraro Pasquale	Vico rotto S.Carlo, 15–16 (takes it over in May, turns it over in July)	f.988
Giannoccoli Francesco	Vico Campane, 7 (son of the late Pasquale), 37 years old, formerly of Ferraro Pasquale	f.988
La Vecchia Antonio	Largo Carità, 3 (son of the late Giovanni), 32 years old—takes over the business from the widow of San-giorgio Salvatore (deceased)	f.989/I
Lo Masto Angelo	Vico Maiorani, 52 (son of Felice), 26 years old, born in Benevento	f.989/II
Piccirillo Antonio	Vico Tre Regine, 42—takes ove a "country" trattoria at Pedamentina San Martino, 39	f.989/II

1859

Avallone Emanuele	Str. S.Monica, 18—pizzeria and wine shop	f.940
Correale Raffaele	Vico Carcerri S.Felice—move from Via Pellegrini, 27–8	f.1023
Della Monica Anna	Vico Monteroduni, 4 and 23 (son of the late Carmine), 40 years old, oven for bread and foccacia	f.1024/I
De Marco Giuseppe	Borgo S.Antonio Abate, 205 (son the late Gennaro), 23 years old	f.1023
Galluccio Giuseppe	Vico Fico a S.Biagio dei Librai (son of Antonio, wine shop keeper), 32 years old, pizzeria and trattoria	f.1024/II
Giudice Nicola	Via Pellegrini, 27–8 (son of the late Giuseppe), 42 years old, formerly of Correale Raffaele	f.1023
Torino Antonio	Vico Teani a S.Aniello dei Grassi (son of the late Francesco), 60 years old, formerly of Aiello Antonio	f.1023

SOURCES—NEAPOLITAN PIZZERIAS FROM 1860 TO 1901

ITALIAN STATE ARCHIVES OF NAPLES—CENTRAL POLICE COMMISSIONER—GENERAL ARCHIVE, 1ST SERIES

1860

Arpaja Bernardino	Str. S.Monica, 18 (son of Aniello, son of Ottaviano), 52 years old, pizzeria and wine shop formerly of Avallone Emanuele	f.940
Russo Luigi	Str. Infrascata (Via Salvator Rosa), 239—takes over from father Antonio, deceased—in the request, "cakes" are written, but the license reads "pizzas, in addition to a wine shop and "country" trattoria"	f.940

1861

Mirto Alfonso	Vico Monaco a Porto, 4 (an orphan raised by Ottaiano Nicola, pizzaiuolo), 25 years old, shop of his uncle Vincenzo?	f.1002

1862

Paparcone Pasquale	Str. Pignasecca, 48 (mentioned for the collection plate monies of Santa Maria Vertecoeli)	f.1036

1863

Aprea Angela Rosa	Porta S.Gennaro, 42 (son of the late Tommaso), 58 years old	f.1042
Aragone Antonio	Supportico Nasti, 3 (son of the late Pasquale)	f.1068
Bruno Gaetano	Largo Pentite alla Pignasecca, 49 (old numbering)	f.1068
Calicchio Ferdinando	Calata S.Anna di Palazzo, 1 (pizzeria) and 30 (wine shop), son of the late Pietro—fined because without license (perhaps had not renewed)	f.1037/bis
Calicchio Ferdinando	License renewed	f.1042
Carbone Paolo	Str. S.Teresa, 52 (?) (listed only as a bakery)	f.1068
Carpentieri Raffaele	Vico Nunzio, 2 (son of the late Pasquale), 34 years old	f.1042
Cennamo Fortunata	Str. Speranzella, 150 (son of the late Antonio), 70 years old	f.1042
Ciaramella Carmine	Salita Sette Dolori, 25 (shop with a well)	f.1042
Cuccurullo Ferdinando	Vico Fico al Purgatorio, 26 (son of the late Angelo), 38 years old	f.1042
Esposito Domenico	Str. Tribunali, 33–4 (son of the late Salvatore), 50 years old	f.1042
Giannoccoli Francesco	Vico Campane, 7—pizzeria and trattoria	f.1042
Giudice Nicola	Str. Barretta, 28 (son of the late Giuseppe)	f.1042
Imperatore Michela	Str. Foria, 89 (?) (listed only as a bakery)	f.1068
La Vecchia Antonio	Largo Carità, 3 (son of the late Giovanni), 52 years old, pizzeria and trattoria	f.1042
Ottaiano Nicola	Str. Porto, 9—fire prevention inspection and suggestion to renovate	f.1068
Paparcone Ferdinando	Str. Pellegrini, 43	f.1068
Paparcone Pasquale	Str. Pignasecca, 48 (son of the late Domenico), 81 years old	f.1042
Piccirillo Antonio	Vico Tre Regine, 48 (son of the late Gaetano), 45 years old	f.1042
Romano Pasquale	Str. Materdei, 2	f.1068
Testa Giuseppe	Str. Tribunali, 35—description of shop, three rooms as in 1822	f.1068

1868

Pennino Maria	Salvator Rosa, 34 (moglie di Aloja Gennaro), pizzeria and wine shop	f.1187

1869

Del Gaudio Antonio	Largo Antignano (son of the late Raffaele), pizzeria and wine shop	f.1186
Salvi Pasquale	Largo S.Tommaso, 7 (son of the late Gennaro), pizzeria with consumption of wine by the glass	f.1182

1870

Stajano Luigi	Porta Piccola al Carmine, 15 (son of the late Aniello)	f.1192

1872

Soccoia Ferdinando	Str. S.Maria della Neve, 19 (son of the late Filippo), pizzeria and wine shop	f.1172

1873

Aloja Gennaro	Salita Stella, 59 (son of the late Andrea), husband of Pennino Maria	f.1187
Del Gaudio Antonio	Largo Antignano (son of the late Raffaele), pizzeria and wine shop—taxes not paid	f.1171
De Marco Giuseppe	Str. Foria, 222—pizzeria and trattoria—taxes not paid	f.1171
Manciarullo Salvatore	Via Chiavettieri, 93—taxes not paid	f.1171
Mattozzi Luigi	Largo S.Demetrio 16–17—taxes not paid	f.1171
Molone Gioacchino	Vico 1° Gravina, 4—pizzeria and wine shop—taxes not paid	f.1171
Palumbo Gaetano	Vico 1° Gravina, 4 e	f.1171
	Str. Speranzella, s.n.—licenses not picked up after renewal	
Sarsano Raffaele	Vico Baglivo Uries, 7 (son of the late Lorenzo)	f.1182
Spadaro Luigi (Sparano)	Vico Pacella, 4, taxes not paid	f.1171
	(also in the list of those who had not paid their taxes are Caflish Luigi, bottled wine ship at Via Roma, 253/254 and 315, and Thevenir Francesco, Caffè d'Europa, in Piazza San Ferdinando)	f.1171

1875

(Di) Bello Giovanni	Str. Materdei, 3 (son of the late Giovanni)—sale of wine in a shop used as a pizzeria—in the renewals sometimes "Largo Materdei" is listed	f.1191
Mattozzi Luigi	Largo S.Demetrio, 16–17—substitution of an old license issued in 1869—mistakenly, San Demetrio, 20–1 is listed, which corresponds to the Church of San Demetrio. In renewals, sometimes "pizzeria with wine" is written, other times "pizzeria and wine shop"	f.1189

1876

Amitrano Elisabetta	S.Caterina Spina Corona (son of Vincenzo)	f.1174
Ammirati Vincenzo	S.Antonio ai Monti, 32 (son of Luigi)—pizzeria, wine shop	f.1201
Aprea Angela Rosa	Porta S.Gennaro, 35 (son of the late Tommaso), pizzeria and sale of wine by the glass	f.1173
Aragona (Dragone)	Antonio—Supportico Nasti, 30 (son of the late Pasquale)	f.1183
Caldarelli Antonio	P.za Tribunali, 76 (son of the late Pietro) pizzeria and wine shop—after 1877 solo wine shop	f.1186
Ceso Gaetano	Via Lavinaio, 160 (son of Luigi) pizzeria and sale of wine by the glass	f.1201
Cesa Luigi	Vico 5° Duchesca, 15 (son of the late Gaetano) in June requests to move to Strada SS.Giov. and Paolo, 13	f.1184
Corcione Francesco	Vico Baglivo Uries, 62 (son of the late Andrea)	f.1199
Corso Filomena	Str. Speranzella, 150–1 (son of the late Domenico)	f.1185
De Felice Carmine(a)	Str. Arena Sanità, 23 (son of the late Angelo) pizzeria and wine shop	f.1173
De Marco Giuseppe	Via Foria, 222 (son of the late Gennaro), wines and pizzeria	f.1199
Ferrante Filomena	Str. Tribunali, 35 (son of the late Pietro) pizzeria and sale of wine by the glass	f.1176
Son of the latesco Luigi	S.Maria della Scala, 63 (son of Gennaro)	f.1186
Imparato Vincenzo	Vico Fico al Purgatorio, 36—sublet to Pace Luigi	f.1173
Izzo Gennaro	Porta S.Gennaro, 104 (son of Francesco) the more credible address of Via Foria 104 is written on renewals	f.1198
La Vecchia Antonio	Largo Carità, 3 (son of the late Giovanni) since 1863	f.1191
Malato Luigi	Strada Porto, 75 (son of the late Giuseppe), 47 years old, husband of Ottajano Angela Maria—shop that before was used to store coal	f.1208
Mangiarulo Salvatore	Via Chiavettieri, 93 (son of the late Carlo)	f.1200
Miranda Aniello	Vico Pietrasanta, 35 (son of the late Giovanni), pizzeria and wine shop	f.1181
Mirto Alfonso	Str. Porta Medina, 43 (ivi domiciliato, son of the late Nicola Ottajano), 43 years old, move from Vico Monaco, 4	f.1204
Molone Gioacchino	Vico 1° Gravina, 4 (son of the late Angelo), tax not paid	f.1171
	In December asks permission to move to Vico Nunzio, 2	f.1194
Muratore Gennaro	Via Pellegrini, 27–8 (son of Gaetano)	f.1197
Ottaiano Angela	Str. Porto, 9 (son of the late Nicola), pizzeria with sale of wine by the glass	f.1173
Pace Luigi	Vico Fico al Purgatorio, 36 (son of the late Lorenzo)—closed but did not turn in the license—Imparato Vincenzo took over the business	f.1173
Pennino Maria	Salvator Rosa, 34 (pizzeria and wine shop), wife of Aloja Gennaro	f.1187
Piccirillo Antonio	Vico Tre Re, 20 (son of the late Gaetano and son of the late Esposito Rosa), 56 years old, new shop, on the license to open is written "pizzivendolo"	f.1197
Pierro Nicola	P.za Cavour, 22 (di Salvatore), 25 years old, from Benevento	f.1203
Riccardo Pasquale	Vicaria Vecchia, 19 (son of the late Antonio), pizzeria and wine shop	f.1174
Romano Francesca	C.so Garibaldi, 94–Portici (son of the late Francesco) in 1877 moved to Resina	f.1181
Sarnello Vincenzo	Selleria al Pendino, 35 (son of the late Gennaro)	f.1180
Scafaro(Cafara)	Vincenzo Piazza Cavour, 67 (son of the late Giovanni)	f.1182
Soccoia Ferdinando	Str.S.Maria della Neve, 19 (son of the late Filippo), pizzeria and wine shop	f.1172
Spadaro Luigi	Vico Roselle alla Conceria Vecchia, 4 (son of the late Gennaro)	f.1186
Stajano Luigi	Porta Piccola del Carmine, 15 (son of the late Aniello)	f.1192
Urciuoli Raffaele	(son of the late Gaetano, di Ottaviano), pizzeria and trattoria	f.1182
Volpe Luigi	Vico Campane, 7 (son of the late Gaetano)	f.1194

1877

Ammirati Vincenzo	Str. Selleria al Pendino, 12 (son of Luigi), pizzeria, wine shop—moved from Sant'Antonio ai Monti, 32	f.1201
Aragona Antonio	Piazzetta di Porto, 13 (son of the late Pasquale), from Supportico Nasti 30	f.1183
Brandi Giovanna	Strada Porto, 125 (son of the late Pasquale and Ottajani Luigia), 28 years old—before had a wine shop at Via Nardones, 37	f.1193
Cesa Luigi	Via Magnocavallo, 21 (son of the late Gaetano)	f.1184
Ciaravola Giuseppa	Borgo S.Antonio Abate, 125 (di Pasquale), 24 years old	f.1212
De Felice Carmina	Str. Arena alla Sanità, 23 (closed for "domestic reasons")	f.1213
(D')Esposito Raffaele	Vico rotto S.Carlo, 16 (son of the late Giovanni), 30 years old, shop previously run by a coffeemaker (?)	f.1211/3
Fusco Luigi	S.Maria della Scala, 63 (son of Gennaro), license renewal	f.1186
Malato Luigi	Strada Porto, 75 (son of the late Giuseppe), license renewal	f.1208
Mirto Alfonso	Largo Montesanto, second shop without a street number (son of the late Nicola)	f.1214
Parise Francesco	Vico Carrozzieri a Toledo, 12–13 (son of the late Giuseppe), 57 years old	f.1201
Sarsano Raffaele	Vico Baglivo Uries, 7 (son of the late Lorenzo), license renewal	f.1182
Spadaro Luigi	Vico Roselle, 4 (son of the late Gennaro), license renewal	f.1186
Vezza Giuseppa	Str. Arena alla Sanità, 23 (also domiciled there, son of Salvatore), 21 years old—formerly of De Felice Carmina	f.1213

1878

Ammendola Maria	Vico 1° Gravina, 4—wife of Caldarelli Salvatore who has wine shop at n.6	f.1182
Ammirati Vincenzo	Str. Selleria, 12—fine for complaints from: 1) Sarnelli Vincenzo, son of the late Gennaro, at n.25—2) Russo Luigi, son of Giuseppe at n.42—License revoked	f.1201
Cesa Luigi	Vico Barrettari, 74 (son of the late Gaetano), from Via Magnocavallo, 31	f.1184
Ciaravola Giuseppa	Borgo S.Antonio Abate, 125 (son of Pasquale), license renewal	f.1212
Corcione Francesaco	Vico Baglivo Uries, 7–8 (son of the late Andrea), pizzeria and wine shop—move from n°62	f.1199
(Di) Bello Giovanni	Via Materdei, 3 (son of the late Domenico), license renewal	f.1191
Orciuolo Gennaro	Via Gennaro Serra, 20 (son of the late Gaetano), pizzeria and restaurant—closes in March and turns the license back in	f.1215
Parise Francesco	Largo Ferrandina a Chiaia, 7 (son of the late Giuseppe), move from Vico Carrozzieri and trasformation into a trattoria (February), then into a pizzeria (July)	f.1201
Riccardo Pasquale	Vicaria Vecchia, 19 (son of the late Antonio), license renewal	f.1174
Sarnello Vincenzo	Selleria al Pendino, 35 (son of the late Gennaro), license renewal	f.1180

1879

Aloja Gennaro	Salita Stella, 59 (son of the late Andrea), license renewal	f.1187
Aprea Angela Rosa	Porta S.Gennaro (son of the late Tommaso), move from n.35 to n.42	f.1173
Aragona Antonio	Piazzetta di Porto, 13 (son of the late Pasquale), license renewal	f.1183
Caldarelli Savatore	Vico 1° Gravina, 4–6 (husband of Ammendola Maria), requests both licenses be made out to him, so issued	f.1182
Calicchio Ferdinando	Salita S.Anna di Palazzo, 1 and 30 (son of the late Pietro), pizzeria at n.1 and wine shop at n.30—licenses renewed	f.1193
Ceso Gaetano	Via Lavinaio, 160 (son of Luigi), license renewal	f.1201
Cesa Luigi	Str. Borgo Loreto, 48 (son of the late Gaetano), from Vico Barrettari, 74	f.1184
Corcione Francesco	Vico Baglivo Uries, 7–8 (son of the late Andrea), license renewal	f.1199
Corso Filomena	Str.Speranzella, 150–1 (son of the late Domenico), license renewal	f.1185
Del Gaudio Antonio	Largo Antignano—license renewal	f.1186
De Marco Giuseppe	Via Foria, 222 (son of the late Gennaro), license renewal	f.1199
Ferrante Filomena	Str. Tribunali, 35—license renewal	f.1176
Izzo Gennaro	Via Foria, 104—license renewal	f.1198
La Vecchia Antonio	Largo Carità, 3 (son of the late Giovanni), license renewal	f.1191
Mangiarulo Salvatore	Vico Chiavettieri, 93 (son of the late Carlo), license renewal	f.1200
Miranda Aniello	Vico Pietrasanta, 35—license renewal	f.1181
Molone Vincenzo	Vico Nunzio, 2—license renewal	f.1197
Muratore Gennaro	Via Pellegrini, 27–8 (son of Gaetano), license renewal	f.1197
Ottaiano Angela M.	Strada Porto, 9 (son of the late Nicola), license renewal	f.1173
Parise Francesco	Largo Ferrandina, 7—pizzeria and trattoria—license renewal	f.1201
Pierro Nicola	Piazza Cavour, 22 (son of Salvatore), license renewal	f.1203
Stajano Luigi	Porta Piccola al Carmine, 15 license renewal	f.1192
Urciuoli Raffaele	Trattoria and restaurant	f.1182
Volpe Luigi	Vico Campane, 7 (son of the late Gaetano), license renewal	f.1194

1880

Carpentieri Raffaele	Largo Montesanto, 48 (son of the late Pasquale)	f.1293
Salvi Pasquale	Largo S.Tommaso, 7—license renewal	f.1182
Vezza Giuseppa	Str. Arena alla Sanità, 23—license renewal	f.1213

1881

Soccoia Ferdinando	Str. S.Maria della Neve, 19—license renewal	f.1172

1882

Carpentieri Raffaele	Largo Montesanto, 48 (son of the late Pasquale), license renewal	f.1293

Albano Felicia	S.Pietro Martire, 46	f.1313
Aloja Gennaro	Via Stella, 59 and Via Fonseca, 25 (son of the late Andrea), pizzeria and wine shop	f.1313
Aprea Angela Rosa	Porta S.Gennaro, 42 (son of the late Tommaso), 80 years old	f.1313
Aragone Antonio	Piazzetta di Porto, 13 (son of the late Pasquale)	f.1313
Battaglia Pasquale	Via Carlo Poerio, 5	f.1313
Brandi Giovanni(a)	C.so Vittorio Emanuele, 588	f.1313
Brandi Giovanni	Via Tribunali, 292 (son of the late Pasquale)	f.1313
Caldarelli Salvatore	Vico 1° Gravina, 4 (son of the late Francesco)	f.1313
Calicchio Ferdinando	Salita S.Anna di Palazzo, 2 (son of the late Pietro)	f.1313
Cappitelli Pasquale	Via Salvator Rosa, 106 (son of the late Giuliano)	f.1313
Carpentieri Raffaele	Vico Nunzio, 2 (son of the late Pasquale), moved from October from Largo Montesanto, 48	f.1293
Cesi(o) Luigi	Str. Lavinaio, 160	f.1313
Cirillo Antonio	Vico Nunzio, 2—ceded to Carpentieri	f.1313
Corcione Gaetano	Vico Baglivo Uries, 6–7 (son of the late Andrea, anni 33), pizzeria and trattoria	f.1287/10
Corsi Filomena	Strada Speranzella, 150	f.1313
Corvino Teresa	Corso Garibaldi, Strada Ferrovia	f.1313
Criscio Carmela	Via S.Pantaleone, 21 (son of the late Crescenzo), 40 years old	f.12889/1
De Felice Lazzaro	Vico Fico al Purgatorio, 26 (son of the late Giuseppe)	f.1313
Del Mastro Felice	Vico Cinquesanti 12 (son of the late Angelo), 30 years old, pizzeria and cooked foods	f.1293/1
	In September gets a notice to close, but clarifies that he is working in the place of Vanacore Gabriele	f.1318
De Marco Giuseppe	Via Foria, 222 (son of the late Gaetano)	f.1313
De Piscopo Pasquale	Vico Campane, 7 and 55 (son of Francesco)	f.1313
Esposito Raffaele	Via Gennaro Serra, 21 (son of the late Giovanni), in April moves to Salita Sant'Anna di Palazzo, 1–2	f.1289/1
Ferrante Filomena	Via Tribunali, 35 (son of the late Pietro)	f.1313
Ferrante Giuseppe	Via Port'Alba, 18 (son of the late Raffaele)	f.1313
Son of the latesco Luigi	S.Maria La Scala, 65	f.1313
Germano Luigia	Vico Sedil Capuano, 27 (son of the late Alfonso), 25 years old, wife of Luigi Mattozzi	f.1292
Larenza Pasquale	Str. Banchi Nuovi, 17 (previously Largo S.Demetrio, 17)	f.1313
Lemma Gaetano	Borgo S.Antonio Abate, 125 (son of the late Lorenzo)	f.1313
Mangiarulo Gennaro	Vico Chiavettieri, 92 (son of the late Salvatore), 23 years old, takes over for deceased father who had run the shop since 1846	f.1316
Mattozzi Luigi	Strada Chiaia, 166 (son of the late Michele)	
Mazzarelli Anna	Porta Piccola al Carmine, 16	f.1313
Monaco Carolina	Largo Carità, 3	f.1313
Muratore Gennaro	Via Pellegrini, 28	f.1313
Ottaiano Angelo)a)	Strada di Porto, 9	f.1313
Pace Luigi	Via Foria, 104 (son of the late Lorenzo)	f.1313
Pagano Francesco	Str. Pignasecca, 12 (son of the late Vincenzo), 46 years old	f,1313
Palumbo Assunta	Via Conte di Mola, 36 (son of the late Domenico)	f.1289
Palumbo Vincenzo	Vico Nunzio, 3	f.1313
Pierro Nicola	Piazza Cavour, 22	f.1313
Sarnelli Luigi	Vico Roselle alla Conceria Vecchia, 4 (son of the late Gennaro), 28 years old	f.1287/10
Spadaro Luigi	Vico dell'Antica Conceria, 6	f.1313
Succoia Ferdinando	S.Maria della Neve, 24	f.1313
Trotti Francesco	Via Port'Alba, 19—pizzeria and restaurant	f.1316
Vanacore Gabriele	Vico Cinquesanti, 12 (turns over to Del Mastro Felice)	f.1293/1
Vezzi(a) Giuseppe(a)	Via (Arena) Sanità, 23 (son of Salvatore, wine shop owner)	f.1313

1884

Albano Felicia	S.Pietro Martire, 46	f.1313
Aragone Antonio	Piazzetta di Porto, 13 (son of the late Pasquale)	f.1313
Brandi Giovanna	C.so Vitt.Emanuele, 589 (son of the late Giovanni), pizzeria and bottled wine shop	f.2262
Brandi Giovanni	Str. Tribunali, 292 (son of the late Pasquale), 24 years old—"Pizzeria of the friends"	f.1313
Buongarzone Francesco	Via Port'Alba, 19 (son of the late Antonio), 58 years old—pizzeria and restaurant formerly of Trotti Francesco	f.1316
Carrino Vincenzo	C.so Garibaldi, 13 (son of Giuseppe)	f.1329
Corcione Gaetano	Vico Baglivo Uries 6–7 (son of the late Andrea), pizzeria and trattoria	f.1313
De Felice Lazzaro	Vico Purgatorio ad Arco, 26 (Vico Fico a)	f.1326
Ferrante Filomena	Str. Tribunali,35 (son of the late Pietro), 40 years old—with the sign "Monzù Testa"	f.1313
Son of the latenaro Maria	Vico Cinquesanti,12 (son of the late Giovanni), 36 years old—pizzeria and wine shop	f.1313
	The shop has another entrance at Vico Gigante 53, later closed	f.1318
Germano Luigia	Sedil Capuano, 27 (son of Alfonso), wife of Mattozzi Luigi	f.1313
Larenza Pasquale	S.Demetrio ai Banchi Nuovi, 16–17 (son of the late Salvatore)	f.1313
	Closed without notification, Mattozzi Luigi returns	f.1319
Launo(Lemmo) Gaetano	Via S.Antonio Abate, 125—license renewal	f.1318
Mancini Antonio	Strada Fuori Porta Capuana, 41	f.1318
Mattozzi Luigi	Str. Banchi Nuovi 16–17—appeal for wrongful closing because of cholera epidemic	f.1314
Nappi Eugenio	Vico 1° Gravina, 6–7–8 (son of Biagio), pizzeria and bottled wine shop	f.1325
Ottaiano Angelo(a)	Strada di Porto, 8 (in reality n.9)	f.1313
Pierro Nicola	Piazza Cavour, 22 (son of Salvatore), 41 years old	f.1313
Ruoppo Girolamo	Vico Pergole all'Avvocata, 18 (son of the late Luigi), in business since 1850—in May closes and turns the license back in	f.1319/1
Salvato Gennaro	Vicaria Vecchia (Forcella), 19 (son of Antonio), 44 years old, born in Acquarola, domiciled in the shop, in two rooms and a kitchen for his own use	f.1319/5
Teodanno Elisabetta	C.so Garibaldi, 98, Portici (son of the late Tobia), widow, 55 years old, from Portici	f.1317

1885

Annunziata Aniello	Vico 1°Gravina 4–6–7 (son of Pasquale, cobbler), from Ottaviano, 32 years old, manager for Luigi and Pasquale Rescigno, pizzeria and trattoria	f.1326
Bari Anna	Vico Cinquesanti, 12 (pizzeria) and Vico Gigante, 53 (wine shop) (orphan), 45 years old, formerly of Funaro Maria	f.1327
Basile Vincenzo	Str. Cavallerizza a Chiaia, 44 (son of the late Antonio, carpenter), 33 years old	f.1329
Calicchio Ferdinando	Salita S.Anna di Palazzo, 30—wine shop, left the pizzeria at n.2	f.1313
Caprez Baldassarre	Vico Rotto S.Carlo, 14 (son of Baldassarre)	f.1313
Carrino Vincenzo	Corso Garibaldi, 13 (son of Giuseppe), In April renovates into a cafe and bottled wine shop	f.1329
D'Andrea Giuseppe	S.Maria la Neve, 2 (son of the late Gaspare), 60 years old, fined for lack of license	f.1328
De Chiara Rosa	Via Tribunali, 201 (son of the late Carmine), 55 years old, widow of Esposito Raffaele	f.1328
Del Mastro Felice	Str. Tribunali, 292 (son of the late Angelo, pizzaiolo), 32 years old	f.1374
De Luca Domenico	Vico 2° Pozzari, 6 (d son of i Nicola, bettoliere), 28 years old	f.1328
Esposito Raffaele	Salita S.Anna di Palazzo, 1–2 (with the sign "Pizzeria della Regina d'Italia"), pizzeria and wine shop	f.1313
Ferrante Filomena	Via Tribunali, 34 (son of the late Pietro) sign with "Monzù Testa"	f.1313

Gavino Gaetano	Salita Magnocavallo, 27 (di AGP, allevato da Attanasio Nicola and Setola Caterina), 38 years old	f.1332
Germano Luigia	Vico Sedil Capuano, 27—closes and turns license in	f.1325
Liccardi Francesco	Vico Sedil Capuano, 27 (son of the late Antonio), 45 years old, domiciled at n.26, sublets from Germano Luigia	f.1313
Mangiarulo Gennaro	Vico Chiavettieri, 94 (son of the late Salvatore)	f.1313
Miranda Alfonso	Via Gennaro Serra, 21 (son of the late Santalo)	f.1313
Nappi Eugenio	Vico 1° Gravina, 6–7–8—pizzeria and bottiglieria—does not renew license	f.1318
Pierro Nicola	Piazza Cavour, 22 (son of the late Salvatore)	f.1313
Sarnelli Luigi	Vico Roselle alla Conceria, 4 (son of the late Gennaro)	f.1313
Terriano Anna	Vico Fico al Purgatorio, 25 (son of the late Salvatore, Fontanaro), 28 years old, sublets from De Felice Lazzaro	f.1326

1886

Ceso Gaetano	Via Lavinaio, 160 (son of Luigi)	f.230 3
Son of the latesco Luigi	Vico Chiavettieri al Pendino, 94 (son of the late Gennaro, snack hawker), 47 years old	f.1380
Miranda Alfonso	Via Gennaro Serra, 21 (son of the late Santo), pizzeria and bottled wine shop	f.1378
Pace Luigi	Via Foria, 104 (son of the late Lorenzo) renews license	f.1374
Palumbo Luigi	Vico Conte di Mola, 32 (son of the late Pasquale, painter), 32 years old	f.1376
Passaro Carmina	Strada Chiaia, 166 (son of the late Domenico, coppersmith), 71 years old—pizzeria and restaurant	f.1381
Piccolo Grazia	Portici-C.so Garibaldi, 98 (son of Bartolomeo), 22 years old, formerly of Teodanno Elisabetta license reqeuested in May, issued in August	ff.1379 and 1380
Sarnelli Vincenzo	Conceria Vecchia, 4 (son of the late Gennaro), pizzeria and wine shop	?
Vezza Giuseppa	Str.Arena Sanità, 23 (son of Salvatore, bettoliere), pizzeria and sale of wine, shop with only one exit, sleeps there with husband	f.1379

1887

Aprea Angela Rosa	Via Porta S.Gennaro, 35 (son of the late Francesco), license renewal	f.1374
De Chiara Rosa	Via Tribunali 201 (son of the late Carmine), license renewal	f.1374
Franchini Giuseppe	Via Salv.Rosa, 311 (son of the late Pasquale, laborer), 50 years old, pizzeria, wine shop, and homemade food	f.1391
Mattozzi Luigi	Via Banchi Nuovi, 16–17—license reissued after loss	f.1383
Volpe Antonio	Vico Carminello a Toledo, 24 (son of the late Gaetano, fruit seller), 56 years old	f.1390

CENTRAL POLICE COMMISSIONER—GENERAL ARCHIVE, 2ND AND 3RD SERIES

1888

| Allocco(a) Luigi | C.so Vitt.Emanuele, 589 (orphan, recognized as the natural-born child of Allocco) | |
| | Francesco (son of Ottaviano and Giovanna Brandi) 23 years old, resides in the mezzanine floor for which he pays £20 a month in addition to the £40 for the shop—requests permission to change the wine shop of his mother into a pizzeria-bottled wine shop | f.2262 |

Annunziata Aniello	Vico 1° Gravina, 4–6–7—pays taxes on distilled spirits	f.2321
Buongarzone Francesco	Str. Port'Alba, 19 (son of the late Antonio), taxes on distilled spirits	f.2321
Corcione Gaetano	Vico Baglivo Uries, 6–7 (son of the late Amedeo), pizzeria, trattoria and sale of wine by the glass—pays taxes on distilled spirits	f.2321
De Luca Domenico	Vico 2° Pozzari, 6 (son of Nicola, wine shop keeper), 32 years old, license renewal	f.1328(1 ^ Serie)
Franchini Giuseppe	Via Salvator Rosa 311—in April requests permission to move to S.Nicola dei Caserti, 22	
	But because the shop is too narrow, opens just a wine shop, then moves back to Santa Maria Apparente, 40, in July, where he adds a pizzeria to the wine shop	
	Then moves to Vico S.Anna a Capuana, 21 (in December) wine shop	f.2335
Passero Carmina	Via Chiaia, 166—on 4 May closes and turns the license back in	f.2400
Pavone Vincenzo	Via Chiaia, 166 (son of the late Giovanni, fishmonger), 37 years old, found guilty	f.2401
Pisciotti Giovanni(a)	S.Maria la Scala, 65 (orphan) renews his old license obtained in 1884 from Fusco Luigi	f.2410
Volpe Luigi	Salita Conte di Mola, 5 (son of the late Gaetano), with rooms upstairs—moved from Vico Campane because of the construction of the new Galleria Umberto I	f.2469

1889

Albano Giovanni	Via Firenze, 49 (son of Raffaele, manual laborer), 44 years old, from Bracigliano	f.2260
	Already has ovens for bread at numbers 50–1, requests license for a pizzeria at n.49	
Casaburo Francesco Paolo	Porta S.Gennaro, 42 (son of the late Odoardo), from Cava dei Tirreni, 48 years old	f.2298
Ceso Luigi	Via Lavinaio, 160 (son of the late Gaetano), 72 years old, asks that his son Gaetano's license be reissued in his name	f.2303
Ciuccio Biagio	Vico Cupa Riviera di Chiaia, 12 (son of Cristofaro) already has a wine shop, asks permission to add apizzeria	f.2307
De Luca Domenico	Via Genova, 23 (son of Nicola) move from Vico Pozzari, 6	f.2363
De Tommaso Antonio	Largo Pignasecca, 20 (son of the late Pasquale, tailor)	f.2455
Ferrante Filomena	Via Tribunali, 372 (son of the late Pietro) moved from Via Tribunali, 35	f.2329
Russo Antonietta	Borgo S.Antonio Abate, 125 (son of Mauro, wine shop keeper), 23 years old	f.2426

1890

Bottone Alfonso	Riviera di Chiaia, 154 (son of Luigi), pizzeria and wine shop	f.2285
Criscio Carmela	Str. S.Pantaleone, 21 (son of the late Crescenzo), returned license because of death of holder	f.2315
De Tommaso Antonio	Str.S.Pasquale a Chiaia, 25—move from Largo Pignasecca, 20	f.2455
Estremo Giovanna	Strada Corsea, 96 (orphan), 33 years old, married to Gallo Salvatore	f.2325
Son of the latesco Luigi	Vico Chiavettieri, 94—in July closes and turns pizzeria over to Scialò	f.2336
Izzo Gennaro	Salita Conte di Mola, 5 (son of the late Francesco, pizzaiolo), 40 years old, takes over pizzeria of Volpe Luigi, deceased	f.2355
Mattozzi Luigi	(son of the late Michele) Str. Bernini, new neighborhood Vomero, letter Z, property of Signor Cardone	f.2376
Mercadante Pasquale	Via Tribunali, 372 (son of the late Giuseppe, cook), 42 years old, formerly of Ferrante Filomena	f.2379

Mucci Tobia	Via S.Pantaleone, 21 (son of Vitangelo), son of Gioia Sannitica, 47 years old, husband of Criscio Carmela, fined because without license	f.2387
Pedata Angela	Via S.Pantaleone, 21 (son of Antonio, day laborer), from Sant'Antimo, 29 years old, wife of Basile Vincenzo, obtains license	f.2401
Perato Teresa	Via S.Pantaleone, 21 (son of Antonio), 29 years old, fined because without license	f.2404
Scialò Luigi	Vico Chiavettieri, 94 (son of the late Francesco, bucciere), 43 years old, succede a Fuco Luigi	f.2438
Scognamillo Giuseppe	Str. Portamedina, 40 (son of Salvatore, oyster seller), 23 years old, pizzeria and restaurant	f.2439

1891

Conte Luigi	Via Salvator Rosa, 109 (son of Raffaele), 33 years old, pizzeria, wine shop	f.2309
Coruzzola Amalia	Vico 1° Gravina, 4—wine shop	f.2394
Fiorentino Salvatore	Vico Nunzio, 2bis (son of Biagio, cod seller), 34 years old, pays £30 monthly for the shop and another £30 for his domicile	f.2332
Malato Giovanni	Via Porto, 9 (son of the late Luigi, navigator and son of the late Ottajano Angela Maria) takes over for his mother, deceased	f.2366
Masi Maria della Saletta	Vico Conte di Mola, 5 (son of the late Salvatore, stable hand), 25 years old, takes over the business from Izzo Gennaro	f.2375
Mattozzi Luigi di Luigi	Vico Carrozzieri a Toledo, 12—22 years old	f.2376
Palumbo Teresa	Nuovo Rione Vomero, Palazzo Cordani or Cardone (son of Pasquale, stablehand of the Royal House)	f.2397
Scognamillo Giuseppe	Vico Rosario a Portamedina, 35—move from Portamedina, 40	f.2439
Talamo Cesare	Vico 1°Gravina, 4-6-7 (son of the late Pietro, day laborer), 24 years old	f.2452
Ventriglia Alfredo	Porta S.Gennaro, 42 (son of the late Gennaro), 25 years old, fined for selling wine without a license	f.2464

1892

Cappitelli Pasquale	Via Salvator Rosa, 106 (son of Giuliano)	f.2293
Ciuccio Biagio	Vico 2°S.Maria in Portico, 8—move from Vico Cupa, only wine shop	f.2307
Estremo Giovanna	C.so Vitt.Emanuele 412—move from Strada Corsea, only wine shop	f.2325
Pepillo Concetta	Via Genova, 23 (son of the late Pasquale), 23 years old, married to Lombardi Antonio	f.2401
Russo Antonietta	Nuovo Corso Garibaldi, 164—move from Borgo Sant'Antonio Abate, 125	f.2426
Talamo Cesare	Vico 1° Gravina, 4-6-7 (son of the late Pietro) arrested for fight and assault, shop closed	f.2452

1893

Imparato Vincenzo	Vico Rosario a Portamedina, 35 (son of the late Giovanni) on May 4 takes over the shop from Scognamillo Giuseppe	f.2439

1894

Ceso Luigi	Via Lavinaio, 160 (son of the late Gaetano)	f.2303
Conte Luigi	Via Salvator Rosa, 109 (son of Raffaele), pizzeria and bottled wine seller	f.2309
Son of the latesco Luigi	S.Maria della Scala, 65 (son of the late Gennaro)	f.2321
Mazzarella Anna	Portapiccola al Carmine, 16 (son of the late Luigi)	f.2321
Palumbo Teresa	Via Poerio, 11—move from the new Vomero neighborhood	f.2397
Sarnelli Vincenzo	Vico Roselle alla Conceria, 4 (son of the late Gennaro)	f.2321

1895

Ceso Gaetano	Via Lavinaio, 160 (son of the late Luigi), 49 years old, takes over upon father's death	f.2303
De Tommaso Antonio	Str. S.Pasquale a Chiaia, 25 fined for wine bought elsewhere, judged, found innocent	f.2455

1896

Aloja Pasquale	Borgo S.Antonio Abate, 123 (son of the late Luigi, wine shop keeper), 30 years old	f.2262
Cappitelli Pasquale	Via Salvator Rosa, 109 (son of the late Giuliano), license renewal	f.2293
Lieto Vincenzo	Via Porto, 161 (di Giuseppe, pizzaiuolo), 29 years old, sublets in August from Lombardi Errico	f.2359
Lombardi Errico	Via Porto, 161 (son of the late Tommaso), obtains a license in March Via Porto, 9—moves from n.161 taking over from Malato Giovanni	f.2361
Merlino Girolamo	Via Foria, 104 (son of the late Luigi, public servant), 48 years old, in August asks permission to have Palumbo Gaetano represent him, takes over from Pace	f.2379
Pace Luigi	Str. Banchi Nuovi 16–17 (son of the late Lorenzo), moved from Via Foria, 104—lives in the rooms above, sublets temporarily from Mattozzi Luigi	f.2394
Ruggiero Pasquale	C.so Garibaldi vecchio, 334 (son of Gaetano), 24 years old, pizzeria and osteria	f.2425

1897

Pagano Francesco	Via Sette Dolori, 61—move from Strade Pignasecca 12, because of rent that was too high	f.2394
Scarpati Luigi	Riviera di Chiaia, 25 (son of Pasquale, falegname), 20 years old	f.2436

1898

Brandi Ciro	Via Salvator Rosa, 109 (son of Vincenzo), 37 years old, fined because without license	f.2286
Pagano Francesco	Via Tribunali, 350 (è 35), move from Via Sette Dolori, 61 because of crumbling of street	f.2394
Sciortino Antonino	Via Sergente Maggiore, 55–6 (son of the late Giovanni, traveling musician), from Girgenti, 34 years old, pizzeria, bottled wine shop and restaurant	f.2438

1899

Sciortino Antonino	Via Roma, 143, first floor—move from Via Sergente Maggiore—two of the seven rooms for a domicile for the family	f.2438

1900

Basile Vincenzo	Via Bisignano move from Via Cavallerizza a Chiaia, 43	f.2321
Nocera Maria	Via Gennaro Serra, 21 takes over from Miranda Alfonso, deceased	f.2321
Ruggiero Pasquale	Via Cesare Rossaroll, 334 pizzeria and wine shop, license renewal	f.2321
Sarniolo Raffaele	Porta S.Gennaro, 42 (formerly called Corso Garibaldi vecchio), warned for not having renewed his license	f.2321

1901

| Di Pietro Salvatore | Portici, C.so Garibaldi, 76 (son of the late Michele, sharecropper), 43 years old | f.2408 |
| Guida Andrea | Via Cesare Rossaroll, 28 formerly at n.334 (son of the late Domenico, cart driver), 52 years old, pizzeria and wine shop | f.2349 |

SOURCES—NEAPOLITAN PIZZERIAS CITED IN COMMERCIAL GUIDES FROM 1880, 1881, 1886, 1888, AND 1900

Name	Address	Year
Albano Giosuè	Str. Chiaia, 146	1880 until
Ambrosio Francesco	Port'Alba, 18	1900 1932
Amirante Vincenzo	Str. Forcella, 61	1886
Amirante Vincenzo	Via Duomo, 242	1888
Amitrano Raffaele	Str. Loggia di Genova, 67	1881
Aragona Antonio	Piazzetta di Porto, 12	1880–1881–1886–1888
Aragona Antonio	Str. Corsea, 96	1900 1903
Arpaia Giosuè	Str. Chiaia, 166	1880
Arpaia Domenico	Str. Chiaia, 166	1888
Avolio Anna	Str. Foria, 104	1900
Battaglia Salvatore	Via Carlo Poerio, 5	1880–1881
Battaglia Pasquale	Via Carlo Poerio, 5	1886
Bergamo Maria	Via Foria, 178	1900
Bernardo Concetta	Via Piedigrotta, 9	1900
Brandi Giovanni (a)	Via Gennaro Serra, 21	1880–1881–1886
Brandi Giovanni	Strada di Porto, 125	1880
Brandi Giovanni	Str. Speranzella, 150–1	1880–1881–1886–1888
Brandi Giovanni	Vico Baglivo Uries, 9	1900 1915
Buongarzone Francesco	Port'Alba, 18	1886
Calicchio Ferdinando	Salita S.Anna di Palazzo, 1–2	1880–1881
Capone Salvatore	P.za Belle Donne	1886
Cappiello Gaetano	Salita Magnocavallo, 27	1900
Cappitelli Pasquale	Via Salvator Rosa, 106, poi n° 75	1880–1881–1886–1888 1907
Carrino Giuseppe	C.so Garibaldi, 13–14–15	1880–1881
Caruso Stanislao	Via Lavinaio, 160	1886–1888
Cerillo Antonio	Str.Conte Di Mola, 36 (Cirillo)	1881–1886
Cerillo Antonio	Vico Nunzio, 2 (Cirillo)	1881
Ceso Gaetano	Str. Lavinaio 160	1900
Cesi(o) Gennaro	Str. Tribunali, 292	1886
Ceso Luigi	Str. Lavinaio, 160	1881 1888
Colarusso Luigi	S.Nicola da Tolentino (C.so V.Em.), 588	1888
Corcione F.Lli	Vico Baglivo Uries, 7	1880–1881–1886–1888
D'Anna Maria	Str. Montesanto, 48	1881
D'Anna Pasquale	Borgo S.Antonio Abate, 125	1886–1888
De Angelis Luigi	Via Piedigrotta, 9	1900 1903
De Felice Carmela	Str. Foria, 144	1880
De Felice Lazzaro	Vico Fico al Purgatorio, 26	1880 (De Felice G.) 1911
Del Mastro Felice	Str. Tribunali 292	1888–1900 1912
De Prisco Pasquale	Vico Campane, 7 (De Piscopo)	1880
De Tommaso Antonio	Salita Magnocavallo, 27	1886
De Tommaso Antonio	Cavallerizza a Chiaia, 43	1888
De Tommaso Antonio	Via Bisignano, 1	1900
Diano Nicola	Vicaria Vecchia, 19	1900 1903
Di Napoli Pasquale	Str. Porta Capuana, 5	1886–1888
Esposito Raffaele	Salita S.Anna di Palazzo, 2	1886–1888–1900 1917

Ferrante Filomena	Str. Tribunali, 35	1881–1886–1888
Ferrara Luigi	S.Maria la Scala, 65	1900
Ferraro Guglielmo	Port'Alba, 18	1888
Ferrara(o) Vimcenzo	Vico 2° Spina Corona, 1	1881–1886–1888
Festa Gennaro	Str. Selleria. 12	1880–1881–1886
Fiore Vincenzo	Str. Carmine, 16	1900 1903
Frezza Agnello	C.so Garibaldi, 87	1886
Fusco Luigi	S.Maria La Scala, 65	1881–1886 (Alfonso) 1905
Fusco Vincenzo	S.Maria La Scala	1888
Gargiulo Luigi	Cesare Rossaroll, 324	1900
Giudice Maria	Via Pellegrini, 28	1881 1888
Guglielmi Angelo	Str. Cedronio, 16	1886
Imparato Gaetana	Str.Materdei, 2	1900 1909
Imparato Vincenzo	Str. Loggia di Genova, 67	1886 1900 1907
Imparato Vincenzo	Vicaria Vecchia, 19	1888
Izzo Luigi	Via Bonafficiata Vecchia, 3	1881–1886–1888
La Vecchia Antonio (widow)	Largo della Carità, 3	1880–1881
Lisci Gennaro	Vicaria Vecchia, 19	1886
Longo Gennaro	Via Loreto, 48	1880–1881
Magna(o) Angelo	Str. S.Pantaleone, 21	1886–1888
Malato Luigi	Strada Porto, 9	1886
Mattozzi Gennaro	Via Tribunali, 202	1900 1932
Mattozzi Luigi	Str. Banchi Nuovi, 16–17	1880–1881–1886–1888
Mattozzi Luigi	Str. Chiaia, 166	1881
Mattozzi Vincenzo	Str. Banchi Nuovi, 16–17	1900 1924
Mazzarella Anna	Via del Carmine, 16	1886–1888 1910
Mellone Salvatore	C.so Garibaldi, 334	1900 1904
Migliorati Carmine	S.Giovannniello, 113	1900
Milone Gioacchino	Vico 1° Gravina, 4 (Molone)	1880–1881–1886–1888
Miranda Alfonso	Via Gennaro Serra, 21	1888–1900 1904
Monaco Carolina	Largo Carità, 3	1888
Nocera Gelsomina	Str. Loreto, 63	1880–1881–1886–1888
Ottajano Angela Maria	Strada Porto, 9	1880–1881 1888
Pace Raffaele(è Luigi)	Str. Foria, 104	1888
Pagano Francesco	Pignasecca, 12	1888
Pavone Alfonso	Largo Carità, 3	1900 1915
Petrillo Rosa	Vico 2° Molo Piccolo, 4	1900
Pezza Luigi	Vico 1° Gravina, 4	1900
Pezzella C.	Via Sanità, 25	1900
Piccirillo Antonio	Conte di Mola, 36	1888
Pierro Nicola	Piazza Cavour, 22	1880–1881–1886–1888–1900 1905
Pinto Nicola	Strada Porto, 161	1900
Pisciotti Giovanni	S.Maria la Scala, 65	1900 1901
Riccio Raffaele	Str. Materdei, 2	1888
Roma Nicola	Via Rosario a Portamedina, 35	1900 1903
Ruopolo Girolamo	Vico Pergola all'Avvocata, 18 (Ruoppolo)	1881
Sarnelli Vincenzo	Vico Antica Conceria, 3 (4)	1886–1888 1909
Scannapiecoro Felice (widow)	Vicaria Vecchia, 19	1880–1881
Scarpati Luigi	Riviera di Chiaia, 25	1900 1903
Sorano Concetta	Vico Calzettari, 44	1900 1901
Spadaro Luigi	Vico dell'Antica Conceria, 4	1881
Stajano Luigi	Str. del Carmine, 16	1880–1881 (nephew) 1932
Tedesco Luigi	Via Speranzella, 69	1900 1905
Terracina Raffaele	Str. Porta S. Gennaro, 42 (Terracciano)	1880–1881–1886–1888
Terracina Raffaele	Str. Foria 104	1886
Tremalaterra Gennaro	Via dei Pellegrini, 28	1880
Uciuolo Raffaele	Port'Alba, 18	1880–1881
Volpe Luigi	Vico Campane, 7	1881–1886
Volpe Luigi	Conte di Mola, 5	1888
Zeraldi A.	Vico Fico a Foria	1900

NOTES

AUTHOR'S PREFACE

1   Matilde Serao, *Il ventre di Napoli*, Treves, Milan 1884. All translations of quotations, unless otherwise noted, are by the translator.

2   Roberto Minervini, *Storia della pizza*, E. P. T., Naples, 1956

3   Alexandre Dumas, *Il Corricolo*, edited by Gino Doria, Naples, 1950.

4   It was first a "federated city" (ally) then a *municipium* (city with autonomy but incorporated into Roman citizenship).

5   Johann Wolfgang von Goethe, *Italian Journey*, Princeton, NJ: Princeton University Press, 1994.

6   For an example of this method of describing Neapolitan life and customs through realistic and picturesque sketches—something that had man followers in the nineteenth century but which one can still see today when journalists try to capture Neapolitan life—see Edmondo Cione, *Napoli Romantica*, Naples: Morano, 1957, 296 and *passim*.

7   The historian Giuseppe Galasso, in his essay "Professioni, arti e mestieri della popolazione di Napoli nel secolo decimonono" published in 1961–3 in volumes 13 and 14 of the *Annuario dell'Istituto Storico Italiano per l'età moderna e contemporanea*, says that "the extended study of a whole region or country permits a global vision […] but much more difficult is a concrete vision of the declared professional activities […] whereas a study restricted to a single city or place or rather several territorial entities offers in general the opposite, always assuming that the data available are sufficiently detailed." The risk then of the present microhistory of pizzerias and pizzaioli is in the possible insufficiency of data available, but the advantages of operating in such a restrained space are clear.

8   These authors will be cited in the pages that follow.

9   The twentieth-century publications about pizza begin in the postwar period with Roberto Minervini's *Storia della pizza*, cited above. In this pleasant little volume there are however a number of urban legends about pizza and pizzerias, legends that subsequent authors that wrote about pizza then repeated, as we will see in the various chapters of this book.

1—THE ORIGINS OF PIZZA AND THE PIZZERIA

1   The fact that neither "pizzeria" nor "pizzaiolo" appear in lists of Neapolitan trades in the second half of the eighteenth century confirms my supposition about the chronology of the origin of Neapolitan pizza.

2 In 1956 Roberto Minervini (in the book already cited above) confirmed what Serao had said about the failed attempts up to that point of Neapolitan pizzaioli to "open shop outside of [Naples]": almost all failed or were condemned to just getting by.

3 F. P. Rispoli, *La provincia e la città di Napoli*, Naples, 1902, 114.

4 Salvatore Di Giacomo (1860–1934), a great Neapolitan poet, writer, and dramaturge was the author of many songs, among them "Quanno sponta la luna a Marechiaro" and "E spingule frangese."

5 E. De Renzi, *Sull'alimentazione del popolo minuto di Napoli*, Naples, 1863.
A. Spatuzzi and L. Somma, *Saggi igienici e medici sull'alimentazione del popolo minuto di Napoli*, Naples, 1863.

6 Until the end of the nineteenth century Naples had the highest population in Italy. In 1861 (the year of Italian unification) it had 447,000 inhabitants, Turin had 204,700, and Milan just 196,100.

7 Cione points out correctly that pizza, in the *Dictionary* of the Academy of the Crusca, "was not the marvelous food we eat today [...] but rather a type of cheese that was called by that name" (ibid.: 99). Other northern Italian dictionaries also give the definition of "a type of cheese in the form of focaccia or egg" for the word "pizza." Indeed, even many Neapolitan dictionaries give different meanings. In M. Cortelazzo and C. Marcato's etymological dictionary, they report that in the dialects of Calabria, southern Puglia and Sicily, the word "pizza" means "masculine member."

8 G. B. Basile, *Lo cunto de li cunti overo lo trattenemiento de' peccerille*, Naples (posthumous), 1634–6.

9 Benedetto Croce, *Aneddoti di varia letteratura*, II series, 73. Ettore De Mura, *Poeti napoletani dal Seicento ad oggi*, Naples, 1963, 4. There are only a few fragments of the poet Velardiniello and the apparent contradiction of the presence of pizza in the mid-sixteenth century is belied by the fact that (as critics have showed) the poem was later reworked by anonymous subsequent authors.

10 "Take a half dozen Tomatoes, that are mature; put them above the coals, to cook, and after they're toasted, diligently remove their skins, cut them up with a Knife, add some Onion cut fine, as much as you wish, some Bell Pepper also cut fine, Hot Pepper in a small quantity, mix it all together, garnish with a bit of Salt, Oil & Vinegar, which will make a tasty sauce, for boiled meat, or for other things." From Antonio Latini, *Lo Scalco alla moderna overo l'arte di disporre i conviti ...*, Naples, 1694.

11 Vincenzo Corrado, *Il Cuoco Galante*, Naples, 1773.

12 M. F., *La cucina casereccia*, Naples, 1807. Reprinted in 1993 by Editore Grimaldi, Naples, edited by Leyla Mancuso Sorrentino.

13 Ippolito Cavalcanti, *Cucina teorico-pratica*, Naples, 1837.

14 Nunzio F. Faraglia, *Storia dei prezzi nel Regno di Napoli dal 1131 al 1860*, Naples, 1878, 291.

15 Salvatore Di Giacomo, *Storia del teatro S.Carlino, 1738–1884*, preface by Gino Doria, Naples, 1967, ix–x.

16 Given that we are discussing a phenomenon that developed over a long period of time, I have preferred here to follow the chronological succession rather than separate the two parallel themes.

17 Francesco De Sanctis, *La giovinezza, memorie postume ...*, edited by Gennaro Savarese, Turin, 1961, 32.

18 Grated cheese, basil, slices of mozzarella, and tomato: incontrovertible proof that the Pizza Margherita already existed. See Emanuele Rocco, "Il pizzajuolo," in *Usi e costumi di Napoli e contorni descritti e dipinti*, edited by Francesco De Bourcard, Naples, 1857–66, vol. II, 123–7.

19 The *Vocabolario della Crusca* (Dictionary of the Crusca) was a work published by the Academy of the Crusca, an association of linguistic purists that began in Florence in 1583. Its mission was "to separate the flour from the chaff [*crusca*] in the Italian language."

20 Alexandre Dumas, *Il corricolo*, 93.

21 Edmondo Cione, *Napoli romantica*, Morano, Napoli, 1957, 308. Another possibility is that Valeriani suffered from Celiac's Disease.

22 Carl August Mayer, *Neapel und Neapolitaner oder Briefe aus Neapel in die Heimat*, Oldenburg, 1840. There is a copy of this work in the private library of Benedetto Croce, a copy I was able to consult thanks to the interest of Lidia Croce Herling, whom I thank for her encouragement in the course of this research.

23 Niccolò Tommaseo and Bernardo Bellini, *Dizionario delle lingua italiana*, Turin, 1871. Luciano Scarabelli, *Vocabolario universale della lingua italiana*, Milan, 1878.

24 Emilio Peruzzi, *Una lingua per gli italiani*, Turin, 1961.

25 "La pizza: quand le casse-croute des miserables passe à table," in *Mutations*, Revue Mensuelle n. 206, July 2001.

26 G. Princi Baccini, "Etimo germanico e itinerario italiano di pizza," in *Archivio Glottologico Italiano*, Florence, 1979.

27 "Etimologia semitica dell'italiano pizza e dei suoi corradicali est-europei, turchi, e dell'area semitica levantina," in *Quaderni di Semantica*, a. XXVIII, n. 1, June 2007.

2—CENSUSES AND STATISTICS

1   Archivio di Stato di Napoli (Italian State Archives in Naples), hereafter ASN, Ministero della Polizia Generale, 1799, f.131, n. 194.

2   ASN, Ministero della Polizia Generale, 1792, registro n. 1.

3   Benedetto Croce, *Storia del regno di Napoli*, Laterza, Bari, 1958, 253.

4   *Bollettino delle leggi*, Legge sul diritto di bollo, May 9, 1807, n. 124.

5   ASN, Ministero Finanze, 1807, f.2327.

6   Raffaele De Cesare, *La fine di un regno*, Longanesi, Milano, 1969, 661.

7   Giuseppe Galasso, *Professioni, arti e mestieri*, 140.

8   De Cesare, ibid.

9   Benedetto Croce, "L'agonia di una strada," in *Napoli Nobilissima*, I serie, III, 177–80.

10 ASN, Prefettura, 3° Rip. For the documents relative to the pizzaioli cited here, see "Sources—Neapolitan Pizzerias in the 1800s (Bourbon Period)" at the end of the book.

11 Biblioteca Nazionale di Napoli, Manuscript Department, "Classi della popolazione," Palat. Banc.II -81/8 e segg.

12 *Bollettino delle leggi*, Legge, n. 712 of July 27, 1810.

13 Marcelin Pellet, *Napoli contemporanea, 1888–92*, translated and reprinted in Naples, Pres. di E. Corsi, 1989. It is sad to note that even today the Prefect of Naples has declared that "in Naples there are 150,000 people who have to figure out how to survive every day." The tribulations of Naples because of the camorra is now known all over the world thanks to Roberto Saviano's bestseller, *Gomorra*.

14 It is important to remember that we are referring to a period in which the social division of labor was distinct.

15 This is perhaps the explanation for the fact that many names appear only for a few years in these registers before disappearing completely from the panorama of pizzaioli.

16 Francesco Mastriani, *Ciccio, Il pizzaiuolo di Borgo Loreto*, Napoli, 1880.

17 With her research, Daniela L. Caglioti has published several lists of goods belonging to failed merchants (see *Il guadagno difficile*, already cited above), but these are more serious merchants, in other words those who bought and sold products of a certain importance. In another essay ("I fallimenti del Tribunale di Commercio di Napoli," in *Società e Storia*, anno XII, 44, April–June 1989) she asserts that even though there were bankruptices in the food sector, the most numerous examples are in the luxury goods sector (p. 450).

18 G.Valeriani, "Porta Capuana," in *Napoli in miniatura*.

19 The French writer came to Naples towards the end of 1835 and found in the city "a full overlap between tastes and interests, an almost irrational transport of those in love, a reciprocal, overall indulgence, and a disproportionate admiration of nature not critical but passionate" as Gino Doria has written in the introduction to *Il corricolo* (cited above). It must have been his own adoption of "passionate and not critical" that made him misunderstand the "pizza a oggi a otto" and make him write not that one ate it today and paid eight days later, but rather that "there are, for small pockets, pizzas from last week, which can substitute perfectly, if not pleasantly, hard tack" (*Il corricolo*, 94).

20 P. A. Allum, *Potere e società a Napoli nel dopoguerra*, Einaudi, Turin, 1975, 52.

3—LICENSES AND THE LAW

1 ASN, Prefettura di Polizia, 3° rip., anno 1821, f.1454.

2 ASN, Prefettura, 1822, f.1455.

3 ASN. Prefettura, f. 1455. Copper utensils (much used in the past in cooking) produce a very toxic substance when in contact with the air. To prevent this happening on the inside of bowls, they had to be covered with tin. The partial or total lack of this "tinning" was quite dangerous.

4 ASN, Prefettura, f.1455, n. 29.

5 ASN, Prefettura, f.1460/I, n. 15.

6 Ordinance of June 20, 1815 on closure of shops on holidays ("sulla chiusura delle botteghe ne' dì festivi"), ASN, Prefettura, f.1456/II, n. 26.

7 Circular letter of December 13, 1822. ASN, Prefettura, f.1455, n. 3.

8 ASN, Prefettura, 1828, f. 1462/II. This solicitations to the commissioners to be vigilant about the renewals of licenses can be found frequently in the successive years as well.

9 ASN, Prefettura, 1840, f.1491/I, f.1491/II, f.1492/I.

10 ASN, Prefettura, f.1495/I.

11 ASN, Prefettura, f.1492/I.

12 ASN, Prefettura, f.1493/I.

13 ASN, Prefettura, f.1492/II.

14 ASN, Prefettura, f.1462/II.

15 ASN, Prefettura, f.1465, nn. 24 e 32.

16 ASN, Questura, Archivio generale I° Serie, 1884, f.1314.

4—INSIDE THE PIZZERIA AND BEHIND THE COUNTER

1 ASN, Prefettura, 2° Rip., 1842, f.484.

2 Quotation from Giuseppina Laurito, "Comportamenti matrimoniali e mobilità sociale a Napoli," in *Quaderni storici*, new series 56, n. 2, 1984, footnote 15.

3 F. P. Rispoli, *La provincia ...*, 96–7.

4 From Commissioner's Office of San Ferdinando, July 20, 1849: "After the fire which occurred in the storage pit of the shop used as a pizzeria, for which reason the aforementioned shopkeeper Pietro Calicchio has been kept from his shop, the vice-mayor of this zone met with myself and a commission of architects, among whom was present also the police architect Signor Baccigalupi and the head of the fire brigade Signor Del Giudice in order to find the means with which to secure this locale from fire. A report that then drafted in which all the necessary steps to render less likely any future fire. The work was then done according to the present codes and after the assurances made to me by Signor Baccigalupi, the oven was reactivated." ASN, Prefettura, 2° Rip., 1849, f.697, n. 741. Unfortunately both the initial and final reports are missing from the dossier.

5 R. De Cesare, *La fine di un regno*, 237.

6 ASN, Prefettura, 2° Rip. 1857, f.985/II, n. 430. The fire brigade, created by Murat in 1810, was disbanded down by Ferdinando I in 1815. In 1833 a new fire brigade was created by Ferdinando II.

7 ASN, Questura, 1896, f.2394.

8 ASN, Prefettura, II Rip., f.486.

9 ASN, Prefettura, II Rip., f.480, 495.

10 ASN, Prefettura, II Rip., f.525/II.

11 M. Stefanile, *Partenope in cucina*, Azienda Autonoma Cura e Turismo, Naples, 1954.

12 M. Pellet maintains that "despite many reasons for impairment, [our] breed [*sic*]

is resistant [...] In a city in the north [of Italy], a population subject to the same conditions would be decimated every year." *Napoli contemporanea*, 33.

13 Achille Spatuzzi, *Saggio sull'alimentazione del popolo minuto di Napoli*, Naples, 1863, 37.

14 Errico De Renzi, *Sull'alimentazione del popolo minuto di Napoli*, Naples, 1863, 59.

5—UNCERTAINTY AND CONTINUITY IN HARD TIMES

1 From the death registers (*1853 Deaths*, San Ferdinando, 705) we see that on October 19, 1853 "in his house, at Salita Sant'Anna di Palazzo 23, Pietro Calicchio died, seventy-four years old, profession pizzaiolo, son of Francesco, a roasted chestnut vendor, and Antonia Saporiti, and husband of Antonia Paravicino, with five male sons."

2 ASN, Questura, Archivio Generale, I ^ Serie, f.1013, n. 81.

3 In the documents consulted, Cesa father and son do not always have the same final vowel in their surnames. One finds Ceso, Cesa, and even once Cesi, but always in reference to the same people.

4 There has been much research about social mobility and occupational and matrimonial choices, and not just for Italy. After the theoretical framework of the American S. Thernstorn, who did research on the verification of the myth of the "land of unlimited opportunity" ("Notes on the Historical Study of Social Mobility," in *Comparative Studies in History and Society*, 1968), there were also a number of other specific studies of J. Kocka on the working class in Westphalia, ("The Study of Social Mobility and the Formation of the Working Class in the 19th Century," in *Le Mouvement Social*, 1980), by D. Crew on the workers in Bochum in Germany ("Definition of Modernity: Social Mobility in a German Town 1880-1901," in *Journal of Social History*, n. 1, 1973) and by W. H. Sewell Jr. on workers in Marseille Marsiglia ("Social Mobility in a Nineteenth Century European City: Some Findings and Implications," in *Journal of Interdisciplinary History*, n. 2, 1976), to cite only a few. For nineteenth-century Naples a number of scholars have done work, among others Giuseppina Laurito, who in the article cited above ("Comportamenti Matrimoniali e Mobilità Sociale a Napoli," in *Quaderni Storici* 56 a. XIX, n. 2, August 1984) agrees with other researchers. Laurito underlines the minimal competition and the tendency across trades to remain in one's own work environment: in a city that suffered from continuous stagnation the occupational homogeneity between father and son stands out, not only in commercial and artisanal activities but also even in the public administration and professional categories. Thus we cannot be surprised that even among pizzaioli there was his tendency not only to not abandon one's trade and to be sure to pass it on to one's son, but also to not abandon one's work evnironment by marrying a woman who did not belong to the trade.

5 ASN, Questura, 1886, f.1378, n. 241.

6 The majority of the dates recorded are susceptible to error given the lack or precise references to when the business changed hands.

7 See the second list of *Sources* at the end of this volume.

8 ASN, Questura, 2 ^ e 3 ^ Serie, f.2335.

6—THE DISTRIBUTION OF PIZZERIAS ACROSS THE CITY

1   All of the scholars who have studied this topic (the citations would be quite lengthy and inopportune to include here) have underlined this particular aspect of the problem.

2   These continuous moves are evident in the sources at the end of the book.

3   On rainy days Via Toledo became veritable river. The *lazzaroni*, perennially under-unemployed, took advantage of the situation and, to earn a few *carlini*, became "ferrymen," carrying people across the street. Of all of the anecdotes of the various visitors and writers, one that is quite funny is one that happened to Emanuele Bidera and which he recounts in the work cited above. During one of these cloudburst he was in Via Toledo, waiting for the waters to calm so that the street was again passable. Nearby was a group of women servants who had gone out to do shopping. Invited by a *lazzarone* to be helped across the street, he laughed at the guy and (seeing that he was a bit scrawny) said that he was too heavy to carry. But the boy insisted and put Bidera on his shoulders almost by force. The author continues: "Ah, I who had foreseen my fall so clearly! The impish servants who started to exclaim 'Oh that guy! Now he's gonna fall! He's falling! Uh! He fell!' And indeed with that universal acclaim this dolt, bending more and more, delivered me into the lava. He remained underneath me, and, drawing up his head from the dirty waters, he asked me to stand up. Me, the old man, with one hand busy holding my umbrella, couldn't find my balance. 'Oh, sir, having fun?' 'Let me just get my balance.' And finally, God willing, I was able to get up and those nasty servants, faking compassion, laughed at me." See *Passeggiata*, 106–7.

4   The streets in Naples were crowded at all hours of the day and night, some in particular. Foreign visitors were always shocked by this. Samuel Sharp, talking about the Via del Tribunale and nearby streets, writes: "The first time that I went to the Vicaria [courthouse], I was mortified to have set out so late from home [...] but notwithstanding the difficulty of threading the multitude, who were pouring out in such numbers, I found, when I had pushed into the hall, almost as much pressing as we usually meet with the first night of a new play in our *London* theatres." *Letters from Italy*, 2nd edn, R. Cave, London, 1767, 135. Before him (just to cite one other comment) was the wife of Prince Gonzaga; in a letter written in 1789 to one of her correspondents in Marseille, she said "The movement in this city is prodigious. It is not the action, the activity of the men, who produce it, but rather their number. It is a crowd that never dissipates, neither by day nor by night." *Il Settecento a Napoli*, edited by the Municipality of Naples, 1914, 250.

5   ASN, Questura, Archivio Generale, 2 ^ e 3 ^ Serie, f.2376, n. 28. "Commissariat Vomero, June 12, 1890: Luigi Mattozzi, son of the late Michele, shopkeeper of a pizzeria with the sale of wine by the glass at Via Banchi Nuovi 16–17, wishing to move his business to the Strada Vernini [*sic*] at Nuovo Rione Vomero, letter Z, property of Andrea Cardone, requests the relevant license." This was duly issued on July 14, 1890.

7—HISTORIC PIZZERIAS

1   This date is given by Gabriele Benincasa, *La pizza napoletana: Mito, storia e poesia*, Naples, Guida, 1992, 157. Immediately after the date he adds that "two years

after, in 1750, at Porta San Gennaro the Pizzeria Capasso opened." The Capassos only started as pizzaioli in 1919. In addition, he states that "at that time [the end of eighteenth century!] the families that we can call the first generation of pizzaioli [started in the business]: Ambrosio, Autunno, Brandi, Calicchio, Capasso, Condurro, Lombardi, Martano, Mattozzi, Nappi, Pace, Pagliarulo, Testa and Triunfo …" (ibid.: 56). It is like putting Masaniello and Michele il Pazzo (both rebel leaders) who both had tragic ends, together: the first was killed in 1647 and the second hung in 1799. Pietro Calicchio also gets backdated, to 1760—twenty years before his birth. Other dates are proposed as well, all without a shred of documentary evidence. Despite this the book, for other aspects, is quite well done: its great failing is the lack of facts for the pizzaioli. The author, however well he wrote, trusted pizzaioli a bit too much.

2   In 1850 a new ordinance changed many names that seemed vulgar or in any event not very decent, such as Chianche ("slaughterhouse") or Sciuscelle ("carob bean"), all names that were dialectical in origin and indicated unseemly situations in some way in the nineteenth century. It was a need that apparently was also felt by the more sensitive part of the population, as before the ordinance even was announced we find some requests of that nature. One example is Vico Gagliani: in the Marchese map cited earlier we see a Vico Lordo between Vico I Foglie and Vico II Foglie a Santa Chiara. The name "Lordo" was infamous in Neapolitan history, as it was essentially an outdoor water closet for the poor in the area at the time. We find, in a heretofore unpublished document of 1829 a letter to the Prefect from Francesco Gagliani, one of the marquis of San Mauro. The letter informs the Prefect that the marquis had bought the palace between Vico Foglie I and Vico Foglie II and had had the street repaved and cleaned. He then requests that "the street sign with the indecent name Vico Lordo be substituted with another [name]." The request was accepted and the street was renamed "Vico Gagliani," and remains so today. ASN, Prefettura, f.1463, n. 9.

3   From the daily *Il Roma*, May 22, 1889. This letter confirms that why pizzerias lasted so long: even when they change hands, it was rare that they were completely dismantled.

4   Annuario Napoletano, *Grande Guida commerciale, storico-artistica, scientifica, statistica, amministrativa industriale e di indirizzi della città di Napoli e Provincia*, edited by Alliata Bronner and Cipriani. 1880 and 1881, as well as in ASN, Questura, 1 ^ Serie, f.1313.

5   Annuario Detken, *Guida amministrativa, commerciale, industriale e professionale della città e provincia di Napoli*, Naples, 1915.

6   *Giornale Costituzionale delle Due Sicilie*, June 26, 1849.

7   ASN, Prefettura, 1857, f.957, n. 4.

8   The existence of a pizza with mozzarella, tomatoes and basil since the first decades of the nineteenth century has been amply documented in the preceding pages.

9   The translation of the document is as follows: "House of Her Majesty, Capodimonte, June 11, 1889—Inspection Office of the Mouth—Most esteemed Sig. Raffaele Esposito Brandi. I confirm that the three types of pizza prepared by you for her Royal Highness the Queen were found to be excellent.—Please believe me to be, Most devoted, Galli Camillo, Head of the Services of the Table of the Royal House." According to a recent article, the document may be a forgery. For a further analysis of the veracity of the story and the relevant archival evidence, see Zachary Nowak,

"Folklore, Fakelore, History: Invented Tradition and the Origins of the Pizza Margherita," *Food, Culture and Society: An International Journal of Multidisciplinary Research* 17 (March 1, 2014): 103–24.

10 Archivio di Stato Civile, Registro Matrimoni, anno 1877, Porto 50. The marriage certificate was not signed by the bride and groom as they were "unlettered."

11 Annamaria Ghedina, *Quando il Re scendeva da Brandi a Chiaja a farsi una pizza*, V. Pironti, Naples, 1997, 39–41.

8—A FAMILY AFFAIR

1 From the interviews with some of these descendants, it was clear that their "historic" memory does not go beyond the second generation. In other words, it is difficult to get back to the memories of their grandparents. The habit of backdating the beginning of the family business was also quite common.

2 The name is from the province of Rome, probably from the town of Artena. Artena today has around 12,000 residents, with over seventy families with the last name Mattozzi. There is a document in the town archive (a seventeenth-century manuscript) that recounts the histories of the old families of Artena. In it the Mattozzis are mentioned, so they go back at least to that century.

3 "16 May 1892. Pepillo Concetta, daughter of Pasquale and of Margherita Russo, from Naples, 23 years old, married to Lombardi Antonio son of the late Tommaso, with pizzeria at Via Genova 23, requests permission to have a bottled wine shop." ASN, Questura, Archivio Generale, 2 ^ e 3 ^ serie, f.2402.

4 Archivio Stato Civile. Reg. Matrimoni, 1892, Stella 10.

5 Apparently somewhere in the EU there is a law being formulated to substitute wood with some other "ecological material."

6 This information is from his birth certificate. Archivio Stato Civile, Registro Nati, 1838, Chiaia 264.

7 ASN, Questura, Archivio Generale I ^ Serie, f.148.

8 ASN, Questura, Archivio Generale, 2 ^ e 3 ^ Serie, f.2394, n. 6.

9 Archivio Stato Civile, Reg. Matrimoni, 1849, Chiaia 172.

10 G.Benincasa, *La pizza* ..., 159.

11 This is how he was listed in his daughter's death certificate: M. Giuseppa. Archivio di Stato Civile, Reg. Morti, anno 1842, San Lorenzo, n. 1898.

12 ASN, Prefettura, 2° Rip., f. 844.

13 Archivio Notarile di Napoli. Notaio Pasquale Mele, June 6, 1858.

14 *Grande Guida Commerciale storico-artistica, scientifica, amministrativa, statistica, industriale e d'indirizzi di Napoli e Provincia*, edited by Cesare Alliata-Bronner, 1881–2.

15 ASN, Questura, Archivio Generale 1 ^ Serie, f. 1292, n. 393.

16 ASN, Questura, Archivio Generale 1 ^ Serie, 1884, f.1314.

17 In 1885 Mattozzi had bought his first wife's mother's house, which was next to their house and where the old woman lived until her death.

18 ASN, Questura, 2 ^ e 3 ^ Serie, f.2376, n. 29.

19 In the *Guida commerciale Stellacci* from 1932.

20 In the *Guida Commerciale Detken-Prestreau* from 1909, on page 77, we find: "From number 11 to number 105 (of Via Depretis) all [buildings] are still under construction."

21 *Guida Generale Stellacci di Napoli e Provincia*, 1925, 1130.

YESTERDAY'S PIZZA, TODAY'S PIZZA

1 During the festival, a competition subdivided into three categories takes place: "Pizza Napoletana STG" for which the rules of the Verace Pizza Napoletana association have to be followed, "Pizza Classica" in which ingredients from different ethnic origins can be used, and "Pizza Primavera" for which only seasonal ingredients can be used. Ryo Kageyama, "Even Top Italian Pizza Makers Bow to Skills of Japanese Woman in Nagoya Pizzeria," *Asia & Japan Watch by The Asahi Shimbun*, November 1, 2014, http://ajw.asahi.com/article/behind_news/social_affairs/AJ201411010013 (accessed November 21, 2014). A recent book on the transnational flow of pizzaioli between Japan and Italy helps explain some of the Japanese talent in the world of pizza. See Rossella Ceccarini, *Pizza and Pizza Chefs in Japan: A Case of Culinary Globalization*, Leiden and Boston: Brill 2011.

2 Harvey Levenstein, *Paradox of Plenty: A Social History of Eating in Modern America*, Oxford and New York: Oxford University Press, 1993. Donna Gabacccia notes that restaurant and eating guides mentioned pizza (which demonstrates its existence prior to World War II) but routinely "misunderstood" it, calling it an "inch-thick potato pan-cake sprinkled with parmesan cheese and stewed tomatoes." Donna Gabaccia, *We Are What We Eat: Ethnic Food and the Making of Americans*, Cambridge: Harvard University Press, 1998, 170, citing Rian James, *Dining in New York*, New York: John Day Company, 1930, 34. There is also extensive documentation of immigrant pizzamakers in Connecticut, where Greek pizzeria owners dominated the market from the 1920s until the 1970s. See Joel Denker's *The World On A Plate: A Tour Through the History of America's Ethnic Cuisine*, Boulder, CO: Westview Press, 2003, 62–3. Denker cites a sociological study, done by Lawrence Lovell-Troy, that later became the book *The Social Basis of Ethnic Enterprise: Greeks in the Pizza Business*, New York: Garland Publishing, 1990.

3 Eric Schlosser, *Fast Food Nation: The Dark Side of the All-American Meal*, Boston: Houghton Mifflin, 2001.

4 Carol Helstosky, *Pizza: A Global History*, London: Reaktion, 61–2. Helstosky is also unconvinced by the "GI thesis" of pizza's post-war popularity.

5 Gabaccia, *We Are What We Eat*, 197.

6 Franco La Cecla, *Pasta and Pizza*, Chicago, IL: Prickly Paradigm Press, 2007, 59–60.

7 In an otherwise light-hearted celebration of pizza, food writer Ed Levine, in a chapter called "The Pizza Police," discusses the Vera Pizza Napoletana's efforts to "regulate" pizza. See also Florence Fabricant, "Italian Pizza Police Offer Rules for the Real Thing," *The New York Times*, June 7, 1995, sec. Home & Garden. http://www.nytimes.com/1995/06/07/garden/italian-pizza-police-offer-rules-for-the-real-thing.html. As we have seen, efforts to standardize pizzas manufacture goes against

its history. *Pizza: A Slice of Heaven*, New York: Universe, 2005, 322–4. That said, it is hard to imagine the horror of Neapolitans when they see the assembly lines that produce "their" pizza abroad, and the "exotic" ingredients (so foreign to Naples) that go on top of them.

8   I owe this term to Peter Naccarato and Kathleen LeBesco, *Culinary Capital*, London and New York: Berg, 2012.

BIBLIOGRAPHY

BIBLIOGRAPHY IN ITALIAN

Allum, Percy A. *Potere e società a Napoli nel dopoguerra.* Einaudi, Torino 1975.

Basile, Giambattista. *Lo cunto de li cunti overo lo trattenimiento de' peccerille.* Napoli, 1634–6.

Benincasa, Gabriele. *La pizza napoletana. Mito, storia e poesia.* Guida, Napoli, 1992.

Bidera, Emanuele. *Passeggiata per Napoli e contorni.* All'insegna di Aldo Manuzio, Napoli, 1844.

Caglioti, Daniela Luigia. *Il guadagno difficile. Commercianti napoletani nella seconda metà dell'Ottocento.* Il Mulino, Bologna, 1994.

Caglioti, Daniela Luigia. "I fallimenti del Tribunale di Commercio di Napoli," in *Società e Storia*, XII, 1989, n. 44, 443–53.

Cavalcanti, Ippolito. *Cucina teorico-pratica*, Gemelli, Napoli, 1837.

Cione, Edmondo. *Napoli di ieri e di oggi.* Morano, Napoli, 1954.

Cione, Edmondo. *Napoli romantica.* Morano, Napoli, 1957.

Corrado, Vincenzo. *Il cuoco galante.* Stamperia Raimondiana, Napoli, 1778 [1st edn 1773].

Croce, Benedetto. "L'agonia di una strada," in *Napoli Nobilissima*, I Serie, III, 1894.

Croce, Benedetto. "Varietà intorno ai 'Lazzari,'" in *Napoli Nobilissima*, I Serie, XIV, 1905.

Croce, Benedetto. *Aneddoti di varia letteratura, II serie.* Laterza, Bari 1954.

Croce, Benedetto. *Storia del Regno di Napoli.* Laterza, Bari, 1958.

Cucina Casereccia (La). Giordano, Napoli, 1828.

De Cesare, Raffaele. *La fine di un regno,* Longanesi, Milano, 1969 [1st edn 1895].

De Mura, Ettore. *Poeti napoletani dal Seicento ad oggi,* Marotta, Napoli, 1963.

De Renzi, Errico. *Sull'alimentazione del popolo minuto di Napoli.* Stamperia della R. Università, Napoli 1863.

De Sanctis, Francesco. *La giovinezza, memorie postume seguite da testimonianze biografiche di amici e discepoli,* edited by Gennaro Savarese. Einaudi, Torino 1961.

Di Giacomo, Salvatore. *Storia del Teatro San Carlino (1738–1884).* Arturo Berisio, Napoli, 1967.

Dumas, Alexandre. *Il corricolo,* edited by Gino Doria, Riccardo Ricciardi. Napoli, 1950.

Faraglia, N. Federico. "Storia dei prezzi nel regno di Napoli dal 1131 al 1860," in *Atti del R. Istituto di Incoraggiamento*, XV, 1878.

Galasso, Giuseppe. "Professioni, arti mestieri della popolazione di Napoli nel secolo decimonono," in *Annali dell'Istituto Storico Italiano per l'età moderna e contemporanea*, vol. XIII–XIV, 1961-2, 107–79.

Ghedina, Anna Maria. *Quando il re scendeva da Brandi a Chiaja a farsi una pizza.* Vittorio Pironti, Napoli, 1997.

Latini, Antonio. *La scalco alla moderna del Cavalier Latini.* Parrino e Mutii, Napoli, 1692–4.

Laurito, Giuseppina. "Comportamenti matrimoniali e mobilità sociale a Napoli," in *Quaderni Storici*, nuova serie 56, n. 2, 1984.

Mascilli Migliorini, Luigi. *Il sistema delle Arti. Corporazioni annonarie e di mestiere a Napoli nel Settecento.* A. Guida, Napoli, 1992.

Mastriani, Francesco. *Il bettoliere di Borgo Loreto.* G. Salvati, Napoli, 1880. In later reprints this becomes: *Ciccio, il pizzaiuolo di Borgo Loreto.*

Mayer, Karl August. *Neapel und die Neapolitaner oder Briefe aus Neapel in die Heimat,* Oldenburg, 1840. Italian translation: *Vita popolare a Napoli nell'età romantica,* edited by Lidia Croce. Laterza, Bari, 1948.

Minervini, Roberto. *Storia della pizza.* E. P. T., Napoli, 1956.

Napoli e luoghi celebri delle sue vicinanze. Tipografia G. Nobile, Napoli, 1845.

Pellet, Marcellin, *Naples contemporaine* (1888–92). Paris, 1894. Italian translation by Francesco D'Ascoli. Editrice Copyright, Napoli, 1989.

Pizzerie d'Italia del Gambero Rosso. Gambero Rosso, Roma, 2005.

Rispoli, Francesco P., *La provincia e la città di Napoli. Contributo allo studio del problema napolitano.* Di Gennaro e Morano, Napoli, 1902.

Rocco, Emanuele "Il pizzajuolo," in *Usi e costumi di Napoli e contorni descritti e dipinti.* Edited by Francesco De Bourcard. Napoli, 1857–66.

Rocco, Emanuele. 'Il Vaccaro ed il capraio', in *Usi e costumi di Napoli e contorni descritti e dipinti.* Edited by Francesco De Bourcard. Napoli, 1857–66.

Salerno, Franco. *La pizza.* Tascabili Newton, Roma, 1996.

Serao Matilde. *Il ventre di Napoli.* Treves, Milano, 1884.

Settecento a Napoli (II). edited by Comune di Napoli. Napoli, 1914.

Sharp, Samuel. *Lettere da Napoli.* Stamperia del Valentino, Napoli, 2004. From *Letters from Italy.* London, 1766.

Spatuzzi, Achille and Luigi Somma. *Saggi igienici e medici sull'alimentazione del popolo minuto a Napoli.* Stamperia della R. Università, Napoli, 1863.

Stefanile, Mario. *Partenope in cucina.* Azienda Autonoma Cura e Turismo, Napoli, 1954.

Valeriani, Gaetano, 'Porta Capuana', in *Napoli in miniatura. Il popolo napoletano ed i suoi costumi. Opera di Patrii Autori pubblicata per cura di Mariano Lombardi.* Tipografia Cannavacciuolo, Napoli, 1847.

White-Mario, Jessie. *La miseria in Napoli.* Le Monnier, Firenze, 1877.

BIBLIOGRAPHY IN ENGLISH

Ceccarini, Rossella. *Pizza and Pizza Chefs in Japan: A Case of Culinary Globalization.* Leiden and Boston: Brill, 2011.

Dickie, John. *Delizia!: The Epic History of the Italians and Their Food.* New York: Free Press, 2008.

Donna Gabaccia, *We Are What We Eat: Ethnic Food and the Making of Americans.* Cambridge: Harvard University Press, 1998.

Helstosky, Carol. *Pizza: A Global History*. London: Reaktion, 2008.

La Cecla, Franco. *Pasta and Pizza*. Chicago: Prickly Paradigm Press, 2007.

Levine, Ed. *Pizza: A Slice of Heaven*. New York: Universe, 2005.

Lovell-Troy, Lawrence. *The Social Basis of Ethnic Enterprise: Greeks in the Pizza Business*. New York: Garland Publishing Inc. 1990.

Nowak, Zachary. "Folklore, Fakelore, History: The Origins of the Pizza Margherita," *Food, Culture & Society* 17 (1) (March 2014): 103–24.

Wiener, Scott. *Viva la Pizza!: The Art of the Pizza Box*. Brooklyn: Melville House, 2013.

INDEX

A note on the index. When referring to a footnote, the citation below will list the number of the page and the number or letter of the note. So footnote b on page 104 would be listed as "104 n.b".